To
Terri
With Friendship

S. Daniel Khazzoom
12/14/10.

P9-BJS-399

NO WAY BACK
The Journey of a Jew from Baghdad

J. DANIEL KHAZZOOM

With
Mairin Khazzoom
Ellen Graham

NO WAY BACK
The Journey of a Jew from Baghdad

Published by:

The KOH Library and Cultural Center
2300 Sierra Boulevard,
Sacrament, CA 95825

Copyright © 2010 by J. Daniel Khazzoom

For general information about this book:

Contact the author at:
 Khazzoom@sbcglobal.net
Tel: 916-972-7074

Library of Congress Control Number:
2010911852

ISBN 978-0-615-38332-3

Printed by METRO - Print and Mail Solutions
Sacramento, California
United States of America

NO WAY BACK
The Journey of a Jew from Baghdad

ACKNOWLEDGEMNTS

I owe a debt of gratitude to two special individuals – Mairin Khazzoom for her unstinting help in every stage of writing my memoir during the last six years and to Ellen Graham, former senior writer for the Wall Street Journal, for her labor of love in editing my memoir.

I thank Joan Ominsky and Dr. Steve Ominsky for their incisive comments on the entire manuscript and thank Pat King for guiding my effort at the early stages of my writing. I thank also the many who read and commented on various sections of the manuscript or helped with sources, references and photographs.

Last but not least, I thank Kati Rozak of Metro for her dedication and for generously giving of her time to shepherd the publication of this book.

J. Daniel Khazzoom

NO WAY BACK
The Journey of a Jew from Baghdad

PREFACE

Several times in my life, I have leaped off a precipice into the unknown.

In 1951, at the age of 18, I left my family and the country of my birth, Iraq, to settle in the new state of Israel. Along with more than 850,000 other Jews living in Arab lands, I was escaping persecution and seeking sanctuary in the Jewish homeland after Israel's war of independence. With the rise of Arab nationalism during the nineteen thirties and forties, the everyday hatred directed toward Baghdad's Jews by our Muslim neighbors snowballed into fearsome terror. Still, we didn't decide to upend our lives lightly. Most of us who joined this migration left behind homes, loved ones, businesses and bank accounts in order to live in peace and security among fellow Jews.

One of my aims in writing my story is to document a way of life that vanished with this exodus: the rich Babylonian Jewish culture that had flourished since ancient times in Iraq. I also want to put the current bloodshed in Iraq in a larger historical context. Though not on a scale comparable to that in present day Iraq, much of the torture, assassination, bombing, kidnapping, hand cutting and beheading that dominate today's headlines (and that mistakenly many tend to attribute to the presence of our troops in Iraq) – much of that is what we lived through and endured, except that at the time there were no TV cameras and no reporters to report to the world on what was happening. Iraq was always, and remains, a violent society. Saddam Hussein was not a' aberration. He was a product of that culture of violence. I witnessed this inherent violence of Iraqi society over and over as a child. However much I tried to erase it from memory, terror is imprinted on my soul. What remains—what I have been unable to shed—is a harrowing instinct to be prepared to flee at any moment.

For decades after I left Iraq, I faced a quandary every morning when dressing. I would pause to consider whether I should put on both my socks before slipping into my shoes—or, instead, first put on one sock and shoe before putting on the other sock and shoe. The source of this irrational obsession? Trying to decide whether, if I were forced to flee just then, would I be better off wearing at least one shoe or flee in my stocking feet. And only in the past few years have I stopped hiding money under the rug in my study-- ready cash should I suddenly need to run.

I was young and had little to lose by way of material assets when I left Iraq. But my departure marked the first of many tearful partings and separations that would be my family's fate amid the incessant turbulence in the Middle East. For seven years after leaving Baghdad, I had no contact with my parents who I'd left behind. To communicate would have put their lives at risk. Eventually, they and my siblings followed me to Israel. But it was 22 years before I was reunited with my oldest sister, who had to remain in Baghdad with her husband until 1972.

Life in Israel was a huge comedown for the refugees that streamed in from Arab lands, swamping the new nation's ability to provide jobs, housing, and even food. More painfully, we encountered discrimination, were often branded Arabs and derided for our language and customs. So in 1958, I once more ventured into the unknown. I again took leave of my family-- to attend graduate school, start a family and build a career in the United States and Canada.

The price of freedom has been almost unbearably high. The dispersal from our homeland, the expropriation of our assets by the Iraqi authorities, the years of anxious separation and the demoralizing economic strains of life in Israel would ultimately tear at our once-close family bonds. The passage of time has helped repair the breach, but it came too late for some of my relatives. They died penniless and alone in Israel.

I am an American now, living a comfortable life as a retired academic in beautiful, sun-splashed California. But even in this free and open society the dark frights of the past have ambushed me at unexpected moments:

On Sunday, January 27, 1969, I was engulfed by a strange feeling that I had never experienced before. I had an inexplicable but overwhelming sense that something terrible was about to happen, that the few of us left in Baghdad were about to be taken away from us. Try as I might, I was unable to shake that feeling. My immediate family was safe with me in Montreal and the news reports contained nothing unusual. Unable to sleep, I even called my father in Israel. He reassured me that nothing untoward had happened there. Yet our conversation did nothing to dispel my mounting sense of dread. What was causing this premonition of impending doom?

The very next day, I received my answer.

Baghdad's radio informed a horrified world that a military tribunal had convicted nine Jews of espionage for Israel and had ordered them summarily executed. The prisoners were publicly hanged in Liberation Square in Central Baghdad before jeering mobs. Just before their hangings, the gallows were inspected by Saddam Hussein, then Iraq's vice president, who toured the square in an open car.

That day was declared a day of national celebration in Iraq. Dancers were summoned to perform under the gallows. People were provided free rides in trams and buses, so that they could come and celebrate under the corpses. Loudspeakers announced that at 4 p.m. the bodies would be brought down so that the mob could deal with them in the streets.

NO WAY BACK
The Journey of a Jew from Baghdad

The news of the hangings shattered me. To this day, I shiver at the thought that the wave of terror might have led the battered remnant of Baghdad's Jewish community to disavow its sons. To this day I wonder: who went to claim the bodies of the nine "spies", after they had been dragged in the streets of Baghdad, without fear of being murdered as a spy sympathizer? Were there ten courageous souls left in Baghdad's Jewish community to recite in public our ancestral *kaddish* in memory of the victims of Iraqi savagery?

During the Gulf War, news reports of Iraq's brutality in Kuwait again reopened old wounds, resurrecting frightening memories of Baghdad's Jewish community crumbling under Iraqi atrocities.

During the third week of August 1990 a correspondent for the Washington Post who had managed to escape from Kuwait was interviewed on PBS's "The McNeil-Lehrer Report." She told of the terror she had experienced while living under the Iraqi occupation.

"Once they see you," she said of the Iraqi forces, "they get ideas about what to do with you. To stay alive, you stay indoors, you never go out, and hope they won't come after you. But the nights brought the greatest fear."

So it was with my family, as we huddled inside our Baghdad home in 1941, listening as a rampaging mob moved closer to our neighborhood, bursting into homes and massacring Jews.

"This woman is telling our story," I told my wife.

I was visiting Israel in September 2000, during the outbreak of the Palestinian intifada against Israel. When I watched televised images of the mobs throwing stones and surging forward with hate blazing in their eyes, it once again summoned up our dark days in Baghdad. I was so disturbed that I could not sleep. I cut short my trip to Israel and flew back to the States, grateful to escape the abhorrent scenes of raw hatred. In Baghdad, when I was growing up, there was nowhere to go. We were trapped.

When the U.S. invasion of Iraq began in 2003, people asked me how I felt about it. I could only say that I hoped Iraq would move toward becoming a more humane society, and in the process serve as a catalyst for the transformation of the Arab world. But as I write this, such an outcome seems elusive.

Sometimes people ask me if I would not want one day to visit Baghdad, my birthplace. My answer is—and always will be--an emphatic "Absolutely Not." I left Baghdad in April 1951 and I will never return.

--Sacramento, California, 2010

PART ONE - IRAQ

BY THE RIVERS OF BABYLON

AN ANCIENT COMMUNITY

I was born a Jew in Baghdad, in the Muslim country of Iraq. My roots there go back centuries: Legend has it that our first Khazzoom ancestor was born in Baghdad six hundred and fifty years ago.

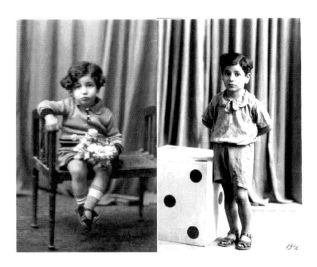

Daniel - April 7, 1934   *Daniel -two years later - June 11, 1936*

Even though Iraq was a land of plenty, I was painfully aware from an early age that it wasn't my promised land. And because of my experiences growing up there, I have never identified myself as Iraqi, but rather as a Jew from Baghdad. The community that nurtured me was a cloistered, self-contained enclave within the often-hostile city at large. Although Baghdad's Jews were not confined to a walled ghetto, we lived in what might be described as a cultural or spiritual ghetto, within a repressive state. We had minimal contact with the Muslims around us and were subject to separate restrictive laws. There were quotas limiting the number of Jews who could serve in Parliament, for example, and for most of my youth we were not permitted to leave the country. Sometimes, in my younger years, the exit regulations could be bent with a bribe, but there was no recourse for the whim of clerks who, willy-nilly, denied permission to travel abroad. It was a country ruled by men, not law.

In Baghdad, my world consisted of family, synagogue and school, tightly bound by ancient tradition and the seasonal progression of religious holidays.   The outward security that this close-knit world provided, however, was illusory.   For outside the safety of my family's embrace lurked ever-present threats: We didn't set foot in exclusively Muslim neighborhoods.   In Baghdad in those times, Jewish children were frequent victims of harassment or theft on the street--or worse, kidnappings or beatings. Even as a small child, I internalized the anxiety that came from knowing we could never let down our guard, and that at any moment it might be necessary to flee for our lives. These fears proved all too prescient, when the pervasive, almost routine, sense of alienation and dread culminated in full-scale terror: the 1941 *farhood*, or massacre of Baghdad's Jews that my family and I narrowly escaped.

In school, we were taught how some of the world's earliest and greatest civilizations took root in the lands that make up modern Iraq, which acquired its present name when the Arab Caliph Omar conquered it from the Persians in 634 CE. I never developed a feel for the true size of the country until I traveled with my parents from Baghdad to Basra in Southern Iraq when I was twelve. The trip took twenty-four hours by train. Much later I learned that Iraq is more than three times as large as New York State and twenty times as large as Israel.

Pinning down facts about the country of my birth was always a dubious proposition, because the government controlled the flow of information and it was a highly unreliable source. In the early forties, the official estimate of Iraq's population was 4.5 million. Two years later, the estimate had jumped to 14.5 million—with no explanation or investigation of the obvious discrepancy. The information vacuum and our starvation for news would worsen in the following years, intensifying our sense of peril.

Iraq produced most of the food it needed, but had very minimal industrial capacity and most industrial products were imported. Oil was first discovered in Karkouk, in northeastern Iraq, in 1927. Early estimates put the country's oil endowment in excess of one hundred billion barrels. By the mid-1930s, the Iraq Petroleum Company (IPC) had acquired sole rights to develop the oil fields in Northern Iraq in return for paying royalties to the Iraqi government, and IPC opened a pipeline from Mosul to Tripoli in Lebanon and to Haifa in what is now Israel, and the export of oil began in earnest. Soon Iraq became one of the world's leading producers and exporters of oil, with oil revenues contributing roughly fifty per cent of the gross domestic product. Little of this sudden wealth trickled down to the population, however. In the corrupt regime of Iraq, which wallowed in bribes and kickbacks, a good chunk of the oil revenue went to line the pockets of public officials, cabinet members, the royal family and their cronies, instead of being channeled to meet social needs and enhance the welfare of Iraq's citizens.

Though oil was cheap in Iraq, the very poor couldn't afford it and used cow dung and wood as fuel. They seldom used lamps, rising and going to bed with the sun except on nights when the moon was full.

The city of Baghdad was founded in 762 CE by the Muslim Abbasid Caliph al-Mansour. Prior to that, Baghdad was a suburb of Ctesiphon, the capital of the Sassanid dynasty. My father told me that Baghdad is a Persian word meaning "beautiful orchard," that a small Jewish community was known to have lived there some five centuries before the Abbasid dynasty chose it as its capital, and that over time the community grew to become the center of learning for world Jewry.

Growing up, the history of Iraq and Baghdad didn't concern or interest me particularly. Rather, I identified with the history and achievements of the Babylonian[1] Jewish community, the oldest Jewish community in existence, whose history goes back two thousand six hundred years and predated the arrival of Arabs in these lands by many centuries.

My ancestors were exiled from Palestine, our Promised Land, to Babylonia after the destruction of the First Temple in Jerusalem in 586 BCE. They settled along a canal in a region called Kebar near Babylon, about fifty miles southwest of present-day Baghdad. And it was there that they composed the ode that Jews recite the world over to this day: "By the rivers of Babylon, there we sat and wept, as we remembered Zion." In Iraq when I was growing up, it was customary to read this ode only once a year, on *tish'a be'ab*, the day when we remember the destruction of Jerusalem and the Temple's torching. And we read it from the depths of our souls. The ground under our feet was where it had all happened. There was the Tigris—one of the rivers of Babylon—before our very eyes, less than a hundred yards away from the synagogue in which I grew up. For us, Babylonian Jews, the calamity was a living thing - not something that had happened in the distant past. We were where we were because our ancestors were exiled here. We were the exiled.

Those early settlers went on to establish other new towns in Babylonia not long after they arrived. One town, called Tel-Aviv, became the communal and spiritual center of the elders of the Jewish community. "And I came to the exile community that dwelt in Tel Aviv by the kebar Canal, and I remained where they dwelt. And for seven days I sat there stunned among them." (Ezekiel 3:15). Tel Aviv is significant not only because of the prominent people who resided there, but also because of the message that underlay its name: We are down today, but we are not giving up. A brighter future lies ahead. Tel Aviv is made up of two Hebrew words: Tel, which means a mound of ruins -- and that is

---

[1]*Historically the Jews of Iraq were referred to in Jewish sources as Babylonian, never as Iraqi or Jews of Iraq. I follow the same practice. In Iraq, the Jewish community was known as alta'ifa alIsraeliya – the Israelite group (or minority). The term Israeliya (and Israeliyeen -- plural) became problematic when Israel was established because of its similarity with Israeli. Nonetheless, the term alta'ifa alIsraeliya was never dropped.*

probably how my ancestors saw things when they were led to Babylon, having lost their homeland, their spiritual center, their families, their homes, and their dignity. The second word is Aviv, meaning the spring season, symbolizing revival and rejuvenation. So the name means "it is all ruins now, but it will blossom again; spring is ahead, and we will rebound." Fittingly, on May 21, 1910, the modern city of Tel Aviv in Israel was officially named after the city established by Jewish exiles in Babylonia.

The history of this community, with its theme of hope and invincibility, is the history of the Jewish people. Babylon is where most Jewish practices and traditions originated -- public prayer, the prayer book, the synagogue, and the magnum opus of them all – the Babylonian Talmud.

But what characterized the Babylonian Jewish community more than anything else were its institutions of learning. The Babylonian Academies of *nehardea*, s*ura* and *pumbeditha* were the Ivy League institutions of the Jewish world. It was in those Academies that the Babylonian Talmud was written. The academies' leaders were bold and civic-minded; they were erudite and original thinkers.

The traveler Pethahiah of Regensburg, Germany, who visited Iraq in the late twelfth century, reported on the erudition of the local Jewish community: "There is not an ignoramus throughout the lands of Babylon... who does not know all the twenty-four Books in their punctuation and accuracy ... Babylonia is an entirely different world."

The Jews of Babylon were Sephardim, a term used to include those descending from the Iberian Peninsula, North Africa, and Asia, whose laws, customs, liturgy and language differ from those of the Ashkenazi Jews, who originated in central and Eastern Europe. The vernacular language of my community was Judeo-Arabic, rather than the Yiddish, or Judeo-German, spoken by Ashkenazim. Sephardim tend to be more inclusive and more lenient in their practices than Ashkenazim, and so we have not been fragmented into groups like the Orthodox, Conservative, Reform, and Reconstructionist branches of Ashkenazi Judaism. We Sephardic Jews all pray in the same synagogue, regardless of our level of observance or degree of belief—or non-belief.

A kaleidoscope of colors, a cacophony of sounds, and a myriad of impressions run through my mind when I think of my childhood in the ancient city of Baghdad. Sometimes the pictures form clear images; at times everything is blurred. Even the years seem jumbled together; I know definitely when some things happened; other things I can't place on a definite time line.

In the late nineteen forties, Baghdad's population was reported as 450,000, with most residents clustered into neighborhoods segregated by religion. About 65% of the population were Muslim, 25%—100,000 to 110,000—were Jewish, and about 10% were Christian. My family, along with most of the population, lived on what was known as the *rassafa* side of the Tigris River, where government buildings, commercial offices, schools and hospitals were concentrated. An inviting boardwalk studded with large houses and mansions, cafes and coffee shops ran along the *rassafa* riverbank. But in the shadow of these grand residences was another world entirely: dusty, unpaved alleys crowded with squalid shacks where large families lived without electricity or running water among their cows and sheep. *karkh*, the other side of the Tigris, was wild, green and sparsely populated mainly by poor Arabs living in tin shanties or huts made of cowhide, dung and mud.

When I was in my teen's two modern bridges were erected spanning the Tigris. The two bridges ramped up steeply from the *Rassafa* side and then ramped down just as steeply toward the k side. I remember the climb, because when I rode my bicycle to play tennis on the *karkh* side I was breathless by the time I reached the top. My experience with the floating bridges that these modern bridges replaced was very different.

At the best of times a floating bridge never felt solid under my feet, but under the weight of a moving car it rocked alarmingly. Up and down it went, taking my stomach with it. Staying on the bank was safer. From there I could watch the undulating bridge or the rowboats that ferried people from one side of the river to the other. Sometimes several rowboats were tied together and tugged across the river by a motorboat, serving as a makeshift ferry to the other side of the Tigris.

Baghdad had two wide boulevards. Ghazi Street cut through the lower-class part of town, and we mostly avoided it. *Rasheed* Street ran along the Tigris, and was crowded with hotels, stores, movie houses and restaurants. In my neighborhood, a thick hedge of pink and white oleanders grew along the median. Flowing brooks, fed with water from the Tigris nearby and shaded by stands of towering eucalyptus, separated the wide sidewalks from the traffic. On summer nights, when we slept on the rooftop of our home to get relief from the blistering heat—daytime temperatures often surpassed 110 degrees F. --we were lulled to sleep by the soothing croaking of the frogs that made their homes in the brooks.

Only once in my memory did the thermometer drop to freezing level in Baghdad. I was walking home from school on *rasheed* Street when I noticed a big crowd gathered in a circle, excitedly pointing to something on the ground. When I got closer I could see a thin crust of ice on a puddle of water. I was astonished. It was the only time in my life before coming to the U.S. that I saw frozen water on the ground. That afternoon, the Ministry of Education closed all public and private schools in Baghdad until further notice.

Though automobiles were still a relative rarity, Baghdad's streets roiled with activity during the workday. Hackney carriages, buses, and taxis jostled each other in the bustling thoroughfare, where in lieu of traffic lights, policemen attempted to bring some order to the whirling chaos. Snarls and bottlenecks were commonplace, especially when a carriage horse would stumble and fall. Drivers whipped their horses mercilessly or honked their horns in annoyance, causing other horses to rear up in panic. Tempers flared, and sometimes drivers came to blows—fisticuffs being the all-too-typical way to settle disputes in those days.

We probably had as many paved streets as we did in Baghdad largely because tar, a byproduct of oil refining, was so readily available. My father and I loved the smell of tar and the smell of gasoline, and we often walked on a newly tarred road to enjoy its fragrance. Sometimes we even walked to a gas station to sniff the air.

Trade and finance in Iraq was primarily in Jewish and Christian hands, divided about equally. Some Jewish families owned banks, and many employees at major banks were Jewish—experience that stood them in good stead when they immigrated to Israel. There were also numerous small bankers in the Jewish community, known as sarraf. Some of them would sit outside the banks or other business establishments downtown, rolling money in their hands. Others had large offices and staffs. Not much paperwork was involved; financial transactions were based largely on trust. One of my classmates related how his father, a sarraf, conducted business: Someone would drop a roll of banknotes on his desk worth, say, 100 dinars. (Up until 1948, 1 dinar = $5) His father wouldn't bother to count the money then and there. Nor would the depositor wait to get a receipt.

In the textile and produce markets, peddlers and shoppers haggled at top volume over the price of everything from a single orange to fine jewelry and bolts of silk. Untold hours were wasted negotiating every transaction in a stylized dance of parry-and-thrust between merchant and customer: The shopkeeper's mock indignation when a price was deemed too high or a scale's accuracy was questioned; then exasperation, signified by a turban heatedly flung to the ground; finally the shrug of grudging acquiescence as a lower price was agreed upon. Men—Arabs barefoot in long robes and Jews in mostly Western dress-- congregated in the markets, coffee shops and cafes playing dominoes or backgammon before crowds of onlookers. Women were rarely seen on the street.

While Islam forbade the consumption of alcohol, this stricture was honored mainly in the breach. Spirits were available—sub rosa--at coffee shops, where patrons could quietly indulge while still maintaining an abstemious image at home. It was rumored that some of the wealthier Arabs drank perfume, which presumably didn't violate the letter of the law, but did play havoc with their digestive systems. There was one dry cleaning establishment said to be a secret drinking establishment. Perhaps it was a result of their inhalation of fumes from chemicals, but I observed several people emerge from that establishment in a drunken state.

Amid the hubbub of an emerging modern city, rural ways persisted as they had from ancient times. Tall date palms abounded in our neighborhood. Iraq was then the world's largest producer and exporter of dates—the government claimed some seventy varieties grew there. Dates were cheap, so the poor depended on them for sustenance, often eating nothing more than a date sandwich and tea as their main meal. To harvest dates, workers with hooks strapped to their bare feet and sickles tucked in their belts would scramble up the palms' spiny trunks to harvest the delicious fruit. As the trees bent precariously under their weight, I would watch transfixed, sure they would fall, but they never did.

On Saturdays Baghdad virtually came to a halt for the Sabbath. Arab-owned coffee shops and movie theaters remained open, but most markets and commercial centers were shut down. There was an aura of serenity in the air as the din of traffic fell silent. My father and I were in the habit of strolling the neighborhood on Saturday afternoons. Often, we would simply stand and listen to the pleasant cool water flowing in the brooks and the rustle of the leaves of the fragrant eucalyptus stirring in the wind. I liked to watch fishermen cast their nets from boats close to the riverbank. They worked in pairs: One would walk barefoot along the rocky shore, pulling the boat against the current while the other managed the nets from the boat.

Diseases ravaged the city, and we had to be conscious of dirt and contamination. My parents took every precaution to shield us from those diseases. Every year we were inoculated against typhoid. But there was no inoculation against malaria, and I suffered from recurring malaria four years in a row. I remember being terrified, shaking uncontrollably as I lay in bed, unable to stop my teeth from chattering, while my mother stood by, looking helpless. She put more covers on me, shoved hot water bottles into my bed, and sometimes she just threw herself over me to try and arrest the shaking or stop the intermittent hallucinations. I was treated with quinine, a powerful medication, which damaged my middle ear, causing me even until now to suffer from vertigo.

When I was ten I suffered from a severe case of jaundice, another common disease in Iraq. I was so ill that I did not want to eat or drink. It took me weeks to recover.

Nor were my siblings spared, suffering illnesses ranging from smallpox to chronic digestive disorders.

When I was a boy, my grandmother used to sing "Baghdad *sit leblad*," or "Baghdad the lady of the cities of the world." Was this an instance of the victim identifying with the oppressor? Or was it perhaps a tribute to the only Baghdad my grandmother knew, the Jewish Baghdad of my memories?

NO WAY BACK
The Journey of a Jew from Baghdad

A LOVE STORY

My father, Abraham Kh'doury Khazzoom, and my mother, Looloo Raby, were maternal first cousins. Abraham was born in 1890, the second child of a family of three boys. Looloo, born in 1901, was the second child of a prosperous family of five girls and four boys. Her father was a wealthy banker and businessman, and the family lived in an imposing home in downtown Baghdad.

My paternal grandmother, Farha, had hoped for a girl when my father was born. She was advised that a surefire recipe for fulfilling this wish the next time was to have her newborn son wear earrings. So she had her infant Abraham's ears pierced. The earrings were too heavy for his tender earlobes, but Grandmother Farha didn't waver. She must have been disappointed when she gave birth, a year later, to another boy. In the meantime, the earrings had succeeded in slicing each of her baby's earlobes in two, a scar he would carry for the remainder of his life.

Abraham was left fatherless at age three, when Grandfather Abboudi died in a cholera epidemic that swept through Baghdad. My grandmother and her three young sons then became the responsibility of my father's paternal grandfather, Jacob, a grocer who barely eked out a living. There was no social safety net in Iraq. Though Babylonian Jews did care for the poor, the epidemic had left so many needy widows and widowers that they taxed the resources of the community beyond its limits. Ultimately Farha and her sons moved in with her brother Joseph, who worked as a sarraf, or independent banker. With him, they were relatively better off economically than with Grandfather Jacob, but it was still a life of poverty.

Early widowhood brought with it enormous hardship. My grandmother had no chance of remarrying. Rarely did anyone in Iraq want to marry a widow, certainly not one with three children. She couldn't earn a living - generally, women didn't work outside their homes. Undoubtedly she felt she was a burden to her brother and his family. Every morsel that one of her children ate at Joseph's table was one no longer available for her brother, his wife, or their children. There must have been times when she got the message they were no longer welcome, yet she had nowhere else to go. How does one spend a lifetime under such conditions? The conflicts such dependency undoubtedly caused in the entire family may partly explain my father's sometimes-capricious nature, which led to our frequent clashes as I was growing up.

My father spoke fondly of his Uncle Joseph and the debt he owed him. But he never shared details about his daily life while growing up in his uncle's home. And, although he maintained contact with cousins from his other maternal aunts and uncles, I don't remember him staying in touch with any of Joseph's children. Was there a sense of guilt toward Joseph's family that he couldn't confront? Or was it simply that Joseph's children felt they had had enough of my father and his brothers?

Within his immediate family, Abraham was the most prominent and the best –educated, but he did not always value education. When he was eleven, he told his mother he was going to drop out of school.

"Wonderful," she said. "I feel lonely at home by myself. You'll keep me company. It will be good for both of us. You'll see."

But my father quickly realized he was heading for a dead end. Education was his only way out of poverty. He asked his principal's forgiveness for his foolishness, and the school agreed to take him back. He never cut school after that.

Indeed, after graduation he studied law in Istanbul, Turkey, the center of learning in the Middle East at the time, and went on to become one of the prominent lawyers of his time. One evening, when we were all assembled in our "glass" room, with its glass doors and enormous kerosene chandelier, he read from his memoirs about his long-ago trip to Istanbul. He told a harrowing story of how the horse-drawn carriage that took him and other travelers to Turkey lost its way in a blinding snowstorm. Before the storm subsided, my father said he nearly froze to death on the way to Istanbul's prestigious law school.

Hebrew scripts of Judeo-Arabic
(Notice that it is written under the line)

My mother was the last daughter in her family not to receive a modern education. Her younger sisters attended the same French school that my sisters and I attended. Looloo attended *stayee*, literally meaning "my master," a small private school where she was taught to read the prayers and *sh'bahoth*--the religious paeans—in Hebrew. She also learned to read and write Judeo-Arabic, the language of the Jews of Iraq. My mother never learned to read or write Arabic, and that was typical for most people of her generation. She didn't attend stayee long, and she had few opportunities to practice what she had learned. By the time I was growing up, she could no longer remember how to read Hebrew, but she still remembered a lot of the *sh'bahoth* and some of the prayers by heart.

My father, eleven years older than his cousin Looloo, became attached to her when she was a baby and married her when she turned seventeen. Baba loved to tell us children about Looloo, the toddler he knew and cherished.

"She was a sandwich thief," he would say winking at us. "I would drop by Aunt Aziza's house on the way to school to play with her and do you know what she used to do?"

"No, Baba. Tell us, tell us," we would say, our faces shining with excitement.

"She would grab my schoolbag and rummage through it, tossing every item on the floor until she found my radish sandwich."

"Is that so?" my mother would ask, hiding a smile.

"What would she do with the sandwich, Baba?" we would ask, grinning at our mother. We knew what was coming next.

"She would drop my bag, crawl to the corner of the room with the prize in her hand and eat every last bit of my sandwich."

" And what did you do, Baba? Why didn't you try to get your sandwich back before Mama had eaten it?"

"I couldn't do that. How could I deprive your mother of anything she wanted?"

We were silent then, watching the loving glances our parents exchanged, secure in their love for each other and for us.

But being children we couldn't let the matter rest.

"So what did you have to eat, Baba?"

"I starved the rest of the day," he'd say, rubbing his stomach.

Mama chuckled as we children ganged up and reproached her for leaving Baba to starve.

"Enough, children," Baba would tell us. "Your mother has made up for her thieving ways."

Then he would point to the radishes Mama made sure to have on our Sabbath table every Friday night.

My father and mother continued to meet frequently when they were children, during regular family visits. When Abraham returned from law school in Istanbul, he declared his love for Looloo and asked her parents for permission to marry her. My maternal grandfather, Silman, put his foot down. His daughter's suitor was fatherless, came from a poor family, and his grandfather was only a grocer – clearly an undistinguished pedigree. Even though some saw my father as a rising star, grandpa Silman was not impressed. My maternal grandmother, Aziza, favored the marriage, but women didn't have a voice in such decisions. My mother wanted to marry my father, but she, too, had to keep quiet. Nothing could be done without Grandpa Silman's consent. He wanted to find a more suitable husband for his daughter through the traditional channel – an arranged marriage.

Such unions were facilitated by Jewish matchmakers, mostly women, known as dellalat. The dellalat provided the parents of eligible men with a list of eligible women, describing their family backgrounds and social status. They provided similar information about the bachelors to the women's parents, and helped negotiate the size of the dowry that the prospective groom expected as part of the matrimonial settlement.

Ottoman certification of membership in the legal profession
On top, the logo of the Ottoman Empire; at the lower left,
picture of my father wearing the Ottoman fez

Every detail of family background, history and social status was scrutinized and weighed. When both sides were satisfied that a match was conceivable, a rendezvous was set up, ostensibly to give the eligible man, woman, and their families an opportunity to meet and get acquainted. In fact, however, the meeting was intended to give the young man and his parents the opportunity to look over the woman and decide if she was attractive enough. Rarely did the prospective bride have an equal say, or any say at all, in the choice of a mate.

When the bachelor and his family decided there was a basis for a deal, negotiating the size of the dowry began in earnest. Haggling over price, so ingrained in Middle Eastern culture, naturally came into play when settling on a dowry. (Muslim customs were no less offensive, except that the bridegroom was expected to pay the bride's family for rights to marry their daughter.)

My father detested this custom and wanted no part of it. He loved my mother and rejected the notion that her parents should pay him to marry her. But his feelings were immaterial; both he and my mother were helpless in the face of Grandpa Silman's opposition.

Abraham hoped for a breakthrough. Then opportunity—in the form of a potential disaster-- knocked on his door.

My parents, March 29, 1924
Mama, pregnant with S'haq, is
wearing a diamond necklace she treasured, a present my father had bought for her.

It happened that a few months after my father's return from Istanbul, the Tigris reached dangerously high levels and threatened to flood Baghdad. The Tigris ran through the middle of the city, and the bank was perilously low on the populated *Rassafa* side of the river. In times of flood, people sought refuge on the *karkh* side of the Tigris, where the bank was higher.

When Abraham realized that there was a danger of flooding, he went straight to my mother's home and told her he wanted her to take the boat with him across the Tigris to the *karkh* side, where they would stay until the flood subsided. She agreed to join him.

Her decision was scandalous by the standards of the day. Going out with a man at night without a chaperone was considered disreputable; going away with a man for several days was unforgivable. If what she did became known, no man would ever want to marry her. But that didn't deter either of my parents.

When they returned, the news of what had happened spread like wildfire. Grandpa Silman realized he was outmaneuvered; he had no choice but to give in. My parents were married shortly thereafter. Mama was just 17, and Baba was 28.

THE FAMILY ARMY

The Khazzoom Family, 1934
Front row l to r: Latifa, Helwa, Jacob Meir; second row l to r: Reyna, Muzli,
Baba with two-year old Daniel, Mama, Jamila. My brother, S'haq, isn't in the picture;
my brother, Abboudi, died before I was born; my sister, Valentine, was not born yet

Their love was the talk of the town, even during the time I was growing up. In Iraq it was considered bad taste to show affection in public. My father flouted this custom, too, putting his arm around Mama's shoulders in public. Their behavior drew stares and set tongues to wagging.

My parents had ten children – six daughters and four sons. In the western world a family of this size is uncommon; in Iraq it was not. Women in Iraq married young, and many gave birth to seven or eight children before reaching thirty. Mama had nine children by the time she was thirty-one. In 1896, the rabbis in Iraq issued a ban on marriage when the bride was less than sixteen. Though violations still occurred -- Aunt

Guerjiyi, my mother's older sister, was married in 1913 when she was fourteen -- the ban held pretty well.

My sisters had Arabic, Hebrew, French, and Spanish names, which are variants of beautiful, pretty, pleasant, glorious. (When my sisters immigrated to Israel, Helwa and Latifa changed their names from Arabic to Hebrew -- Yafa and Nava, respectively). My brother and I had Hebrew names only.

Some of my siblings looked at the world differently from me. I loved the Jewish world and wished the Arabs would leave us in peace to pursue our Jewish life. My brother Jacob was not interested in things Jewish. He and some of my sisters liked Arabic songs whereas I loved the Babylonian *sh'bahoth*, the Hebrew religious paeans and, among Arabic songs, I identified only with the old Arabic lullabies my mother sang to me as a child. I was not particularly enamored of movies in general, and did not like Arabic movies. My sisters Muzli and Reyna were big fans of Arabic movies.

My father was the only breadwinner in the family. He literally had an army to feed, clothe and educate. Yet my parents spared no effort, and we lived in physical comfort. I marvel at how they managed.

On a number of occasions my father put on Arab attire. Nine-year old Jacob, Abraham, and four-year old Daniel.

My mother's hazel eyes radiated love and compassion. Unlike my father, with whom I often clashed in a classic father-son power struggle, Mama didn't believe in physical punishment. Only once do I remember her spanking me, and she was seized with remorse afterward. While I knew my mother loved me without reserve, sometimes I wondered if my father loved me at all. Then he would show me kindness, and I would feel secure in his love—though never totally secure.

He was a bundle of contradictions. He fought fiercely against corporal punishment in Jewish schools, but didn't hesitate to beat me. He went out of his way to avoid embarrassing people. But at times he humiliated my brother, some of my sisters, and me. He boasted about my accomplishments to his friends, clients and leaders of the community, but seemed to relish the times when events knocked me down and brought me to my knees. Living in an Arab milieu, he had assimilated some of that culture's rigid patriarchal views about family. Growing up, I was baffled by his behavior, and, when I was younger, I was often afraid of him and the power he wielded over my life.

The happiest times I remember from my childhood in Baghdad are those when the family was gathered together. On winter nights we sat around the *sopa*, or kerosene heater, roasting chestnuts, boiling water for tea, or just watching the flames through the heater's many-colored apertures. When we turned out the lights, the colorful flames illuminated the room, casting dancing shadows on the walls and on the Persian rugs that covered our couches. I nestled into my chair feeling secure and warm, despite the chilly wind that whistled though the cracks in ill-fitting windows and doors. It seemed then as if danger was far away and could never touch us.

Sometimes, in the dark winter evenings, we would hear the turnip vendors, or *abu'l shalgham*, in the street. For children in Baghdad, these peddlers were as eagerly anticipated as Good Humor trucks. We would rush outside and, just as quickly, run shivering back into the house to savor our piping hot, newly purchased turnips in front of the kerosene heater. Cooked with dates, the turnips' sweetness seemed to melt on our tongues.

My parents' second child, Abboudi, died at age two, eleven years before I was born. In Iraq, as in the rest of the developing world, male infant mortality was high. In spite of the superior hygienic conditions within the Jewish community, male infant mortality was high there too, and Abboudi fell victim to it. My mother often spoke lovingly of him, although she never explained the exact cause of his death. I think she never recovered from the devastation of his loss. My brother S'haq, my parents' fifth child, died at seventeen.

I was the next to youngest in the family, and before my birth my parents made a pilgrimage to (what many believed was) the tomb of the Prophet Daniel in northern Iraq, as was customary among Babylonian Jews during *sh'buoth*, the holiday of pilgrimage that commemorates God's gift of the *torah* to the Jewish people on Mt. Sinai. They pledged that if my mother gave birth to a boy they would name him Daniel. I was born a few days later. But because I was named at a time of worsening persecution of the Jews, my parents thought it would be safer to make Daniel my second name and give me Yousif—the Arabic counterpart of Joseph—as a first name. Within the safe confines of our home, however, Mama would sometimes tenderly call me "Dannu." Years later, in Israel,

NO WAY BACK
The Journey of a Jew from Baghdad

I toyed with the idea of dropping Joseph, or Yousif, as reminders of the oppressive times in Iraq when we had to hide our Jewish identity. Eventually I recognized that tyranny would always be an integral part of my history. So I decided to keep only the initial J., as a symbol of my life under Iraqi repression.

My oldest sister, Jamila, was a sort of second mother, teacher, confidant and friend to me. Our mother gave birth to Jamila when she was eighteen, and their relationship was more like that of sisters than of mother and daughter. In Iraq, the eldest daughter was expected to help with housekeeping and caring for the family, and so, by a fluke of birth order, Jamila was robbed of much of her childhood. Although we had domestic help, she was the first one up in the morning to wash the courtyard and kitchen floors, make tea in the samovar, boil the unpasteurized milk, and prepare breakfast.

Jamila had a nurse's healing touch. Once, when I was nine years old I became ill and had a high fever. Our family doctor, *ammu* Guerji, came for a house call - *ammu*, or paternal uncle, being an honorary title, since Guerji was actually my mother's cousin. *Ammu* Guerji looked after all of my family's medical needs, and never took a penny in return.

Ammu Guerji was not sure what could be behind my high fever, and he looked worried. I was scared, and Jamila noticed. If she was afraid of contracting my mysterious illness, no one ever knew. She put her arms around me and lay beside me through the night. I was worried she would catch my disease and die. But deep down, I felt reassured in her arms. I closed my eyes and fell asleep and was back on my feet a week later. We never knew what caused my illness. But I never forgot Jamila's devotion.

In Iraq, families with many children tended to be lax in educating their girls, sending the boys to good schools and the girls to substandard institutions. Not so with my parents. They sent my sisters and me to the *l'Ecole de l'Alliance Israelite*, the elite French school, and the most expensive of all private schools in Iraq. It was my brother Jacob, not my sisters, who was sent to a lesser school. Jacob couldn't take the demanding curriculum of *l'Alliance*.

As a child, Jamila became fluent in French at *l'Alliance*. But because of her duties at home, she had to drop out of school in her mid-teens. When I began attending *l'Alliance*, she walked me through my punishing French homework assignments. Jamila was my all-knowing idol; it seemed there was no French word she had not mastered. As I progressed, I encountered more and more uncommon words, and as usual I asked Jamila for their meaning. When she didn't know, she just said so matter-of-factly. Together we looked up the word in the dictionary. That was the first lesson I learned from her - there was nothing wrong, nothing embarrassing about admitting I didn't know. No one, not even Jamila, could possibly know all there was to know.

Jamila was my father's favorite. She was the only one of his children who ever accompanied him to the King's Palace. In his official capacity as a member of the Governing Council of Central Iraq, Baba was occasionally invited to the Palace to join in celebrations. Usually, only male guests were invited. The Palace made an exception one time, when they invited the famous Egyptian singer, Oom Kalthoom, to perform at a gala celebration of the King's birthday. For that one time, invitees were allowed to bring their wives along. Baba got Palace approval to have Jamila accompany him, along with my mother. It was probably my father's way of letting Jamila know he loved her and appreciated how she put herself out for the rest of us.

Mama and Jamila had long dresses sewn specially for the occasion. They were a dazzling combination of crimson and pink silk. Baba was horrified at how sheer the dresses were, until Mama assured him they were to be worn over very modest under dresses.

My sister Muzli was tall and slender, with straight black hair and an elegant sense of style. She loathed housework, but loved the outdoors, and she found her niche in running the family errands. She would leave mid-morning for the market downtown, where she bought snaps and buttons that Mama needed, took our shoes to the shoemaker, stopped at the watchmaker for a watchband or a repair, and scoured stores for the linens we needed.

Like several of my older sisters, Muzli dropped out of school during intermediate school. I don't remember them getting any argument from our parents about this decision; it was the societal norm. On days when Muzli didn't go to the market, she would loll on the balcony in the sun reading novels. At night she listened to Radio Cairo until it signed off. During those broadcasts, she knit feverishly and with amazing skill, producing all of our sweaters and scarves as well as Baba's socks.

Reyna, the fourth child in our family, was the one who often orchestrated our evenings around the *sopa*, our kerosene heater, making sure we had roasted chestnuts and cups of tea. She was eight years older than I. Mama told me that Reyna had been the most beautiful of all her children, but at an early age, her face had been ravaged by smallpox. Thereafter, she was taunted by her classmates about the scars on her face. Neighbors and friends shunned her. The cumulative effect of the unfriendly world surrounding her took its toll. She distanced herself from almost everyone, and she rejected others before they had a chance to reject her.

Reyna was a great go-getter. No one in our family was a match for her. I suspect that if she had been a man with the same talent, she would have been "forgiven" for her smallpox scars. But in the Babylonian Jewish community there was a double standard. It was acceptable for a man to have scars or to wear eyeglasses - no doors were closed to him. But a Jewish girl who wore eyeglasses was unlikely ever to get married because of this "blemish." To marry her off, her parents would have to literally buy a husband for her. Accordingly, nearsighted girls avoided wearing eyeglasses at all cost. They would stumble and fall, if that was what it took to hide their "blemish." Reyna couldn't hide hers - it was there for all to see, and she was brutally penalized for that.

When Jamila got married, Helwa, my parents' seventh child, became Mama's right hand. She got up early in the morning, prepared our breakfast and our lunches, washed the dishes and swept the floor, and then got herself ready to go to school. The night before, she had polished our shoes. She would line them up by the wall. "Here they are: the shoes of the army," she would laugh. Helwa has always been a clown and inveterate mimic, who brightened our family gatherings with witty impersonations.

Latifa was my parents' mischievous eighth child and my closest companion growing up. Latifa's original name was Doris. When she was a baby, she became very ill and my parents feared she was on the verge of dying. In desperation, they changed her name to Latifa. Their belief was that the heavenly decree of death is issued against a person as he is, with his name being an integral part of his person. By changing the person's name, the heavenly decree would no longer apply to him, and his life would be spared. Latifa didn't die.

In a family as large as ours, we children paired off and tended to be closest to the siblings nearest us in age. Valentine was my father's "old age child", the baby of the family on whom he doted. She was so much younger than the rest of us—six years younger than I —that she didn't have a special playmate in the family. But she was such a sunny, good-natured child—with exotic blond curls—that my sisters liked to take her to school to show her off. My sister, Jamila was present at Valentine's birth, where she witnessed just how deeply devalued girl children were among the Jews of Iraq. Boys were a parent's social security in old age, whereas girls grew up to marry and require dowries. Jamila told me she was aghast when she heard the midwife mutter an expletive at the sight of the infant girl, and declared that she wished she could put her hands around Valentine's neck and choke her to death.

Because there were so many of us, my parents didn't have enough time to fully accommodate the emotional needs of each child. Some of us who had special difficulties, particularly my sister Reyna, suffered from the lack of adequate attention. I know my father was aware of this, and I believe it tormented him. He was knowledgeable about psychology, and often reiterated with obvious regret his inability to give more time to us. Fortunately, Mama's even, gentle nature helped compensate. I owe my resilience and much of my self-confidence to her unconditional love and unrelenting message that I was special.

NO WAY BACK
The Journey of a Jew from Baghdad

My siblings and I were all born in a sprawling house in the older downtown section of Baghdad. Its design was typical of the old-style Jewish homes of that city. It was rectangular, built of brick with wooden columns and steel beams, and featured an open interior courtyard. The courtyard provided security; it was dangerous for Jewish children to play outside on the street. The second and higher-level floors were built around the perimeter of the building, and they had wide walkways that overhung the courtyard. Railings enclosed the walkways and stairs led up from the courtyard to the roofs, where we could stand by the balustrade and look down at the busy street below.

Courtyard, second floor and balustrade of a Baghdadian Jewish home identical in design to the home I was born in.
G. S. Golany, Vernacular House Design
(Or Yehuda, Israel: Babylonian Jewry Heritage Center, 1994).

Viewed from the street, large houses could appear deceptively small behind their high walls. Once my father took me with him to the Baghdad home of a friend and I was astonished to enter a vast interior wood where ostriches, peacocks, and all manner of other exotic birds were kept among tall trees.

The open architecture and hot dry climate invited all manner of unwelcome creatures inside. Like all houses in Baghdad, ours was infested with fat lizards, scorpions and, sometimes, snakes. Once, when Jamila was gathering wood to cook our Sabbath meal, she was bitten by a scorpion hiding in the woodpile. Another time, when I was very small, we found two huge spotted snakes in the house. The man we called to catch them refused the job when it became clear the snakes were mating. "Why do you want to separate them?" he said. "They are just having fun." I lived in dread of those snakes, for I had heard a version of the Adam and Eve story asserting that if a snake bit you on the heel it meant certain death. Ever after, I kept my feet tightly wrapped in a blanket when I slept, even in hot weather.

Exterior view of the houses in the neighborhood in which I grew up - Reyna, with our nephew, Ronny, on the Tigris' boardwalk near our home, 1949

When I was eight, my family moved to the more modern section of Baghdad. I remember Latifa saw the new house before I did. I also remember how excited she was by the prospect of moving.

"You will be so happy when you see the new house," she told me. "We ate sugar when we bought this house."

Babylonian Jews commonly used Latifa's expression of optimism whenever they embarked on a new enterprise. Every new deal was going to be a sweet one. For two days we shoveled sugar into our mouths at every opportunity, savoring the sweetness of moving to a new home.

The night before the move, my parents were up until all hours. They had received cash for the house they had sold, and they needed to count it. What made the task more onerous was that the money—the then-spectacular sum of around $25,000-- was all in one-dinar notes. The buyers transported the cash in a trunk to our new house—an unguarded treasure that could have vanished had robbers chosen that night to break in. The entire family—uncles, aunts, and grandmother—gathered at our home for a boisterous conference about how to safely carry these riches to the bank. After much argument, my uncles divided the money up in small bundles and took it separately to make deposits.

NO WAY BACK
The Journey of a Jew from Baghdad

Before surrendering the old, empty house to the buyer, my father and I went for a last visit. Baba walked into every room, stood silently, slowly moving his eyes over every corner, as if impressing it all to memory. He was quiet, and I didn't want to disturb him. But I realized what must have been going through his mind when we got to what used to be my bedroom. Here was where my bed had stood, and here was where my brother's bed had been. Here was the window through which the sun shone in the morning to cheer us all up, and there was the high ceiling on which the rain drummed during winter nights. It was cozy and secure in that warm room. There was a part of me that would never leave that house; was that how my father felt too?

Because cars and trucks were scarce, and of almost no use in the narrow streets of old Baghdad, laborers had to carry our furniture on foot to the new house. My grandmother had given my parents an enormous wooden chest about 8 feet by 3 feet in size. A Kurdish porter carried it on his back the entire mile or so to the new house. He was a small man, and was struggling for air by the time he arrived. I still can see the sweat dripping from the tip of his nose as he tried to untie the strap around his head to rest the chest on the ground. I just stood and gaped at him. Why did I not even bother to offer him a glass of water? I was the product of a culture that thought of the Kurds as less than human. Yet they were hardworking people – certainly unlike most other Iraqi Arabs, who tended to avoid strenuous physical exertion.

Our new home was actually two houses connected by a corridor. The back house was where the cooking and the laundry were done, but the front house was always immaculate. Rich Persian rugs covered the floors and the chairs in the salon. Though smaller than the old house, the new house was only yards away from the banks of the Tigris. From the front balcony, you could sit and watch the glittering river that played such an important role in our lives. At night the moon seemed to swim in the sky and in the water below. My mother would get up at dawn and watch the sun rise over the river. Sometimes when I sat with her, I wondered if she was thinking about how my father took her across the river during the flood before they were married.

In the spring, the Tigris rose to its full height, sometimes almost overflowing its banks. Looking at the swollen river flowing majestically under the trees, I was awed by its power, by the depth of its mystery. As the river rose, water filled our basement. I liked to think of it as a lake under our house. I used to drag one of our huge laundry tubs to the basement and launch my makeshift boat on our private lake. Using a broom handle to row, I tried to steer my vessel from one side of the basement to the other, and was frustrated when my tub only went in circles.

I told my grandmother about my exploits, and she laughed. "The water came into our basement when I was a little girl," she said.

"My father used to buy several turtles and put them in the water in the basement. He claimed it purified the water."

Although I loved to watch the mighty Tigris as it rose to its full height during the spring, I dreaded the perils associated with the rising river.

When the river threatened to break its banks, it was a dangerous time for men to be on the streets. At times like these, both old and young were pressed into service to stem the rising waters by diverting the flow into reservoirs. A great majority of these men were either Jewish or exceedingly poor. The military picked them off the streets and, under pain of death, compelled them to help with flood control. Sometimes the reservoir walls broke, and had to be repaired. The work was forced slave labor, never paid.

The floods also drew out hustlers, like the Muslim man who would offer to carry people across the street so they wouldn't get their feet wet. Midway across, he'd threaten to dump his passenger in the water unless he paid him more than what they had agreed on.

S'HAQ: OUR HIDDEN BROTHER

My brother S'haq was seven years older than I. He never teased me as my brother Jacob did or hugged me as my sister Jamila did. I remember him sometimes reaching out a hand to me as he muttered something unintelligible. S'haq couldn't speak. He was retarded.

When I think about him now, it is the pain in his eyes that calls to me. I wonder what sense S'haq made of his life, or if he could even think about himself in those terms. Did I imagine puzzlement on his face when he saw me playing backgammon with our father? He clearly was happy when the family sang and, with a big grin on his twisted features, he clapped his hands along with the rest of us. S'haq was part of our family, but he never appeared in our family pictures and I have no pictures of him. He exists only in my mind and in my heart.

My mother had conflicted feelings about S'haq. In addition to being retarded he was also an epileptic, a terrifying disease in those early years. Nobody knew how to treat it, and epileptics were shunned. The Babylonian Jewish community was known for its humanitarian leadership. For example, it established the School for the Blind, a school where students learned trades and received such a rich music education that many of them won leading positions in Baghdad's orchestra. But alongside enlightened attitudes stood the inconsistent and backward view that retardation and epilepsy were punishments from God visited on a family for some sin the parents had committed. S'haq, who had done no wrong, was a blot on our escutcheon and had to be hidden. When company came, S'haq was hustled away out of sight.

Families were large, and it was hard for the community to keep track of every single member, but news of S'haq's existence leaked out beyond our immediate circle. I was sitting in the salon one day when two hard-faced women we barely knew came to call. They sipped their tea, their lips speaking words of no account, their eyes watchful, and their ears alert. Finally, her patience at an end, one of them blurted out:

"We heard you have a crazy person living here."

My mother shook her head.

"There is so such person here."

I wonder how she felt as she denied her son's existence.

Mama and Jamila were responsible for S'haq's daily care. As he grew larger the task became more difficult. He was incontinent, and keeping him clean was a monumental task. My mother looked as if she were bent under the weight of the world when she cleaned him.

"Will this never end? I don't know how much longer I can deal with it," she would say, choking back tears.

Baba, equally despondent, devoted much time and energy to finding a cure for S'haq's condition. He dragged him from doctor to doctor, spending so much time at it that he postponed looking for a husband for Jamila until she was almost past marriageable age.

When S'haq was eleven, my father took him to a hospital in Jerusalem. The doctors there promised to see what they could do to cure his condition. Baba left him in the hospital and went to take care of his own business in Palestine. On his way to catch the bus back to Baghdad, my father stopped at the hospital to visit S'haq carrying several kilos of large sweet grapes he had bought in Jerusalem. S'haq fell on the grapes, devouring the whole bag. It was obvious that S'haq was either refusing to eat or being starved. Baba immediately dressed him and took him back to Baghdad.

While S'haq lived at home for the next six years, my father didn't lessen his efforts to find a doctor who would cure him. We never talked about S'haq outside the family; it was as though he didn't exist. But because Abboudi had died in infancy, S'haq was the oldest son, and my parents were known among close friends as Abu S'haq (S'haq's father) and Um S'haq (S'haq's mother).

When S'haq turned seventeen, my father took him to a Jewish hospital in Beirut. This time he returned home without my brother. The house felt different without him. I missed him sitting at the table with us while either Mama or Jamila fed him. I missed the strange sounds he sometimes made and the odd way he walked as he made his way around the house. I wondered how he felt being in a strange place, so far away from home and everyone he knew.

Three days after Baba arrived home from Beirut, a telegram was delivered from the hospital. All it said was "We're sorry." I learned about the telegram much later. No one told us about it at the time. I saw the stricken look on Baba's face that day and wondered what had happened. Mama's face crumpled as she turned away. Mama and several relatives who came in later that afternoon sat on the floor, a sign of mourning in Jewish tradition. Yet when we asked what had happened, the answer was, "Nothing."

I was confused. My parents seemed to be in mourning, but they never explained why. Gradually I came to realize that S'haq had died— he probably starved himself to death--but I was still afraid to ask my parents about my brother's death. Now I realize that a lot of confusion surrounded his death.

S'haq was seventeen years old when he died, but because he had not learned to speak, he was not seen as having reached the age of *bar miswah*. He had never taken his place as an adult within the Jewish community and, as such, the family was technically not supposed to sit *shib'a*, the traditional seven days of mourning, for him. Nor were my parents required to follow ordinary mourning rituals. Baba, however, chose to mourn S'haq's death fully. He wore a black tie for a year following his death—to work and to the synagogue, where he went every morning to say *kaddish* for S'haq. My parents mourned S'haq's loss; they mourned the man he had never become. They had never talked about him in life; how could they begin to talk about him in death? These days of mourning were a difficult time for them. But they were no less difficult for us children, who didn't know how to behave. A pall hung over the house, and we couldn't see beyond the fog of grief and sadness swirling around us.

One thing, however, was clear to me.

My father saw how S'haq's need for constant care was wearing down my mother, and felt it was up to him to relieve my mother of that responsibility. And so he had taken S'haq to Beirut. It broke my heart when, during this period of mourning, my mother, speaking from the depths of her grief and guilt, said of my father: "He rushed him to Beirut knowing that they would kill him." I believe Baba heard my mother's outburst, but he just turned away in silence. That is what I remember most from this period: Baba's silence. It seemed to me that my father's lips were closed forever.

S'haq is often in my thoughts. Before our first child was born, my wife and I decided to call the baby S'haq if it were a boy. My mother was upset. "It is an unlucky name in our family," she said. I suspect she was relieved when our first child was a girl, whom we named Aziza for my mother's mother. But even though my mother thought S'haq was an unlucky name, she refused to be known as Um Jacob (Jacob's mother) after my brother Jacob, who was her oldest son after S'haq's death. For years thereafter, Mama chose to be known as Um S'haq.

My siblings and I never speak of S'haq now. I believe that I am the last to hold him in my memory. When I donate prayer books to my synagogue I usually dedicate them to a loved one. Several carried this inscription:

In Memory of My Brother S'HAQ

DIED AT AGE 17

In A Hospital in BEIRUT AWAY FROM HOME AND FAMILY.

PROFESSOR J.DANIEL KHAZZOOM.

BABA'S COMPLICATED CHARACTER

I both respected and feared my father. His suffering as an orphan growing up in abject poverty undoubtedly accounted for his contradictory nature: On the one hand, a pious man of wisdom with a keen social conscience; on the other a father who swung from tenderness to cruelty with his own children.

I remember the nights he came home in the evening tired from a long day of work, and marvel at how he overcame his weariness to sit and play the *ood*, or lute, for us. We sang and clapped, happy to enjoy a musical evening with our father.

We used to play *tawlee*, or backgammon, with him, and he loved to be caught cheating. He took cards from the deck surreptitiously, or would upset the game board and rearrange it to his advantage. He cheated so brazenly that he invited discovery by us children, all the while affecting an innocent look. We clamored for payment of a penalty and he would oblige. But he never ceased playing his cheating game, even when he was advanced in years.

The good times, sadly, were tempered by my father's capricious, authoritarian nature, which kept me continually off balance.

Sometimes I felt close to him, like the times I'd put oil in his dwindling hair and played with it, making his hair stick close to his head or stand up in spikes. Then we would laugh together, and I was glad he was my father.

My own hair was thick and curly and I was proud of it. Sometimes my father watched me as I combed my hair in front of the mirror. I knew he was displeased with my vanity, but I never realized the depths of his disapproval.

One day I was at his office when he asked his messenger, Saleem, to take me to the barber. (I do not know Saleem's last name. It was the practice in Iraq for domestic, messenger, construction worker, etc. to be known only by their first name -- perhaps symbolic of their low social status. Saleem worked in my father's office for thirty years, and he was like a member of our family. Still none of us, except perhaps for my father, knew his last name – we knew him only as Saleem). I took no particular notice of the whispered consultation my father had with Saleem, but went to the barbershop trustingly. There, it was Saleem's turn to whisper in the barber's ear. It wasn't until the barber had taken off all my hair, leaving me nearly bald, that I realized what my father had engineered. When I went home, Mama was upset to see what had happened.

"Why did you do that to your hair?"

I didn't know what to say - that I was the victim of a cruel conspiracy my father had orchestrated? I went to the bedroom to look in the mirror. I ran my hand over my shorn head and wept. I felt violated.

L to R: Helwa, Valentine, Latifa; Daniel in back
Passport picture taken several weeks after my hair had been shorn

Two weeks later when school started, my hair had not grown back, and my schoolmates mocked and teased me. I tried to ignore the taunts, but deep inside I felt bitter and angry. My hostility was directed not at my schoolmates, but at my father, who probably had wanted to take me down a peg by asserting his patriarchal authority.

My father and I locked horns frequently and many times it ended in a beating for me. We were both strong-willed and had firm opinions. Neither of us was willing to yield, but my father was stronger than me. I refused to give in despite the beatings, and he punished me by not speaking to me for a week or so. I remember the Friday nights at *kiddush* time when I was being given the silent treatment. We ordinarily kissed our parents' hands on the eve of the Sabbath as a sign of respect. But on those nights, my father would push me away silently and refuse to let me kiss his hands. It took persuasion and intercession on my mother's part before I would be allowed to approach him. Did my father realize how terrifying and hurtful his silence and rejection were? I can only conclude that having no father of his own, he did not realize the terrorizing effects of his wrath on his children.

We struggled constantly over matters as trivial as my sneakers. Our school devoted only one hour a week to gym, at which time we were required to wear sneakers. I looked forward to that hour of physical exercise, but my father forbade me to participate, believing it distracted me from my studies. Still, on gym days, I always put on my sneakers and tried to leave the house without being seen. Occasionally I managed to get away with it. But my father knew me too well. Most of the time, he would wait inside the dining room door until I walked into the vestibule and reached to open the front door. Then he would appear, his face looking like thunder on a stormy day.

"Why are you wearing sneakers? Go back and put on your shoes. You are not allowed to participate in athletics."

I had no choice but to obey, but I didn't obey willingly. We fought repeatedly over my defiance of his ban. "I command you," he roared once. My face then was the one that was as black as thunder.

One particularly disturbing altercation occurred after a bus in which Reyna and Jacob were riding was rear-ended by a car driven at high speed by a member of a powerful family of Muslim multi-millionaires, the Orphalies. When the police arrived, Jacob truthfully described what had happened. Later, my immediate family and some uncles were sitting in the parlor when Jacob returned, looking proud of himself having done the right thing. As he stood explaining what had transpired, my father jumped from his seat, walked toward him and spat in his face. I can still see the terror in Jacob's eyes as he reacted to what was indeed an act of terror. Jacob had acted honestly and legally, just as my father would have. Perhaps my father was worried that our family would be the target of revenge by the Orphalies. Perhaps he needed to show his power in front of those present. In any case, it was a nauseating thing to watch.

Yet sometimes he surprised me. I was seven years old and in the second grade when my father made me a promise: "If you rank first or second in your class, I will buy you a watch."

I wanted that watch, and was terribly disappointed when I ranked eighth in my class. I looked at my report card and hated that eight written in bold script. Before I knew it, my finger went into my mouth and then I was erasing the eight and replacing it with a two written in second-grade script. My father looked at the report card and then looked at me. He could see what I had done, but he could also see how much I wanted that watch.

"I can see I have to buy you a watch, Daniel," he said.

And he did!

As I grew older, my father included me in activities and

expeditions that made me feel grown up. The language he wrote best was Turkish, but he had to write documents in Arabic, and those he asked me to go over and correct his Arabic or write the documents from scratch for him. Then he would brag to his friends and colleagues.

"See this document? My son Daniel wrote it for me. Doesn't he write with a fine hand?"

Another time he took me with him to view a piece of land he had bought. It was in an area inhabited by Bedouins. The Bedouins lived in tents, and I had never seen a tent before. When my father was talking to the man who had sold him the land, I edged closer to one of the tents and peeked inside. All of a sudden four or five enormous dogs appeared out of nowhere and attacked me. I was flat on the ground screaming in terror when my father rescued me. I was never so happy to feel his arms around me. He was my protector, just as he was every night when he barricaded our door against intruders. At times such as those I felt safe with my father.

Baba was a self-made man guided by enlightened ideas and principles, a man ahead of his time. In his public life, I remember his sensitivity to the plight of the poor, the less fortunate, and the rejects of society and his fights on their behalf. I remember his commitment to Jewish ideals, his service to the community, and his belief in equal education for boys and girls. It was from him, and later from my sisters, that I got my first lessons about women's dignity and women's rights.

My father was a man of strong principles. He never bought goods made in Japan during World War II. He bought goods made in England.

"The British are our friends, and I support them," he would say.

Sometimes people scoffed at him.

"What difference can one man buying British goods make?" they would ask.

"I stick to my principles," he would reply.

In 1926 my father was elected to the Babylonian Jewish community's civil council, *mijlis eljismani,* a body of unpaid community leaders that managed the civil affairs of the community. He was appointed the head of its education committee, which oversaw the Jewish school system.

L'Ecole de l'Alliance Israelite was part of an international network of primary and secondary schools established in Paris, and in Baghdad there was one *Alliance* for boys and another for girls. The Jewish community regularly sent messengers to France to recruit the finest teachers for the boys' *Alliance.* As an inducement to a prospective teacher, the candidate's wife might be offered a teaching post at the girls' *Alliance.* Some of the wives turned out to be excellent teachers. Others didn't.

Nine members of the Civil Council (with son of one of the Council members)
My father seated in front row, second from the left.

My father felt *l' Alliance* girls were being short-changed. He proposed that the two schools merge, thus giving girls and boys the same quality of education. This caused an uproar in the Jewish community. Several accused my father of undermining Judaism by advocating coeducation. When he insisted on the plan, my parents' home was cordoned off for nearly two months and there were threats on his life. But he didn't give in. My father was an observant Jew and had no intention of undermining Judaism. He simply saw injustice and wanted it corrected.

A compromise was proposed: Teachers at the boys' *Alliance* would devote half their time to teaching in the girls' *Alliance*. Since my father's interest was in ensuring an equally good education for all students, he agreed to the compromise. Unfortunately, when he left his position in 1928, the compromise fell into disuse, and practices reverted to the earlier system.

My father also fought against corporal punishment in the Jewish schools. On one occasion a teacher beat a student, and the student's mother reported the incident. The teacher was unrepentant. The education committee wrote to the principal recommending that the teacher be dismissed, but the principal, who agreed with the teacher, balked. Since the committee had no jurisdiction over the teacher as long as the principal was in place, the committee dismissed the principal and appointed the committee's chairman—my father--acting principal. In that capacity, he fired the offending teacher.

Once again, Baba had succeeded in stirring up the Jewish community. To many, the education committee's "harshness" was incomprehensible. But eventually most became reconciled to it. Corporal punishment never completely stopped. Incidents went unreported. But when a teacher was caught beating a pupil, it was understood by all that he or she risked dismissal.

I visited with my father in the homes of appellate and supreme court justices and was with him in the company of men of wealth and power. It was from him that I learned early on not to be cowed by titles or awed by wealth or social status, but to judge people by their character and humanity. It was by observing him defy bullies and speak out on unpopular issues that I developed the courage to stand up for my own beliefs.

Some of these traits had begun to rub off on me by the time I was 14, when I tangled with a renowned medical specialist. I developed swollen glands, and my father made an appointment for me with a Muslim doctor. This was unusual. We never went to see Muslim doctors because many were said to have received their doctorates fraudulently, and we weren't sure of their competence. But this one was reputed to be the best in his field. My father couldn't accompany me to the doctor on the day of the appointment and sent my brother, Jacob, with me.

"Explain your symptoms," the doctor said, addressing me in the Muslim dialect and peering down the length of his nose at me.

When Jews conversed with Muslims in Iraq it was understood that both would use the Muslim dialect. Muslims never stooped to use the Jewish dialect. For me, this practice screamed Muslim superiority, and I refused to learn the Muslim dialect. "The Muslim will speak to me in my own language," I vowed.

I then recited my symptoms in Judeo-Arabic.

"The glands on the back of my neck are swollen and they hurt when I touch them or turn my head," I explained.

The doctor shook his head, signaling he didn't understand. I detailed my symptoms again and again, but the doctor just kept shaking his head.

Judeo-Arabic contains Hebrew and Aramaic words and expressions that, to a non-Jew, are incomprehensible. Still, there was enough Arabic in our dialect that a Muslim can understand the gist of what is being said. But my doctor wouldn't admit to understanding a word. He continued to shake his head. Perhaps he felt it was an effrontery that I spoke to him in the language of the despised Jews, and was determined not to admit to understanding anything I said. But I was just as determined. He would admit to understanding my language or we would leave without his treating me.

And that is exactly what happened.

That night, on the roof of our home, where we slept on summer nights, Jacob gave vent to his anger, just as we were about to go to sleep.

"What got into you? Don't you know that you should have spoken to the doctor in the Muslim dialect? Baba had waited for this appointment for two months, and you blew it. You've wasted the visit. He is going to be so mad at you."

Jacob had me worried about Baba's reaction. The next morning when I saw my father he didn't seem angry. I even detected a glimmer of admiration in his eyes as he patted my head.

"You'll have to recover without the help of that doctor, son."

And indeed I did. The bumps in the back of my neck were gone of their own accord within a few weeks.

The charity commandment, or *sedaka*, was instilled in us children early, mainly through Baba's example. Once, a tailor who rented his store from my father took ill and was bedridden for weeks. He was young and had a large family. When the tailor came back to work, he stopped at our home to see my father. He was pale, had lost a lot of weight, and looked frail. He sat on the couch with a worried look on his face. In his hand, he held a quarter dinar bill, the equivalent of about $1.25. In a broken voice, he told my father he had intended to pay his accumulated rent, which I believe was close to ten dinars, but had only a quarter dinar toward what he owed. My father nearly broke down when he saw the tailor extend his hand to offer the small sum.

" I don't want any money," he said. "You don't owe me any money. Take the quarter dinar to your family and feed your children."

Having surmounted the poverty of his youth, my father tried to inspire others who were struggling to get by.

One time he met a friend walking with his wife on *rasheed* Street. He was an electrical engineer who had studied in Berlin and returned with his German wife to practice in Baghdad. The couple appeared dejected. The wife was pregnant; they felt they didn't have the means to support a child, and had decided on an abortion. They were on their way to the hospital, when they met my father and confided their plight to him. He told them, "Don't you know that when God sends a child, He sends his sustenance with him? You have nothing to worry about. Go home and welcome your baby when it is born."

The two looked at each other, looked at my father, then turned around and went back home. They had a baby boy. In time, the engineer's business picked up. He and his wife had more children. Once a year, on the birthday of their first-born son, the engineer and his wife took their son to visit my father, and they thanked him for changing the course of their life on that fateful day.

Occasionally, my father did pro bono legal work, including risky cases involving Jews suing Muslims on criminal charges. These were no-win situations. Either the Jew lost in court, or if he won, the Jew or his lawyer—or both—were subjected to violence; some were murdered. Jewish plaintiffs and lawyers weren't the only victims of such recriminations, but they were most frequently targeted. Not surprisingly, Jews seldom took Muslims to court on criminal charges.

One criminal case may have led to an attempt on my father's life. When he was waiting for a bus one day, a man with a knife attacked him. Baba wrestled his assailant to the ground and stood on top of him until the police came. When he arrived home he was bleeding and furious.

My father in court attire

We never learned the motive for the attack. The police didn't charge the assailant and released him without an explanation. We suspected the crime was an act of vengeance connected to Baba's legal representation of a victim in a criminal suit against a Muslim.

Although I wish my father and I had never butted heads, I suppose, given our temperaments and the generational gap, it was inevitable. But all that pales by comparison to what I now remember of my father. I remember him with much love. I remember my father more for his warmth and caring as a parent and for his commitment to enlightened ideas and principles as a human being than I remember him for his foibles and inconsistencies.

MAMA'S GENTLE STRENGTH

The foundation of my mother's relationship with my father was laid when she risked scandal to cross the Tigris with him during the flood before they were married. I believe that set the tone of mutual trust and caring the two of them shared throughout their life.

Considering the time and place, their marriage was one of co-equals. There was no community property in Iraq, and the family's home was normally recorded in the man's name only. Yet in my parents' case, house ownership was recorded in both names.

My father was responsible for our finances, but my mother was his trusted advisor on major decisions. During the early years of World War II, Baba invested a large sum of money in 100-kilo bags of sugar and rice. Three years into the war, sugar and rice became scarce, rationing was imposed and the price of these two commodities went up. I was present one evening when a friend of the family, a seasoned businessman, came to visit my parents. During the discussion, he urged my father to take advantage of the high commodity prices and sell his holdings of sugar and rice. Instead of responding to his friend, my father turned to my mother to listen to what she had to say. This was almost unheard of in Iraq, where men made the decisions, big or small, without consulting with their wives.

Many times I heard women in Iraq demur when it came to making a major decision—about their own or their family's lives. "I am only a woman," they would say. My mother, however, didn't shrink from asserting herself. There was a clear division of responsibilities, but outside of my father's legal work, I don't think Mama hesitated to exert her influence. When she wanted something she made her wishes known and as often as not my father would go along.

Mama was a wonderful homemaker. Baba never second-guessed her, never complained that she was buying too much, even though I know there were times when he couldn't keep up with all the expenses. Mama tailored her menus to Baba's likes and dislikes. The only times I remember him complaining about her cooking was when the chicken soup had too much tomato for his liking.

During the summer when school was out, we used to wait impatiently for the moment my mother poured the steamy, pearly rice out of the big pot in the late morning hours, uncovering the thick layer of crispy browned rice at the bottom of the pot. It was *h'kaka* time. Everyone took turns helping scrape out the *h'kaka* with an enormous spatula. Each of us children got a piece on a plate. Some of us poured soup over it to soften it; some ate it as is. There was utter silence. One could hear only the crackling sound as we cracked the crunchy *h'kaka* between our teeth.

There were nine of us to care for when I was growing up. And S'haq's illness added an extra burden. Still she made time to be with us, to tell us stories about her childhood, her family, and the old Baghdad of her youth. She taught us the songs that she had learned from my grandparents, and we sat and sang together.

She was sensitive about her lack of a modern education, and it distressed her when her *Alliance*-trained younger sisters came over to help us children with our French homework. Mama often told me how much she regretted not being able to help us herself. "I feel as if I am a useless piece of wood," she would tell me.

Mama devoted a lot of her attention to me, her favorite child. She felt I was special, and she conveyed the message in words and deeds. I loved being singled out, but sometimes it made me uncomfortable.

During the school year our lunch was usually cooked rice and chicken soup, with vegetables and desserts. I never liked chicken soup and would skip it. One day, Mama decided to cook a different chicken dish, just enough for me. For my siblings, she served the usual soup. Mama had an anxious expression when I came to the table. It torments me to this day when I think of the anxiety I must have caused her by being so finicky. Her face lit up when she saw me enjoying the new dish. Before long, Latifa complained that she didn't want to eat chicken soup either, but wanted what I was having. Mama told her there was enough only for me. Now I couldn't enjoy my meal knowing my sister wanted some. So I took half of what I had on my plate and put it on Latifa's plate. Mama beamed with admiration.

My mother never missed an opportunity to praise the positive she saw in me – a good deed, a gentle statement, an organized desk, or neat handwriting. I don't remember her ever criticizing me. When she pointed to a shortcoming, it was always with caring and love.

Mama was a lot more understanding of the needs of growing young men and women than my father was, and she shielded us from my father's wrath whenever we did things that Baba disapproved of. Muzli and Reyna often slipped out to the movies on Sabbath afternoons. That was a violation of the Sabbath and it would have infuriated Baba, but he never knew about it--Mama covered for them. Jacob blew out the kerosene-stove fire one Sabbath day. Muzli and Reyna were aghast; having anything to do with fire on the Sabbath is prohibited by Jewish tradition. But my father never got wind of Jacob's transgression. Mama kept everyone quiet.

Only once do I remember her giving me a spanking. It was in the "*omer*" period, between Passover and *sh'buoth*, when the weather changed unexpectedly from too hot to too cold, and from sunny to rainy. We called that period *omer* el *mijnoon*, the crazy *omer*. During *omer*, it was difficult to decide where we should sleep. Sometimes it was too hot to sleep in the bedroom, but many times when we took our beds to the rooftops we were rained out at midnight.

I must have been eleven on that particular *omer* night. I wanted to have my bed moved up to the rooftop. Mama felt it was too early to do so. It was hot, and I couldn't sleep. I kept going to her room to complain. After waking her up for the third or fourth time, Mama took me back to my bed, and gave me one swat, saying, "You sleep now!" I was taken aback. I never expected her to spank me, and I believe Mama was taken aback, too. She immediately put her arm around me and sat next to me in bed. I fell asleep. The next morning when she saw me she gave me a big hug and asked me if I had slept well. I grumbled. But we made up.

In 1944, when I was twelve, my mother suffered crippling stomach pains and was bedridden for weeks. Our doctor, *ammu* Guerji, diagnosed gallstones and told my father that she needed surgery. Baba wanted her to be hospitalized in Meir Elias Hospital, an institution maintained by the Jewish community. That it was costly was not a consideration, as far as he was concerned. He also wanted the finest in surgeons. *Ammu* Guerji had a colleague in London who specialized in gallbladder, and Baba flew him to Iraq to operate on Mama. By the time she had left the hospital, the cost had nearly exhausted my parents' assets.

Baba, Reyna, uncles, aunts and cousins accompanied her to the hospital. Although my brother and five of my sisters stayed at home, the house felt empty. It felt dark, even though it was daylight. I was out of my wits. Could Mama die? She told me that morning that she had seen her father in a dream the night before. He was dressed in white and held a twig of green myrtle in his hand, which he gave to my mother. Then he disappeared. Mama said she felt reassured. In the traditional interpretation of dreams, white meant peace, green symbolized life and, in the Babylonian tradition, green myrtle symbolized Elijah's blessing. Mama decided that Grandpa Silman was telling her that she would be safe and wouldn't die. But that was only a dream. What if she did die? What would I do?

A week later, Uncle Moshe took me to visit Mama in the Meir Elias hospital. I had never been to a hospital before. Meir Elias was a sprawling facility, surrounded by lush gardens that seemed to stretch for miles. As we walked the corridors, I was fascinated that the floors were made of some material—perhaps cork—that muffled the sound of our footsteps. Mama's large single room overlooked a beautiful field.

I walked toward Mama's bed. Her eyes were closed, and she had a big rubber tube implanted in her stomach that dripped a yellow fluid into a big jar attached to her bed. I learned later that the fluid was bile. Looking pale, Mama opened her eyes slowly. I wanted to run and hug her, but I was afraid I might hurt her or pull the tube out of her stomach. I stood still by her bedside and looked at her. She moved her left arm slowly and put her hand on my shoulder. It felt so good to feel her touch that I cried.

I visited her again two weeks later. She was sitting up, the pink had returned to her cheeks, and she had a smile on her face. A thin tube had replaced the big one.

This time I spent more time with Mama. She told me that when the anesthesiologist came to place the mask on her face, she asked him to wait. She lifted her right hand, covered her eyes, and recited the "*sh'ma yisrael*," the central prayer Jews are taught to try to make the last thing they utter before they die: "Hear O Israel, the Lord is one...." Then she turned to the anesthesiologist and motioned to him that now she was ready.

Unlike the quiet that prevailed during my first visit, this time the hallways near Mama's room were bustling with barefoot people dressed in Arab robes and turbans. Men armed with rifles stood guard at the entrance to the room next door. It seemed that the head of a tribe from Southern Iraq was hospitalized in the room next door. He had hauled the tribe's treasure with him, all cash, stacked in one big suitcase, which he kept under his hospital bed. The armed men were there to protect the suitcase.

The hospital prohibited firearms on its premises. But the sheikh didn't care, and no one could take him on without risking bloodshed. Later we learned from Meir Elias' administrator that, at the end of his treatment, the sheikh and his armed entourage left the hospital without paying the bill.

To my delight, Mama recovered, and all my fears proved unwarranted. She came home to be, as always, the heart and soul of our family, the center of it all. The household again hummed efficiently, thanks to her considerable administrative skill and boundless energy.

Mama oversaw the women who came every two weeks to wash our clothes. They were professional washerwomen who moved from house to house, their wrinkled fingers lifting the clothes in and out of the water, moving them from the washing tub to the rinsing tub, hanging them outside on the roof in the summer and inside in a special room hung with yards and yards of clothesline in the winter. A kerosene heater hastened the drying of the clothes in that room. Sometimes I peeked into that room. The sour smell of clothes drying inside was different from the fresh clean smell of clothes drying in the sun.

When the clothes were dry, my mother examined each piece for signs of wear and tear. It was then that the sewing machine came out, and I would be called upon to assist her. I was in charge of turning the wheel of the sewing machine, and I can still hear the click-clack of the machine and Mama's voice saying: "Turn the wheel now. Stop it. Stop now, Dannu."

Our society was not a throwaway society. We mended everything - clothes, shoes, and household items. A cousin of my mother's had his shoes repaired so often, adding sole after sole, that he unintentionally ended up adding a couple of inches to his height. When I first came to live in the United States, I had difficulty throwing away worn-out underwear.

We bought kerosene from a peddler who walked the streets

dragging a cart that held a large tank of the fuel. Mama often sent me out with a can to purchase the kerosene, and I watched the kerosene flow from the spigot in the tank into my can. We knew there never would be a shortage of that fuel. We used gasoline to clean clothes that couldn't be washed in soap and water. This cleaning was done in the courtyard.

I almost started a conflagration with kerosene when I was about ten years old. Mama left me to watch a fire she had started in a hibachi pot in the courtyard. She had doused the charcoal with kerosene, but the fire began to dwindle after she put me in charge. I decided to improve on matters by pouring additional fuel on the fire. The resulting blaze scared me half to death. Luckily, Mama was keeping an eye on me from the kitchen window. She rushed to pull me back from the wall of flames and held me in her arms. Silently we stood together watching the flames until they receded and the charcoal began to turn red.

It was Mama who supervised the annual production of date syrup, or *silan*. For this major undertaking, a specialized team of professionals came to the house carrying their big pots and heavy equipment with them. The dates were boiled in water until they were reduced to syrup. The syrup was strained and boiled again until it had thickened to the proper consistency. They extracted syrup from a variety of dates—one favorite of mine tasted like sweet persimmons, another like honey. We mixed the sweet *silan* with sesame paste as a dessert, spread it on bread, and poured it over omelets and pancakes. Most importantly, it was mixed with crushed walnuts to make *haroset*, what we called *hillaik*, for our *shettakha* (*seder*) table during the Passover.

There was so much to do to prepare for Passover, and Mama was at the hub of it all. The weather then could be changeable, but spring was in the air and we were relieved to finally come out of hibernation. A week or so before the holiday, we began to move beds to the roof in preparation for sleeping on the rooftop. All the dark, heavy drapes came down, and in their place we hung beautifully embroidered white curtains that wafted in the breeze. We replaced the Persian rugs on our sofas and benches with white embroidered covers. We didn't own a vacuum cleaner, so Mama always hired four or five Kurds to roll up the rugs and lug them up to the roof to shake out the dust. The job was hard even for a team of this size, for the rugs were extremely heavy. But in their usual fashion, the Kurds worked without a break until all the rugs were clean, mothballed and put into storage for summer. Mama spent the whole day under the searing sun on the rooftop, ready to lend a helping hand to the workers and making sure they had enough water to drink. When they were finished, the shiny white floor tile was exposed to view and our house was ready for summer.

Roses came to full bloom around Passover time. And it was the season to make rosewater, or *miwaghd*, for use in cooking. The week before the *miwaghd* was distilled, sacks of rose petals stood in the corner of our storeroom from which the smell of roses drifted out to permeate the house. When the team arrived with their distilling equipment, it was a momentous occasion. I watched the steam rise from the boiling water steeped with rose petals. The steam was condensed and the distilled rosewater was bottled for future use. The bottles stood on the shelf long after the perfume had faded from the house, but just looking at them summoned up the scent of roses. It seemed to me that the smell of rosewater was at the core of our lives, spilling its fragrance everywhere.

Mama always bought us new clothes for Passover. It was especially important that our new shoes squeak to demonstrate beyond doubt they were brand new. One of our neighbors had six boys, and they regularly passed by our house on their way to the synagogue. The father walked ahead and the children marched in a column behind him - nothing unusual, except during Passover they sounded like a marching regiment: One big pair of squeaky shoes followed by six other pairs, each with its own peculiar squeak.

On their holidays, Arabs bought squeaky new shoes, too. But more often than not, Arab men walked barefoot carrying their shoes, called *yamanee*, in their hands. They were proud of their *yamanee* and didn't want them to get dirty. Clean feet were not, apparently, a priority.

A week before the Passover, we baked our *massah*, thin round crackers of unleavened bread, twelve to fourteen inches in diameter. My mother, my siblings and I rolled the dough. Wearing a thick head cover and with hands and arms covered, my sister Jamila stood in front of a large wood-burning clay oven and stuck our thin-rolled dough directly on the hot walls of the oven. She pulled those that had already cooked and lay them on a large table to cool. We had to be careful not to bring food to our work area, for fear of getting the unleavened dough in contact with leavened food. On the eve of the Passover itself, we baked a dozen thick, soft *massah* for use on the *shettakha* plate.

Passover was a time for mutual visits and renewed friendship, and Mama oversaw the preparations for the occasion. Friends dropped in to wish us a happy Passover. My father, mother, and my siblings and I came out to greet them and join them in the living room. They sipped Turkish coffee we served in demitasse and munched on *masafan* (star-shaped marzipan), *hajji bada* (round shaped marzipan), and other goodies Mama had prepared for the occasion. We sat and chatted together. No one stayed long. There were too many families to visit. Sometimes it was a madhouse trying to keep the fresh Turkish coffee coming with every new wave of visitors or, as sometimes happened, with a bunching up of visitors.

Baba's greeting card
We left the card behind when the family we went to visit was out-
Card depicts a handshake with the biblical blessing "Happy Holiday"
and a personal blessing commonly used by the Sephardim "May You Be
Credited with Many Happy Years".

My own family's greeting card 5730 (1970)
patterned after my father's

We, too, went to pay visits to friends. Sometimes we ran breathlessly from one place to another trying to make the whole list. Most of the time we returned home exhausted. I still loved those visits. I enjoyed the sense of renewed friendship they elicited, and I loved to cross paths with the throngs of visitors, constantly coming, constantly going.

Those mutual visits were something special. They were unique to the holiday, and they did a lot to reinforce our festive feel of the day.

Some practices at the *shettakha* table are unique to Babylonian Jewry. We follow the kabala, or rituals Jewish mysticism, and break the *massah* into a large piece in the shape of the Hebrew letter *wow* and a smaller one in the shape of the Hebrew letter *daleth*.

The cutting of the *massah* was one of the highlights of the evening. We sat up straight, eyes fixed on our father's fingers, as he painstakingly cut the unleavened bread into the proper shapes. When he succeeded we all let out a triumphant cry, as he lifted each piece up high.

"Is this a *wow?*" he'd ask.

"Yea," we would all clap.

"Is this a *daleth*?"

"Yea," we would all scream.

Baba wrapped the wow piece in a large white linen cloth, tied the linen across his back and shoulder, and recited in Hebrew: "This is how our ancestors came out of Egypt - they hurriedly bundled what they possessed and carried it on their shoulders." Then he would run around the table to reenact the Israelites' hurried exodus, as we all shouted, "Go! Go! Quick! Quick!" He then untied the bundle, turning it over first to Jacob and then to me to follow suit. Being the youngest son, I got the honor of keeping the linen tied to my back until it was time to distribute pieces of the *massah* to everyone at the table. On the last day of Passover my father and I ritually took leftover *massah* to the fish in the Tigris. I laughed to see their gaping mouths appear like magic out of the water, waiting to be fed their *massah*.

We chanted the *haggadah,* or Passover story, both in Hebrew and Judeo-Arabic. The Babylonian Rabbis who fought fiercely over the ages against any encroachment of Jude-Arabic on the Hebrew liturgy made an exception (one of only three known exceptions) and allowed the translation of the *haggadah* into Judeo-Arabic to make sure that everyone understood what was being said and appreciated the miracle of the Exodus. But the Judeo-Arabic translation of the *haggadah* is anything but helpful. It is as opaque as they come, and it reads as if it were designed more to obfuscate than clarify. It doesn't help that the vocabulary is very old, dating back probably to the ninth or tenth century, and is replete with words whose meaning no one can understand any longer. Worse, the translators seem to have merely gone through the motion of translating. They never seem to have striven to convey the meaning, the thrust of what was being said. Words seem to have been slapped together without ever making sure the sentence made sense. But we still loved it. We relished every word of the Judeo-Arabic text and chanted it at the top of our lungs. I guess it was more the happy occasion than what we read or understood.

We took turns chanting the *haggadah* in order of age–first Jamila, the eldest, then Muzli, all the way to Valentine, the youngest. When Valentine had finished reading her portion, we started over. Some portions of the *haggadah* were lively and had beautiful tunes. But everyone hated the portion about the "*rasha*" the wicked son who disdains his traditions and ancestors. That portion followed another that portrayed the "wise" child who honors his heritage.

Since Jamila was the oldest, she always got to read about the wise child. Muzli, the second child, always got saddled with the portion about the despicable, contemptible, ignominious *rasha* - the wicked son. She protested bitterly but no one else would trade with her. She was the second child, this was the second portion, and that was it! So it went every year until Jamila got married and left the house to celebrate with her husband. Then Muzli became the first in the family. She got to read about the wonderful wise child!

Years later, my siblings and I gathered in Israel for Passover celebration. This time we shared the reading of the *haggadah*, not by birth order, but by our random seating order around the table.

It was all peaceful and pleasant at first. But wouldn't you know it – when it was Muzli's turn to read, what section did she draw? It was none other than that of the despicable, contemptible, ignominious *rasha*, the wicked son -- Muzli's old nemesis.

Muzli had a fit. Somber faced, she stood up, put on her sweater, picked up her purse, and got ready to walk out. My goodness, I thought! We needed to do something to keep *"shlom bayit"* – to keep peace.

It was then that my wife, Mairin, made her move.

"Don't go Muzli. Stay here," Mairin said calmly. "I will read the *rasha* portion. You won't have to read it"

Muzli looked incredulous, as Mairin started reading the *rasha* section. And then there was a big smile, maybe a triumphant smile, on Muzli's face. Muzli put down her purse, took off her sweater, and took back her seat at the table

And, to the relief of all of us, there was *shlom bayit* for the rest of the evening.

FAMILY CIRCLE

My siblings and I attended Jewish schools and all of our friends were Jewish. There were also a few Christian children, and occasionally some children of diplomats, but none happened to be in my class. My best friend was Abboudi Yousphan, whom I met on my first day in kindergarten and with whom I studied every year through my last year in high school. I had limited contact with the Arabs around us and, indeed, sought to avoid contact as much as possible. I dreaded violence and never felt safe in the presence of the Muslims who lived in our neighborhood. I was happy in my Jewish world and did not want to move outside it. I knew that in the poorer sections of Baghdad some Jewish children attended public schools, which were largely Muslim schools and, more importantly, free.

When Jacob attended the Royal College of Pharmacy, he was the only Jewish student in the college and he did make Muslim friends there. As it happened, his friendship with one Muslim fellow student served him well. When Jacob and his friend graduated, the friend's father bought a pharmacy for his son. The son hired Jacob to run the shop, gave him a free hand and paid him well.

My sister Helwa attended a convent school during her last two years of secondary schooling. The school happened to be within a five-minute walk from our home. The hours my sister would have spent commuting back and forth to Shamash school, a downtown Jewish secondary school, she spent doing household chores. Helwa, however, did not make close friends in her new school, though I do think it was Helwa's nature to stay within the family circle. Latifa's friends from school, all of them Jewish, often came to visit, filling our salon with girlish laughter or taking Latifa with them for extended walks by the river. Muzli's friends, on the other hand, often formed a knitting circle as they sat together discussing the latest movies or listening to Egyptian music.

We were a large family and, in the main, our social interactions were with each other and with members of the extended family. Every Saturday evening when *shebbath* was over, we gathered at my grandmother's house to drink tea, munch on pastries and other goodies, and listen to stories from the elders of our family. Extended family gatherings were the focal point of our social life. My cousin Abboudi, though younger than I, was one of my special friends. Every day one of my uncles or aunts dropped in for a visit. We children were always welcome in our aunts' and uncles' houses, too, where hospitality and kindness warmed our hearts.

Many Jewish men in Baghdad spent their leisure hours in all male coffee shops and clubs, playing domino, backgammon or billiard, but not Baba. He turned to the family for most of his social interactions. Most of his friends were drawn from the leadership of the community, and the subjects of discussion were generally serious.

We paid my father's Muslim friends formal visits on Muslim holidays to wish them joy. These friends were all Sunnis, all from the legal field, and among them there were two Appellate judges and two justices of the Supreme Court. Usually I, and sometimes Jacob as well, accompanied my father on those visits. The visits were short, lasting no more than ten or fifteen minutes. The only exception that I can remember was our visits to appellate judge alOrphali, which sometimes lasted as long as two hours. A tall, soft-spoken middle-aged individual, Judge alOrphali received us in his huge, beautifully furnished parlor. I do not remember any time we visited when the parlor was not at least half full with visitors and well-wishers. Every now and then, a house servant would walk in with a glittering golden pot full of freshly brewed Turkish coffee, to make sure no one would sit with an empty cup in front of him. What I loved most about our visits with Judge alOrphali were the subjects discussed – never small talk, always serious legal issues that made me think, and usually a quiet, thoughtful exchange of ideas. I used to look forward to our visits with Judge alOrphali, and always felt enriched as we left.

I don't remember any visits with Shiites and have no recollections of Shiites being friends with my family. Any Shiite I knew considered Jews to be unclean and would never eat or drink from dishes used by Jews, no matter how well these dishes were washed. If a Shiite accidentally brushed against us in the street, he cursed us. One Shiite told a school friend of mine: "The clay the Jews are made of is dirty. Nothing can make a Jew clean."

Our visits with my father's Muslim friends never blossomed into deep family friendships. Occasionally we had a Jewish friend visit us with his wife and children or join us with his family for a meal on a Jewish holiday, and they in turn reciprocated. But interactions with my father's Muslim friends never reached this level. It was as if there was an invisible red line that was never to be crossed – up to here and no more. Why was that? Was it because we lived in a society where people's first commitment was to their sect rather than to people outside the sect? Was there fear of getting too close and opening oneself up for betrayal by a friend from another sect or ethnic group? Or was it the Muslim's circumscription that women were not to be seen without a veil? I do not remember the wives or daughters of any of our Muslim friends ever joining our hosts in welcoming us on our visits, nor did Mama accompany us to Muslim homes. In direct contrast, our social interactions within the Jewish world included women.

The dietary laws that prohibit a Jew from eating food that is not *kasher* could have been another impediment. The only time from my childhood that I remember having dinner in a non-Jewish home was when we visited a Christian family from Baghdad that Mama had met in Beirut. While our hosts had a full meat dinner that evening, we munched on watermelon cuts only – and even with that we were not quite comfortable, knowing that the knives we used to slice the watermelon might have been used one time to cut non-*kasher* meat. It was so awkward that we never met again, though we liked our Christian friends and they seemed to like us too.

My connection with a British Christian family in Baghdad came about when the parents hired me to tutor their three daughters in math. Regrettably I no longer remember their names. I enjoyed my time with the girls and I was impressed with how courteous all three were. Their parents always made me feel welcome in their home, but I didn't eat with them. I do remember them inviting me into their parlor to see their Christmas tree. It was artificial and just a couple of feet tall, but it was ablaze with flickering candles and shiny ornaments. I can still see the family, their faces shining, huddled around that tree and I remember feeling a special kinship with them. They had created their own island of peace and were just as isolated from the culture surrounding them as we were, strangers in a land that could never be theirs.

HEARTBREAK AND MARRIAGE

As the next to youngest child, I was often perplexed by the family dramas unfolding around me, particularly when it came to my older sisters and matters of the heart.

In the summer of 1939, Baba arranged for Mama, Muzli, Reyna and Jacob to spend the summer in Beirut. He felt that a change of scene might help cure my three siblings of a chronic stomach ailment that was afflicting them. Beirut was known for its beauty, its gorgeous mountains, and its majestic view of the Mediterranean. Uncle Moshe, who accompanied my mother and my siblings on the trip, wrote to us fairly regularly about the great time everyone was having in Beirut.

When they all returned home at the end of August, I peppered my sisters and brother with questions.

"What is it like in Beirut?" I asked.

Reyna and Jacob merely shrugged, but the light in Muzli's eyes could have lit up the world. She danced around the house, clapping her hands to the music emanating from the radio.

"It was wonderful, wonderful! Beirut is wonderful!"

Later I went to my mother.

"Why is Muzli so happy?"

My mother looked up. All she would say was that Muzli lived in a dream world and wouldn't be happy for much longer.

"We have to follow the traditions. Muzli has to understand that. What would happen to Jamila if Muzli were to get married before Jamila?"

It was very puzzling, but, as usual, it was Latifa who explained it all to me. She was only ten months older than I, but her eyes and ears missed nothing. We were together in the courtyard pumping the spinning top my mother had brought me from Beirut.

Latifa tapped my shoulder.

"You know why Muzli is so happy?"

"No," I replied.

"Do you want another turn with the top?"

I was feigning disinterest, for I knew Latifa would have to be coaxed to tell if she realized how badly I wanted to know.

"Never mind the top," she said impatiently. "When Mama, Muzli, Reyna, and Jacob were in Beirut they used to go to a café to spend the evenings. There, a man from Jerusalem used to join them to play cards. But he really was not interested in cards--he was interested only in Muzli. He wanted to marry her. And Muzli liked him, too."

"Muzli is getting married? Will she be going to Beirut? I would like to go to Beirut, too."

Muzli, right, and Reyna, left, by a waterfall in Beirut, 1939

"No, silly. Jamila is older than Muzli and she isn't married yet. Mama wouldn't allow her to get married before Jamila."

Latifa went back to spinning the top. I went back to my mother.

"Is it true that someone wanted to get married to Muzli in Beirut?"

"Yes," Mama explained. "But I told him that he couldn't marry Muzli because Muzli is younger than Jamila. If we let Muzli get married first, people will think there is something wrong with Jamila, and nobody will want to marry her."

"And what happened?"

"He kept coming back," Mama continued. "And I told him the same thing every time he asked to marry Muzli."

My mother looked proud of herself for sticking to tradition.

"And what happened to the man?"

"I don't know. He probably went back to Jerusalem."

Muzli's smile faded as the days went by. She talked wistfully of her time in Beirut, but she never talked about the man.

Twelve years later, Muzli married Naim. Years after that, when we were sitting together in a park near Muzli's home, she told me sadly about a dream she had the night of her wedding. The man she had met in Beirut appeared in a dark alley holding a kerosene lamp. There was no one else in the alley – just the two of them. He walked slowly toward Muzli. He had a sad look on his face. He stopped in front of her, raised his lamp and took a long look at her face; said nothing. Then he turned off the lantern and vanished in the dark.

Our community's rigid insistence that daughters be married off in order of age—oldest first—was but one of the harsh marriage customs that cast a pall over my family for years, as pressure mounted to find husbands for my sisters. Unmarried women were not highly regarded by

Babylonian Jews. Marriage bestowed respectability and desirability on a woman. The families of future husbands often took advantage of the situation and demanded huge dowries from the bride's family— humiliating for the women and often reducing their families to penury.

Marrying off a daughter imposed strictures on the bachelors, too. Bachelors were expected to postpone marrying until all of their sisters were married off. Otherwise, rumors would spread that the single sister was unmarriageable, that she had a "blemish." Bachelors also were expected to pay their sisters' dowries when the father was deceased or didn't have adequate funds. My maternal uncle, Sion, never married. By the time his youngest sister, my Aunt Nazeema, was married off, Sion was in his fifties and considered himself too old. He died not long afterward. I mourned his life, and what his surrender to those traditions had done to him. He was a compassionate man and would have made a loving husband and a nurturing father.

My parents had married for love and by mutual agreement. There was no dowry and no talk of money. They had always impressed on us children that it was demeaning to make marriage conditional on money. But then I watched as they suffered through the despised dowry and bargaining route, in order to get Jamila married off. I resented what it did to them and to Jamila. I resented it no less when it was time to find a mate for Reyna.

Uncle Moshe oversaw the search for Reyna's husband after they had immigrated to Israel, because my parents had stayed behind in Baghdad. The months went by, but whenever a match seemed near at hand, the deal fell through - either because of Reyna's smallpox scars, or the prospective bridegroom's demands for horrific dowries, which were probably not unrelated to the smallpox. Reyna was hurt. She wept and stopped eating.

And then the inevitable happened. Helwa and Latifa, who were younger than Reyna, met men they wanted to marry. I supported them in their plans to marry before Reyna. Reyna was hurt by this, believing that if her younger sisters married ahead of her it would dim her own chances of marriage. Because I so despised these outlandish rules, I was dismissive when Reyna broached the subject with me, and I very much regret that now. I wish I had been more understanding of her plight.

Helwa and Latifa went ahead and married before their older sister. Then Reyna met a man she liked, the first one she had ever opened up to. Like Reyna, he had been afflicted with smallpox as a child. Reyna fell in love, and they talked about getting married. But his parents forbade the match unless our family came up with an exorbitant dowry. The couple stopped seeing each other and Reyna was heartbroken. I believe the young man cared for Reyna, but lacked the backbone to stand up to his parents. He wrote Reyna a letter after their breakup, and addressed the envelope to "Reyna Khazzoom the Precious."

Not long after the breakup, we learned that he was scheduled to marry a woman his parents had found for him. But the story had a tragic ending. On the day of his wedding, he got out of his taxicab to cross the street. A car ran a red light and struck him. He died that night. Reyna sat in mourning. She withdrew more into herself.

I believe that was the only man she ever loved.

Two years later, Reyna married Saleh, a soft-spoken mailman. It was arranged marriage. Reyna and Saleh had a son, Gideon. For a while she seemed happy—her in-laws adored her, and made no secret of the fact they felt honored to have their son marry into our family. But Reyna's relationship with Saleh quickly deteriorated. They remained married, but led the life of two divorced people under the same roof. Reyna wouldn't consider divorce, for fear she would never remarry.

Heartbreak aside, the dowry system - and the enormous financial stakes involved - sewed discord and treachery within families, including ours. Jamila's marriage to Ezra Hay was arranged in the late nineteen forties, and my father promised that she would have a dowry of five thousand dinars, the equivalent of $25,000. However, the money that Jamila spent on her trousseau and furnishings for her new home could be deducted from the total. Because of this, Jamila had to keep a strict accounting of every penny she spent.

No sooner was Jamila's marriage arranged than my father gave her money to go shopping. It was then that my manipulative aunt, *khala* (maternal aunt) Toya, stepped in. She volunteered to help Jamila select a trousseau.

"And now a dress for me," *khala* Toya would say to Jamila as they browsed in a store. "Your father can well afford it."

My father had always disliked *khala* Toya, considering her a troublemaker, which indeed she was. But I don't think even he knew the extent of her perfidy. Jamila was unable to refuse her, even when *khala* Toya bought wedding clothes for her sons with my father's money. Jamila was afraid to confess to my father: How could she tell him that *khala* Toya had appropriated the money, without creating deep divisions within the family and casting a dark shadow over the coming wedding?

Later, I overheard my father and Jamila going over her trousseau account.

"Jamila, what has happened to you?" he scolded. "What has happened to the money? I gave you one hundred dinars yesterday, and you can only account for seventy. I want you to have the best that money can buy, but this is money for which I must account to Ezra's family. If you can't account for the missing money, I will have to make it up when I hand over your dowry. Did you lose it? Are the bills incorrect? Were you cheated by some wily merchant?"

I could hear the despair in Jamila's voice, as she twisted her skirt between her fingers and looked at the ground.

"I will do better, Baba. I am really sorry."

"Do try, Jamila."

But every time Jamila went shopping it was the same story, and I grew to hate *khala* Toya when I heard Jamila stammer her excuses to my father.

In Iraq, children lived with their parents at least until they got married. When daughters married they often remained in close proximity to their parents. In the old section of Baghdad, some parents bought newlyweds a house across the street from their own, and built an enclosed bridge to connect the two residences. One family who lived in a huge house across the street from us had four of their married sons with their wives and children living with them in the same house.

When Jamila got married, the nuptial agreement stipulated that my parents rent a house for her in our neighborhood where her husband Ezra, his parents, his five brothers and his sister would come to reside with the newlyweds. My parents paid a huge sum of money for the rent. Jamila's in-laws paid nothing. They occupied six rooms and the whole first floor in the house. My sister and Ezra occupied only two small rooms.

HARD BARGAINING

In our Baghdad neighborhood, we were surrounded by family. All my aunts, uncles, cousins and grandmothers lived within a radius of a few blocks. And for the most part, the extended family pulled together. In our world, women never shopped for fruits and vegetables; the men folk did that. But in our family, it was Uncle Moshe, and not my busy father, who did our shopping.

Every evening Uncle Moshe would make a list of what my mother needed him to buy at the market the next day. He usually hired an Arab porter to help him carry his purchases. Often, he'd buy a dozen or so watermelons for us. They were placed in a large cloth, knotted into a bundle, and one end of the cloth was tied around a porter's head so that he could carry them. My uncle walked by the porter's side to ensure the watermelons reached their destination safely. There was the assumption that one or more of them might be sold en route to passers-by on the street.

My uncle was a commodities broker. The Baghdad market was a loose, unruly system. My uncle had a list of merchant clients who wanted to buy or sell certain commodities and he generally knew where to find the potential seller or buyer. He served as the intermediary to arrive at a mutually acceptable price. Usually this involved shuttling back and forth many times between all the parties involved, using every trick in the book to cajole, pressure, plead and haggle to seal the deal.

He never went to work before eleven on any given day; his mornings were spent marketing for us. I remember times when he said he had a hot deal and would have to go to work early (still meaning no earlier than nine a.m.). On those rare occasions, he didn't do the daily purchases for us.

His partner often called us in the mornings, looking for Uncle Moshe, saying he needed to finalize a deal and wanted Moshe's extra push. But Uncle Moshe was busy doing our shopping. The partnership didn't last. Apparently Uncle Moshe still made enough to live comfortably with his wife, *khala* (maternal aunt) Guerjiyi, my mother's older sister. They didn't have children and lived alone in a huge house. Uncle Moshe was our second father, as we were his surrogate children.

The only shopping for food my mother did was from street peddlers. If, for example, she ran out of tomatoes, she would hail one of the peddlers. Then the fun—the inevitable ritual of haggling --would begin. My mother would point to the tomatoes she wanted, and the peddler would place them on one side of his scale, with a large stone on the other side.

"Just two kilos," he would tell my mother, holding out his hand for the payment.

My mother would shake her head.

"No! No! I want you to use proper weights."

It was the peddler's turn to shake his head, as he stared at my mother, amazed and outraged by her request.

"By Allah I swear, this stone weighs exactly two kilos."

"I'm sure it does, but I still want you to use proper weights," my mother would insist.

In the end, my mother won -- the peddler producing his weights but still raising his eyes to heaven, his arms thrown wide to emphasize his outrage at his honesty being questioned, and by a woman at that.

We never bought *laban* (yogurt) on the street, since my mother always made ours. But the Arab women who sold it fascinated us. The *laban* was packed into huge tubs about two feet in diameter, and the *laban* sellers carried these containers on their heads. Even my father was mesmerized by the ability of these women to walk and run with the tubs on their heads and, as often as not, a baby strapped on their backs. I remember one day Baba shaking his head in disbelief as he counted twelve tubs on one woman's head.

As a sanitation measure, our unpasturized milk was always boiled as soon as we brought it into the house. Once when I was four years old, I spotted a jug of newly boiled milk covered with muslin on the kitchen table. The steam was escaping through the muslin, and I wanted to investigate. I pulled on the tablecloth to help me climb on the table. Before I knew it, I was covered in boiling milk, and the jug lay in pieces on the floor. My skin was blistered and everyone in the house was near hysterics.

We bought our milk from Arabs who lived in settlements about eight blocks from our house. Usually one of my sisters and I walked there carrying our own bottles with us, bottles into which the cows were milked directly via a funnel. Sometimes the cow wouldn't let the milk down, and a calf was put to the cow's teat to induce her to give milk. As soon as the milk began to flow, the calf was pushed away from its mother. Even though we were waiting for our milk, my sympathies were all with the hungry, lowing calf.

Many of the Arabs who owned the cows had several wives. I remember one man in particular who had two wives. The first was extremely plain, and she was the one who milked the cows. His second wife was young and beautiful. I still remember her name – Shamsiya. I could see how much the man valued Shamsiya. Everyone in the settlement knew she was her husband's favorite. I felt sorry for the sullen, silent first wife, who had to do all the work. Then one day I realized neither woman had an easy life.

My sister Latifa was with me, and we were watching the first wife milk a cow. Suddenly a woman's screams rang out in the quiet evening air. I was frozen, as I watched the Arab repeatedly kick and beat up his young wife, who was on the ground trying to protect herself with her hands. I thought the first wife might interfere. But she looked terrified, and continued milking. I was horrified.

"What happened?" I asked Latifa.

"The young woman had just walked out of the hut, where she had left her young son asleep. The baby woke up and began to cry, just as the husband appeared on the scene. The husband is beating up the mother for not taking better care of his son."

I was incensed by the man's cruelty.

Latifa shook her head.

"There's nothing we can do about it."

I clenched my hands into tight fists even though I knew Latifa was right.

"Just be happy Mama doesn't have to put up with a husband who beats her," I thought to myself.

That night, as my mother tucked me into bed, I said:

"Aren't you glad you're not married to an Arab?" My mother smiled.

"You say the strangest things, Dannu. I couldn't be married to an Arab. I'm Jewish, and Jews don't marry Arabs. Go to sleep now."

In our family we distrusted the Arabs and seldom did business with them. One day when I was five, we heard a big commotion outside one of the tailor's shops on the first floor of our house. I went up to the third floor to watch what was happening. A big crowd had gathered outside the shop. In the thick of it stood a brawny Muslim holding a suit in his hands, screaming at the tailor, whom he had apparently dragged into the street. The tailor looked frail and his eyes spoke of terror. The Muslim slapped him and seized him by the throat and shook him hard. The tailor's eyes began to bulge in his head and I screamed for my mother.

"Mama, he's killing him. He's killing him."

My mother joined me at the window and put her arm around me.

"It's how they cheat," she said softly.

We learned later that the Muslim had ordered a suit from the tailor a few weeks before a religious holiday. He had chosen the cloth from some the tailor had in stock and had agreed to pay for both the material and labor when the suit was ready. When the suit was finished and the time came to pay, the Muslim claimed the suit was not to his liking.

"Doesn't the man know the tailor would have fixed the suit to the Muslim's liking?" I asked.

"Of course he does," my mother replied, "but it's not what the Muslim wants. He wants a suit without having to pay for it."

We both watched as the Muslim shook the tailor one more time, spat in his face and threw him forcefully to the ground. I flinched at the sound of the tailor's body hitting the ground. Then I saw the Muslim put the folded suit under his arm and walk away.

This was but one of many instances of Muslims exploiting Baghdad's Jewish community. When I was older, I once bought a new Passover suit from a Muslim shopkeeper who didn't have a fitting room in his store. He assured me that I could return the suit for a refund if it didn't fit. When it turned out to be too small and I took it back, he refused to give me my money back.

The tensions between Muslim and Jew were a constant of my boyhood. I especially hated Ramadan, a sacred month of fasting in the Muslim world, for that was the time of the frightful drumming.

Daily, in the wee hours of the morning, men would walk the streets beating drums so that people would wake up to eat and recite their prayers before dawn. Everyone was supposed to be awake at that hour, whether or not he was a Muslim. The relentless, frightening rhythms were the same as those played for Muslim funeral processions. While the drummers were walking the streets and filling the airwaves with their beat, the muezzin, or cleric, would ascend to the top of the mosque's minaret and call the faithful to prayer. In the din, I would lie awake, staring into the darkness, anxiously awaiting the pale morning light.

The Muslim calendar is lunar, so Ramadan can fall during any season of the year. The worst time was when it fell in the summer and our beds were on the roof. No one got much sleep then. The calls and drumbeats began even earlier than in the winter. The fact that Jews and Christians constituted over a third of the population of Baghdad and didn't pray in mosques was of no import.

That reasoning applied to other Ramadan constraints as well. When I was about thirteen, a Jew was arrested for smoking in the street during Ramadan. He was brought before a judge the following day. When told of the so-called crime, the judge raised his eyebrows in horror.

"How dare you? Don't you know that smoking in public during the month of Ramadan is forbidden?"

The judge went on to preside over the case, as the smell of the cigarette on which he was puffing filled the courtroom. The month of Ramadan had not ended at the time.

SABBATH IN BAGHDAD

The Sabbath and the annual cycle of Jewish holidays imparted calm amid danger and drew us closer together in the safety of home and synagogue. Whether during joyous feasts or solemn liturgy, I could picture Jews all over the world being blessed as we were, and felt a connection with every Jew who had gone before us. Even though the practices of Babylonian Jewry differed radically from Ashkenazi Jews, the events we celebrated were the same. It was a long, unbroken chain that linked us one to another.

Preparing for the Sabbath
Baker taking baked Babylonian flat bread out of the clay oven.

On Fridays, the coming of the Sabbath was in the air—in the throngs crowding Jewish bakeries early on Friday morning, in the bustling Jewish barbershops, in the brisk business at candy stores, in the early closings of the textile market and other Jewish shops. Smiling people radiated happiness. The day of rest was around the corner.

Every Friday morning, our classes dedicated the first few minutes to collect *sedaka*, charity, from the students. Sharing our blessings with others was a lesson instilled in us from my *asile* days. Baba would give me a small daily allowance to spend in the school canteen. He never made it a condition, but he always reminded me to set aside part of my allowance to donate at *sedaka* time.

On Friday evenings we celebrated the *kiddush*, a ceremony of welcoming the Sabbath, which began with the lighting of the *kerayee* at sundown. The *kerrayee*, a glass bowl filled with sesame oil and water, hung from the ceiling on three silver chains. A silver Star of David, into which fitted seven homemade palm wicks, nestled on the bottom of the bowl. In the winter, when the sun set early, and we wanted the flame to last several hours into the evening, my mother used more oil than water. In the summer she used more water than oil.

Mama set up the *mady*, as the festive table was known, laying out the customary Babylonian flat bread: four round pieces, each about fifteen inches in diameter laid in pairs back to back so that it seemed there were in reality only two pieces. This method, which was done to simulate the type of bread configuration used in the Temple, is unique to Babylonian Jews. Mama placed the full saltcellar beside the bread, covering the bread with an embroidered cloth. Then she filled the *kiddush* cup with grape juice and set it on the table next to a big bunch of lush green myrtle ready for the *kiddush* ceremony.

Standing in front of the *kerayee* and watching it being lit was a spiritual experience that deepened as I grew older. It evokes in me a sense of peace and fellowship, transporting me beyond the everyday to a new world where tension has melted away. Once Mama had lit the *kerrayee*, my father and I, sometimes my brother and I, headed for Meir Elyahoo synagogue, one block from our home. Services were held whenever a *minyan*, a quorum of ten men, had assembled. Successions of *minyan*eem were formed, as soon as ten men showed up. Each *minyan* met in a separate room in the sprawling Meir Elyahoo building.

There is a Jewish tradition that when the Sabbath arrives at Friday's sundown, every Jew is endowed with an additional soul for the duration of the Sabbath. The added soul, it is said, raises the Jew from the vale of woe, opens a new wonderful world for her and lifts her spirits.

Standing next to my mother, Baba held the *kiddush* cup and recited the traditional prayer to sanctify the Sabbath, just as God had sanctified the day. We all drank from the cup of grape juice, but beforehand we kissed our parents' hands, a sign of respect in the Middle East that always rekindled my connection to our parents.

kerrayee – Babylonian Menorah for Sabbath and holidays.
A replica of my parents' kerrayee, made in Ghana

Babylonian synagogue in Ramat Gan, Israel, patterned after the Babylonian synagogues in Iraq.
The tebah, lectern, is where the services are conducted.
The seats, (covered with Persian rugs) on the tebah are for the elders of the community.
Covered with curtains upfront, the hekhal, Ark of Law, is where the torah scrolls are kept.

NO WAY BACK
The Journey of a Jew from Baghdad

My parents' *kiddush* cup was given to them by my maternal grandmother when they married. At one time, the cup's lid was crowned by six branches, on which a dove of peace perched. With the rise of Arab nationalism in the 1940's, the Iraqi authorities treated any Jew who possessed a Star of David or any other six-cornered object as a traitor. When midnight searches of Jewish homes turned up such items, the penalty for "Zionist sympathies" was a minimum seven-year jail term. So my father had a silversmith remove the six branches. That left the dove wobbling atop the lid—an apt reflection of our shaky situation in Iraq.

My parents' kiddush cup

Every Friday morning, Mama got up while stars were still out to prepare the bountiful meal for that night. There was always *kibba*, a ball of dough made of ground rice stuffed with ground meat, vegetables and cardamom and cooked with mutton or chicken; fried *shibboot*, fish that abounded in the Tigris; and our favorite crispy potato pancakes filled with ground meat, vegetables, lots of raisins, almonds, walnuts and condiments.

We bundled up in the cold winter nights before we sat for *kiddush,* for we didn't light a fire on the Sabbath, as stipulated in the *torah.* For extra warmth, fun and love, we huddled around Mama, burying our hands under her thick furry *robe-de-chambre* and in her armpits. Immobilized, she would laugh and protest, "What are you doing to me, children? I can't even move." Baba wore his camel-skin cloak to keep warm. I remember when I was three or four, I used to sit on his lap at dinnertime and snuggle inside his thick cloak.

For an hour or more we sang *sh'bahoth*, the Sabbath paeans. Then it was time for the *nimnamot*—treats like nuts, roasted watermelon seeds, sheets of dried apricot, and *louzeena* (a diamond-shaped confection made of quince or orange peel cooked in sugar and sprinkled with ground nuts or coconut); *h'lawa* (halva); *sha'ir elbanat* (literally meaning, girls' hair – a crispy confection made of thin strings of halva) and the ever-present *simismiyee* (sesame bar). Often Baba or Uncle Moshe would come home on Friday afternoon loaded with Sabbath treats.

Our father was a good storyteller, and *nimnamot* time was also the time for listening to his stories. He had us wide-eyed and on the edge of our seats with his tale of escaping conscription into the Turkish army during World War I. His plan was to head for British-occupied Basra in the southern part of Iraq. He set out from Baghdad on foot, traveling through primitive tribal areas. At one point he got passage on a riverboat, where a Muslim cleric spotted him as a Jew. When they pulled into port, the cleric told local tribesmen, "There's a dog on the upper deck—get him." My father was rounded up with some other Jewish passengers and marched in a column to a clearing where they were about to be shot. The tribesmen fumbled the job—they attempted to use one bullet to shoot the entire line of prisoners--and in the confusion my father slipped away.

As he told it, it was not long before he encountered another tribal group. This time, he decided to try to outwit them. In this region, the chiefs were identifiable by distinctive turbans decorated with some thirty or forty dangling tassels. Baba knew that according to tribal law, anyone who succeeded in tying two of those tassels together put himself under the protection of the chief, who was honor bound to protect him. He sought out the tribal leader and ducked behind his broad body. As they scuffled, my father managed to tie two tassels together. The tribesmen were forced to let him go.

Once my father reached safety, he began writing a memoir of his escape. In those days, straight pins were used much like paper clips to hold sheets of paper together. My father kept his pins in a cup. Becoming thirsty, he absent-mindedly used the cup full of pins to dip out some water to drink. He was aghast when he realized what he'd done—especially since no pins remained in the empty cup.

"You drank the pins!" we children would scream, amazed that after narrowly escaping a firing squad he might have succumbed to such an ignoble end.

But of course the story had a happy ending. Baba explained that when he had dipped the cup in the water basin the pins had fallen out before he'd taken a drink.

In our synagogue, we held the Sabbath morning services in two shifts early in the day - at five and at seven. Jacob and I attended the second shift with our father, but even that was too early for us. Jacob grumbled and complained and many times Baba, tired of fighting, allowed him to stay in bed. I didn't like to get up early either, but my love of the services overcame my reluctance. Besides, I liked to dress in my Sabbath clothes and wear the watch Baba had given me. Until I reached the age of twelve, the only day I could wear it was Saturday, when my father could protect me from the thieves who preyed on Jewish children walking alone

An open Babylonian sefer torah

On Saturday morning we read from the *sefer torah* the weekly *torah* portion. *Bar miswah* boys and prospective bridegrooms were honored with reading from the *torah*. Afterwards, the congregation went wild wishing them good luck. Women ululated, a sign of happiness in the Middle East, and tossed candies in front of the honorees. On such occasions, we were treated with a visit by Phrayim *abu'l sh'bahoth*, "Ephraim the Singer of Paeans," and his traveling choir.

Phrayim's history intrigued me. Once he had gone to Palestine for an operation while his family waited and prayed for his safe return. His family's hopes were dashed and they shed bitter tears when a telegram arrived saying Phrayim had died. Garments were rent, and the community gathered in Phrayim's house to mourn with the family sitting *shib'a*. In the midst of the wailing and the praying, the door opened and Phrayim walked in. Many of those present screamed and some fainted, thinking he was a ghost.

Mourning turned to joy and the fateful telegram was closely examined, but it yielded no clues identifying its sender. From then on we thought of Phrayim as one who had returned from the dead to celebrate joyous occasions with us.

We didn't eat or drink on the Sabbath morning until after we had returned from services and recited the morning *kiddush*. My parents had a sparkling, tall electric kettle that we used only on the Sabbath morning for brewing tea. They viewed cooking on the Sabbath as a violation of the *torah* commandments against working and lighting fire on that day. I don't know how they reconciled this with using an electric kettle on the Sabbath.

During my youth, Babylonian rabbis tried to convince the Jewish community that turning on electricity was the same as turning on fire. Some especially observant Jews went to extraordinary lengths to obey the torah injunction. Some tied the electric switch to the key that winds an alarm clock and set the clock to go off late on Friday night. When the alarm rang and the key turned back, it pulled the string and turned off the lights.

Our Sabbath breakfast followed tea. Bayth al t'beet, eggs that Mama had set to cook on Friday had by now turned a deep brown color and tasted delicious. On a cold Sabbath day, we would roll the unpeeled eggs between the palms of our hands, put them under our arm pits or stuff them into our pants' pockets. We made sandwiches of bayth al t'beet, parsley, salad, Italian peppers, pickled cucumbers, spring onions, and sliced tomatoes - all rolled in Babylonian flat bread.

On sunny Saturdays, we sat on our balcony to watch the crowds of Jewish families strolling along the Tigris' banks. Jewish residents of mansions along the Tigris filled their balconies, too. Some played *tawlee* or dominos; others sipped tea or Turkish coffee or cracked roasted watermelon seeds; and some simply gazed at the river.

Many times those idyllic scenes were marred by sudden assaults by Muslims. Some of the attackers were young hoodlums; most were not so young, and many were well dressed. Jewish men and women were beaten, some women were stripped of their jewelry, and some girls, including one time my sister Latifa, were sexually assaulted. On those occasions the police were usually nowhere to be seen, and, if they did come, they frequently took up cudgels against the Jews.

Strangely enough--maybe out of denial, undying optimism, or perhaps sheer resignation on the part of Jews--those Sabbath strolls never ceased, even though they thinned out as the noose tightened around the throat of our community during the second half of the nineteen forties. But my sister Latifa's experience by the river is one that probably still casts a shadow over her memories of those walks. I believe I am the only one with whom she shared the story.

Sometimes on Saturday nights in the summertime I went up to the rooftop before it was time to go to bed. I wanted to lie on my bed in the dark and imagine myself moving from star to star through the vast reaches of the impenetrable sky.

Fourteen-year old Latifa joined me that evening. Her soft voice didn't at first disturb my reverie.

"Are you awake, Daniel?" she asked.

"Um, um."

"Something awful happened to me today."

I wasn't giving her my full attention until she began to cry. I sat up and put my arms around her.

"What is it, Latifa?"

"By the river, by the river ---".

Her heart-wrenching cries swallowed her voice. I didn't know how to help her.

"I'll go get Mama."

At this Latifa became almost hysterical.

"No, no. I don't want her to know. I don't want anyone to know. It's awful."

"Sh, sh. It's okay. I won't tell. What happened, Latifa?"

Slowly, through hiccups and sobs, the story emerged. A bunch of young Muslim hoodlums had approached Latifa when she was walking by the river with her girlfriends. For some reason, they singled out Latifa, ran their hands over her body and grabbed her genitals, all the time laughing and daring her to resist.

"I was so scared, Daniel. I was so afraid. When a group of older people from our community came close to us, the boys ran away. "

I rocked my sister in my arms until her sobs lessened and she wiped her eyes. I wanted to rush into the night, find those boys and make them pay for violating my sister. But I was as helpless as she was. I told myself I wanted to be in a place where nobody interfered with the joys of the Sabbath, where we Jews could live in peace. In Iraq, if there was peace, it was an uneasy peace.

At noontime, we usually went to the synagogue for Sabbath *minha*, midday services. I associated returning from these services with my favorite meal of the week – the *t'beet*. We lived in a predominantly

Jewish neighborhood, but many of our neighbors didn't attend minha services. The streets were quiet at that time of the day, and, as we returned home, we could hear through the open windows the clatter of cutlery-- the sounds of our neighbors plowing through their *t'beet*. The urge to pick up speed and hurry home to our own *t'beet* was irresistible.

My mother did all the everyday cooking on a multi-burner kerosene stove. But the *t'beet* was the one meal she cooked the old-fashioned way – over a wood fire. T'beet is a dish made of rice, vegetables, cardamom, raisins, occasionally nuts and condiments, all stuffed in chicken skin sewn into a pouch, and cooked in a big pot filled with rice, chicken, tomato and onion. The pot was placed on a specially built kanoon, an elevated three-walled brick pit, just wide enough to hold the pot securely until the following afternoon. Layers of padded burlap covered the entire pit to hold in the heat.

To cook in advance for a day like the Sabbath when Jews are not allowed to adjust fire intensity required Mama to have the skill of an acrobat and the divination of an infallible seer. Everyone wanted the *t'beet* to come out piping hot, crisp brown. Mama had to balance the wood fire intensity and the amount of food she had put in the pot with her guess of how cold or how warm it was likely to be. There was no weather service in Baghdad, and of course no weather prediction is infallible. Although Mama never talked about it, I believe that *t'beet* making was a source of anxiety for her, and indeed for any woman who had to play that kind of balancing act. We let out a big scream of joy when we sat in our dining room and saw the clouds of steam rising from the crispy brown *t'beet* coming our way. I could see how happy that made Mama. But I can also remember her disappointed look when, of all things, on a cold Sabbath day the fire went out, and the *t'beet* came out lukewarm or cold. No one criticized, but Mama must have felt she had failed to deliver when the cries of joy were muted.

I wish I had been as aware then as I am now of what my mother must have felt on those occasions.

Though I took it for granted at the time, my religion was an important part of my young years and remains so still. I am sure *Hakham* Moshe never realized the deep impression he left on my youthful mind.

From the time when I was eleven or so until he passed away, when I was close to sixteen, *Hakham* Moshe made the trek every Saturday afternoon from downtown Baghdad, where he lived, to our neighborhood's synagogue to give his two-hour *daroosh - commentary - on the weekly portion of the torah. I, too, would make* the trek from our home to the synagogue, just to listen to *Hakham* Moshe. He was a man who spoke to my soul, to my heart, and to my mind.

NO WAY BACK
The Journey of a Jew from Baghdad

Hakham Moshe wore the traditional attire common to Babylonian rabbis – a long robe that snapped in the middle from top to bottom, and a three-inch sash made of silk or wool, depending on the season, which he wore around his waist. On his head he wore the distinct turban, *amama*, worn by Babylonian rabbis, which clearly differentiated a rabbi from a Muslim cleric.

Hakham Moshe was an articulate speaker. His presentation was structured and focused – a rare trait among teachers of Judaism. He was adept at making his audience see the practical relevance of *torah* teaching and its applicability to every day life.

Almost without fail I attended *Hakham* Moshe's *daroosh* on Saturday afternoons. The synagogue was full to overflowing during his *daroosh*. People arrived an hour before his scheduled talk to secure a seat where they would have a direct view of him when he spoke. I learned a lot from *Hakham* Moshe's *daroosh*. I was amazed at how much I gained and how much I was able to retain so effortlessly.

Hakham Moshe died young, and he left young children behind. He had no savings, there was no social security in Iraq, and the Jewish community provided no pension for its rabbinical employees. His family fell on hard times after his death.

I mourned the passing of *Hakham* Moshe. Throughout the rest of my adult life, I searched for someone that could take his place in my life. I met rabbis who had some of his traits, but I have not met his match.

I felt melancholy as the Sabbath came to a close at sundown on Saturday. Sunday was a regular school day for us, and there was always the worry about homework that had to be done that night, or a Sunday exam that loomed large.

After supper I took off my Sabbath clothes and carefully hung them in place until the next week, and polished my Sabbath shoes. Then it was back to my desk and the perpetual wringer of homework and exams.

I no longer experience the unmitigated sweetness of those Friday nights in faraway Baghdad. I am more cognizant now of the inferior role assigned to women in traditional Judaism.

Whenever I visit Israel, I still make a point of attending the Babylonian synagogue nearby. I delight in being at one with the congregation standing up to chant the *lekha dodi*, a hymn sung by Jews all over the world as they welcome the Sabbath: "Come beloved Israel, greet thy bride, welcome the coming of Sabbath tide".

The last time I attended services in the Babylonian synagogue in Ramat Gan, Israel, was in 2004. I closed my eyes and listened as the singing filled the synagogue. Tears filled my eyes, as the soaring song reached into the depths of my soul. But I came back to reality as soon as the *lekha dodi* ended. I looked up and saw the women sitting in the balcony. As in other traditional synagogues, women are required to sit separately from men. The honor of being called to the *torah* is reserved for men only. Why can't women lead the services, if they accept the same obligations that have traditionally been the exclusive domain of the Jewish male?

I love praying in a Babylonian synagogue, and long to go back and connect with my roots unreservedly. But it is a bittersweet experience these days. I am no longer what I was in my teens.

For many years now, I have been attending a conservative synagogue where men and women sit together and where women conduct the services and read the *torah*. This pleases me no end. But the synagogue's liturgy is exclusively Ashkenazi. I long for my heritage, and I long for the way we celebrated the Sabbath. Yet when I go to a Babylonian synagogue, there is a part of me that says I am a stranger to that world. I am in a place that violates my deeply held principles.

It has been painful to deal with the reality that I am neither here nor there.

A CULTURE OF INCESSANT WORK

Education began at a tender age for Jewish boys in Baghdad. My first recollection of schooling goes back to when I was three years old, sitting next to my Hebrew tutor "*m'allim* M'nashee," or Teacher Menasha. An elderly man with a snow-white beard, he wore the traditional fez, a long white robe and a beige cloak called *abayi*. He was my brother's tutor before I was added to his list; he came to our home six days a week to teach me the Hebrew basics and to teach Jacob the Bible.

Every time I pronounced a word correctly or asked about something I didn't understand, *m'allim* M'nashee would shower me with praise. "I am proud of you, my son. You are doing so well," he would say. Naturally I waited eagerly for his arrival every day. Jacob, however, was not interested in religion. He dreaded *m'allim* M'nashee's visits.

After my lesson, our tutor would go in search of him, calling "Jacob, Jacob, where are you?" At this point Jacob would squeal, break cover and run up the stairs to the roof. *m'allim* M'nashee, afraid of tripping, would bunch up his *abayi* behind him with both hands. He would then follow Jacob, trying to run, his head bent over as his body leaned first to one side and then to the other. Even I had trouble stifling my laughter.

If he was caught, Jacob refused to sit still. Halfway through a lesson he would get up and race around the walkway that encircled the second floor of our house. Eventually, our teacher would give up and sink, panting, into a chair.

I felt sorry for our tutor, but Jacob's antipathy to religion was such that he never stopped to think how hard all of this was on *m'allim* M'nashee. To this day, Jacob mocks my adherence to the tenets of Judaism.

As I grew older, *m'allim* M'nashee taught me prayers and the Bible. He stopped coming when his health deteriorated. His difficulty with Jacob may have hastened his retirement. My parents then retained a younger Hebrew tutor. By this time, they had given up on Jacob and hired the tutor just for me.

When I was five years old, my parents enrolled me in *asile*, a two-year kindergarten held in the magnificent girls' school, *l'Ecole de l'Alliance Israelite*. In *Alliance asile*, boys and girls were taught in the same classrooms.

The girls' *Alliance* building was a Moorish-style structure, with massive pillars, arched passageways, airy classrooms, and large courtyards. The philanthropist Sir Elly Kh'doury (1867 - 1944), who lived in Hong Kong and who was a graduate of the boys' *Alliance* in Baghdad, donated the building in 1911 in honor of his wife.

Everything in the girls' *Alliance* was vast, including my <u>asile</u> class. We were taught in French and Judeo-Arabic. Three of our four teachers were graduates of the girls' *Alliance*; the fourth, Mrs. Sabbagh, was French, and a strict, no-nonsense disciplinarian. My other teachers were kind, but my favorite was Mademoiselle Sim'ha. She lived in my neighborhood, and never disciplined students with a stick as Mrs. Sabbagh did.

My overall recollection of my time at *asile* is one of loads of work in the classroom and long daily "*devoirs,*" or homework. Those years were not marked by the play and fun typical of American kindergartens. There was a constant push to cram more and more learning into our heads.

Even at this young age, fear of discipline loomed large. One evening when I was six years old I was roughhousing with Jacob in our courtyard, while my older sister Muzli stood watching from the balcony. In those years I tried to stay out of Muzli's way, for she was bossy and seemed to enjoy making trouble. That evening Jacob challenged me to climb on his back. I grabbed his shirt and tried to climb, but slipped and tore his shirt. Muzli's eyes blazed.

"Wait till you get the punishment you deserve," she scolded. "I am going to write a letter to your teacher and tell her to punish you for your rowdiness."

I had trouble sleeping that night. I worried that my teacher would make me stand in the corner, or make me recite a deprecating statement about rowdy children. She might even hit me with that long stick of hers.

The next day, Muzli handed me the letter to carry to my teacher. For some reason she left the envelope unsealed. My sister Helwa walked with me to school, but neither of us said a word. At school, I opened the letter before we went to class. It was in French, and I couldn't read it, and Helwa could decipher only a few words.

Front of the girls' Alliance Israelite School, Baghdad

Formation in one of the girls' Alliance courtyards before the start of classes

With great trepidation, I handed the letter to my teacher. I was immensely relieved when all she did was tell me gently not to do it again.

When I returned home, Muzli was waiting, and she demanded to know how my teacher had punished me. I balked and ran to my mother and told her what had happened. Mama was furious with Muzli for tormenting me, and for writing to my teacher without her permission.

After two years at *asile*, I moved on to the boys' *Alliance Israelite*.

The boys' *Alliance*, which opened in 1864, was the first modern school in Iraq. The girls' *Alliance* opened three decades later. Both were part of a worldwide network of schools established by *l'Alliance Israelite Universelle*, which was founded by a group of French Jewish intellectuals in 1860. The schools served as links within the Jewish world to channel information about communities in duress and to provide a vehicle for mobilizing help to defend Jewish liberties worldwide.

The visionary behind this educational network was the Sephardic rabbi Judah Alkalai (1798-1878) of Sarajevo. Its formation grew in part out of the 1858 Mortara affair, the abduction of a six-year-old Jewish child, Edgardo Mortara, by papal gendarmes in Bologna, Italy, on the pretext that his Catholic babysitter had baptized him while his parents were gone for the evening.

The boys' *Alliance* that I attended played a major role in alerting the headquarters in Paris when Baghdad's Jewish community was threatened. It also served as a conduit for channeling financial help to stricken communities in Russia and elsewhere in the world. And while rabbis and observant Jews elsewhere tended to send their children to religious schools, Baghdad's leading rabbis sent their children to *l'Alliance*, even though it was secular.

L'Alliance gave us quality education that matched France's best schools. But we students were never told about its international humanitarian work, possibly because our teachers feared a crackdown at a time of rising Arab nationalism.

While impressive, the building that housed the boys' *Alliance* was not as large as the girls', but I still loved it—even though we froze during the winter in our drafty classrooms. The school's magnificent Sasson synagogue was named for Sir Albert David Sasson, a scion of the Baghdadian family known as the "Rothschilds of the East." Sir Albert had donated the school building in 1872 and a large portrait of him hung in our school. Gazing upon it I felt grateful to Sir Albert for his contribution to my education.

L'Alliance was competitive, and so was I. We were required to take three midterm exams and a final every year. We were ranked according to our test scores and given le bulletin, a quarterly report card to take home. The class seating order was rearranged every quarter to reflect our new ranking. Those who ranked ahead got to sit ahead; those who ranked last were placed in the back rows. One of our teachers, *Monsieur* Sabbagh, used to make a show of it. He was wont to remind the one who ranked last, "Mets toi tout a fait au coin, tout a fait au fond de la classe," which means "You sit at the corner, all the way in the back," a humiliating situation for any student. It was harsh, and it fostered cutthroat competition. I usually ranked in the single digits, occasionally first, and in the heedless way of young people, was oblivious to the feelings of those I displaced when I moved ahead in rank.

A view from the teba (Lectern) of the Sasson synagogue in the boys' Alliance

Classes were held six days a week, Sunday through Friday, and, although *l' Alliance* emphasis was on science and the French language (with a smattering of English thrown in for good measure), *l'Alliance* could not continue operation unless it taught classical Arabic and Arab History, subjects required by the Ministry of Education. I became proficient in reading and writing classical Arabic, though I spoke only the Judeo-Arabic dialect. Beginning with my fourth year in *l'Alliance*, we also had a heavy dose of Arab History (basically Muslim History).

Several of my French teachers were Christian French. The religious affiliation of our French teachers never entered my thinking or, as far as I could tell, the thinking of my peers. But we were, I think, more aware of religious affiliation when it came to our Arab teachers. All my teachers of classical Arabic and Arab history were Jewish except for Mr. Abdul Ahhad, who was a Christian Iraqi, and a Muslim teacher who was retained during my last year in *l'Alliance* (1948) to teach Arab History (whose name I regrettably no longer remember),

Our Jewish teachers of classical Arabic were tops, as was Abdul Ahhad. Abdul Ahhad began his teaching career in *l'Alliance* long before I came, and his two boys attended *l'Alliance* too. Our relations with him were good. Still, I always felt on guard in his presence -- I never discussed Jewish topics and particularly Zionist matters when Abdul Ahhad was around. I believe that was also true of my peers, as well. It wasn't so with our Jewish teachers or any of our French teachers, Jewish or not. Our Jewish teachers of Arab History were good, but not inspiring. Our Muslim teacher of Arab History was retained by *l'Alliance*, I believe, to take off some of the pressure on *l'Alliance* by nationalists within the Ministry of Education. Soft-spoken but always correct, maybe aloof, our teacher showed up only to give his lecture in Arab History and left, never staying even during the break. I often wondered if he felt he was hired only to serve as window dressing and resented it. His lectures though were focused and well structured, and I liked his low-key style. I remember asking him occasionally, but with hesitation, a question or two. His answers were usually thoughtful but distant. And it was the same with my friends. It was as if we were miles apart. What was is? Was it he? Was it us? Was it the awful environment of tension and distrust that shrouded our life in Iraq? Was I afraid that he might one day turn me or my friends over to the dreaded Criminal Investigation Department for a slip of the tongue or a question about Arab History that might offend him or other Muslims? Was it basically the sectarianism that dominated relationships among Iraqis, any Iraqis? Was it maybe his feeling that he was hired only as a tool to please the Ministry of Education? Whatever it was, we and our history teacher remained miles apart.

But, no matter who the teacher was, I studied hard, enjoyed learning and resented those who disrupted class. One of my teachers, though an excellent scholar, had no control over his students. Mayhem reigned in his classes, which made it impossible for those of us who wanted to learn to do so. One morning, I came to the classroom before anyone else and wrote on the blackboard: "A committee has been formed to take note of and report to the authorities the names of students who are creating disturbances in this class." Nobody figured out that the committee in question was a committee of one. I could see students looking at one another, wondering who was on the committee, but the end result was that the disturbances came to an end.

There were other class interruptions created by the school. Fees at the *Alliance* were pretty steep, and sometimes parents put off paying them. The school accountant, carrying with him a sheaf of papers, looking self-important as he peered at us over his glasses, would visit the classroom and call out the names of the students whose parents were in arrears. These students would be sent home until their parents came up with the money. Sometimes the students would protest, saying their parents had paid the fees, but these, too, would be sent home to bring back the receipt for the payment. As a general rule, we were never allowed to leave school during the school day, and some students were happy to get a break from their studies under any pretext. I remember Haim, one of my fellow students, always insisting he had to go and get the receipt, though his parents always paid on time, and the accountant never suggested he owed the school money.

NO WAY BACK
The Journey of a Jew from Baghdad

Several of my classmates came from needy families and received scholarships. None of this was publicized to save embarrassing the poor. Poverty was a stigma, and people were even more sensitive about it than today. One day, when I was in the fifth grade, we were all surprised when a few students showed up wearing identical suits. It didn't take long to decipher the puzzle. Those were the students who had received free clothing from the Jewish community. To save on cost, all the suits were made from the same material and cut from the same simple design. The needy students' cover had been blown. But to the community's credit, it rectified the error. New one-of-a-kind suits were made for each student.

Around *purim* and Passover, items donated by the students were auctioned off in class, with the proceeds going to the needy. Roses were always in bloom then and we often auctioned off donated bouquets.

One day a student brought a huge bouquet of red roses from his home garden. The teacher decided to auction it last. The longer it took for the bouquet's turn to come, the more tantalized I got, for I wanted it badly. When the teacher finally held up the bouquet, I immediately bid. I had meant to open with twenty *fils*, the equivalent of about ten cents at the time, but found myself blurting out seventy instead. That stunned everybody, including me, but I was too embarrassed to retract. No one in the class wanted to bid higher, so I had to pay seventy *fils* for a bouquet that sold for less than twenty *fils* in the market. Worse still, I had no one to blame but myself. How was I going to pay for it from my small daily allowance?

Mama came to my rescue. "It is good to help the poor," Mama said as she handed me the seventy *fils*, "but be careful next time."

Our school's emphasis on charity didn't squelch a vexing cultural trait that many Jews in Iraq had absorbed from the Arab world around them: competitive gift giving, and the relentless one-upmanship it inspired. I had an extremely wealthy classmate who regularly treated me to ice cream. I, in turn, was expected to reciprocate with a bigger and better treat for him. He then would top my gesture and so it went, back and forth, quickly exhausting my relatively meager allowance. The unending race upward had nothing to do with generosity, and everything to do with shaming the party who couldn't keep up.

The world beyond Iraq's borders always beckoned to me. My first exposure to that wider world came through my hobby of collecting stamps. When the school initiated a pen pal program, I participated, mainly to acquire foreign stamps.

I remember two pen pals in particular, an American girl and a girl in Switzerland. My Swiss pen pal and I corresponded in French. I envied her descriptions of her country's freedom and her life free from fear. It was not as easy corresponding with my American friend, but Jacob--who went to an all-English school-- helped me with my letters to her.

For some reason I received more letters than any other student in class. I brought all the letters to school to share with my classmates. I was fond of my pen pals and thought of them as my particular friends. One day I received a letter from my American friend telling me she had received a letter from a boy in my class named William. I realized that William, not having any particular luck with the pen pal assigned to him, had copied the name and address of my pen pal when I brought her letter to school. In the way of young boys, I was outraged. I wrote to her immediately, telling her what a thief and despicable character William was. I felt completely justified in doing this; after all, William had encroached on my territory and tried to steal my special friend. I don't remember what happened after that; it is the memory of my reaction to William's imagined perfidy that stays with me

My American pen pal

L'Alliance was an elite sanctuary of learning. But it couldn't entirely shield us from the dangers beyond its gates. What I observed as a child is that disputes between Muslims often ended in fisticuffs. It was not unusual to see two Muslims in a street in Baghdad literally tearing at each other, without anyone taking notice of them. Nor did Muslims need an excuse to make Jews the object of their attacks. My father always stressed what the torah taught us: Justice, justice thou shalt pursue. But there was no justice on the streets of Baghdad, no safety. We never knew when we would be cornered, spat on, or robbed of our book bags or jewelry.

One morning I was waiting in line for the city bus on my way to school. I was in intermediate school at the time and was traveling by myself. The bus was late, and the line grew very long. In front of me in the line was a burly Arab in his mid-forties, dressed in a white gown and the traditional Arab cloak and turban. The bus finally arrived. All of a sudden, everyone in the back pushed forward. I was going over an algebra problem in my head, barely aware of what was happening, when I was hurled against the man in front of me. He whirled around angrily. His huge hand sliced through the air and hit me a resounding blow on the cheek.

I reeled from the force of the blow, and could feel my head spin. As I staggered and fought to regain my balance, I heard the voice of my maternal uncle Sion, behind me. I had not seen him, but Uncle Sion was standing at the back of the line and had witnessed what had happened.

My uncle, a wiry man in his early forties, half the size of the man who had hit me, raised himself to his full height, as he looked my attacker straight in the face. His voice was thick with anger.

Khalu (maternal uncle) Sion March 11, 1984

"What gives you the right to hit him? Who do you think you are? Let me see you raise your hand to him again."

The big bully stood open-mouthed, staring at *khalu* (maternal uncle) Sion, not knowing what to say. He seemed stunned. Finally, he managed to reply.

"Why should it matter to you?"

"It does matter to me," *khalu* Sion responded emphatically. He's my nephew."

khalu Sion put his hand reassuringly on my shoulder, as he renewed his challenge to the bully.

"Let me see you raise your hand to him again."

The man muttered something I couldn't understand as he lowered his eyes and slunk away. *khalu* Sion stayed by my side until the next bus arrived. I stood with him, proud he was my uncle, hoping I would have his courage some day.

Less than a year before this incident, I was rescued by a complete stranger.

I was walking home from school alone. Four or five Arab teenagers approached and formed a circle around me.

"Just a few minutes ago you were on Sa'adoon Street, and you came up to us and spat on us," the tallest one said to me.

I am sure my voice shook when I denied the accusation.

"I wasn't even on that street," I said. "I walked through *rasheed* Street."

"That is right. It was on *rasheed* Street that you spat on us."

They closed in tighter, their jeering faces leaning toward mine.

It was a beautiful balmy spring afternoon. I remember the dry street, the sun, the gentle breeze, and the sour taste of terror rising in my throat and spilling into my mouth, as the thugs tightened their circle around me, leaving no room for escape. I knew I was doomed. The thought flashed into my mind that they might have knives. I wanted to run, but the circle around me was too tight and, besides that, my feet were frozen to the pavement.

Then just as their leader raised his fist, a big Jewish man happened to pass by. Even in my terrified state, I noticed he was tall and muscular, dressed in a dark suit and wearing black-rimmed glasses. The man must have been in his mid- twenties, but to my young eyes he looked very adult. I despaired as he walked past us, but then caught my breath as he suddenly whirled back just as the youths were closing in to strike. He met my eyes for a moment and then put one hand on his hip, as he sternly asked my attackers to move on.

My body sagged with relief, for I could feel my rescuer's strength. I knew he would brook no nonsense, and my attackers got the message, too. They stopped for a moment and scanned the street, only to see it was almost deserted. There was no prospect of a Muslim gang coming to their aid should they choose to tangle with the young man. Their faces fell as they figured they were no match for him. Casting sullen looks at both of us, they scattered.

I thanked my rescuer, and he walked slowly ahead of me, as I proceeded on my way toward the riverbank and home.

At the end of each school year, Iraq's Ministry of Education held national exams for those who had completed the primary, intermediate, and secondary grades. The ministry issued certificates to those who passed the exams.

We heard horror stories about shenanigans that went on with those exams and with the ministry's certificates. There were rumors about people who bought their certificates from the ministry. Bribery for advance disclosure of the exam questions was rampant. One of our Arab neighbors, a high school graduate of a government school, told us how the official test was made available to him for a price, and he described a well-oiled network that orchestrated the operation. To avoid flagrancy, the network revealed only a limited number of questions, just enough to carry a total of sixty per cent of the test score, so that the person who paid the bribe would just squeeze by without attracting suspicion. The advance release time of those leaks was limited to five hours before the start of the exam, to minimize the time available for disseminating the test among students who didn't pay the bribe.

I was dubious about the government tests and certificates, considering them not worth the trouble. I was focused on my French education and, from a young age, dreamed of leaving Iraq. But I wasn't sure I'd ever be allowed to do so, and realized that as long as we lived in Iraq, we couldn't ignore the government exams.

Our teachers had no concept of rest or rejuvenation through relaxation. The message I got throughout was that rest was waste; time had to be filled with work.

The girls' *Alliance* was no different - a similar culture of interminable work and ruthless competition. When my youngest sister, Valentine, was in the fifth grade, my sister Reyna took her under her wing and worked with her non-stop on her homework. Reyna disliked Joyce, a second cousin of ours and a classmate of Valentine's. Joyce was a blonde, blue-eyed girl who exuded self-confidence and ranked first in her class. Reyna was determined to have Valentine dislodge Joyce from top rank, and worked hard with Valentine. Valentine became dependent on Reyna, and in Valentine's mind dislodging Joyce became an obsession.

I remember how tense poor Valentine was the night before the year-end bulletin's release. It was summer time, and we were sleeping on the rooftop. Before she lay down in bed, Valentine lifted her eyes up to the sky and prayed that she would be the first in her class. I boiled with anger at how Reyna had reduced my little sister to a nervous wreck.

The following day, Valentine went off to school to get the bulletin. Two hours into that tense morning, our doorbell rang. Reyna went to the door, but before it swung open I could hear Valentine proclaiming from the other side, "oula! oula!"- "First, First!" She held the bulletin high and her curly blonde hair fluttered in the wind. She jumped and hopped, and looked so relieved. She had been vindicated - Joyce dropped to second place. Reyna won the battle vicariously.

As much as I despised the relentless workload, in time it

became part of me. During my first year in secondary school, I was exempted from the finals because of a perfect score. Nonetheless, I spent the whole week before the exam studying for the finals anyway. I struggled later in life to learn to take time off.

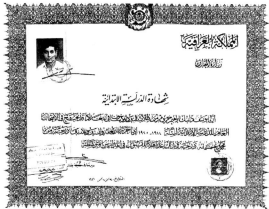

My certificate of primary school education written in the flowery script of the Koran

Graduates of l' Alliance primary, 1944-1945.
Daniel third from left in second row from front.

Respite and Renewal

The Jewish holidays brought us periodic—and welcome--respite.

Hanukkah was peaceful and charming in its simplicity; in a

Muslim country, Christmas came and went without notice, and thus there was no seasonal glitter to emulate as there is in the U.S. I remember *hanukkah* in Baghdad as a quiet holiday that radiated serenity.

My Babylonian hanukkiyah
replica of the hanukkiyah my parents lit in Baghdad

School was out on the first day of *hanukkah*. During the eight days of *hanukkah* Baba came home early to light the candles and spend the rest of the evening with us. My parents had a beautiful half-circular *hanukkiyah* made of silver, which had a mirror inserted behind the candleholders so that the lighted candles reflected in the mirror, creating a mysterious effect.

Baba lit the candles every night with a beeswax candle, as is the practice among Sephardi Jews. When he finished lighting, we all joined together in singing in unison an ancient Babylonian paean "*Yah Hassel Yona Me'hakka*":

> Lord, rescue the dove (Israel) from the fishhook (of captivity)
>> Her tears gushing in prayer to you
>> And she will rejoice in you, her King,
>> In the eight days of hanukkah.

Although it is the practice among Jews to put their lit *hanukkiyah* in their windows for all to see, in Baghdad it was dangerous to do so. We always kept our *hanukkiyah* inside for fear of vandalism by the Muslims. For the same reason we kept our Mezuzahs always on the inside, never on the outside.

NO WAY BACK
The Journey of a Jew from Baghdad

Tu bish'bat, known among Babylonian Jews as *tifkaie elsedgagh* -- the blossoming of the trees – is the day we celebrated as the Jewish New Year of the Trees. School was out on *tifkaie elsedgagh.* Many in our community spent the day in the fields and said a prayer of thanks to God for every blossoming tree they encountered.

On the eve of the holiday we gathered in our living room around a long table set with plates filled with every conceivable fruit of the season; there was also a medley of dried fruits. And there was one fruit that was always a must in my family– a big sweet watermelon. Even though it was not the season for watermelon, *ammu* (paternal uncle) Moshe always managed to find one for us.

We took turns in reciting a blessing over each fruit and thanked God for the bounty of the earth. No one wanted to eat dinner that night. We stuffed ourselves with the yummy mixture of dried fruits that filled the table.

It was cold and windy at night during that time of the year, but we had our protector, our *sopa* (kerosene heater) with the red and blue windows sitting majestically in our midst. Sometimes the whistling wind outside blasted hard, and it rattled our windows. Sometimes we could feel the cold wind whiz inside our room.

Reyna sat by the *sopa* roasting chestnuts and brewing` tea for the rest of us. Every now and then we headed for the sofa to warm ourselves, sip on a cup of tea or grab a roasted chestnut, all courtesy of Reyna.

Mama filled a bagful of dried fruits for each one of us. She had sewed those bags especially for the occasion.

We munched on the dried fruits in our bags all day on *tifkaie elsedgagh* day. I remember spending most of the day sitting in the sun on the balcony with my bag of dried fruits in hand. It was a wonderful, relaxed day. Nothing eventful happened during that day, except perhaps for the lines that formed at the bathrooms. There were only two in our house, but there were eight of us children, all having stuffed ourselves with dried fruit, all of us paying the price for our indulgence.

Our biggest feast of the year came on the traditional New Year, *rosh hashana.* A week or two beforehand, my parents bought a sheep and kept it the courtyard of our backhouse. I'd pet its thick wool and feed it watermelon rind as it regarded me with its soft brown eyes. I had to steal myself from becoming too attached, knowing it was destined to be the centerpiece of our *rosh hashana* table. Then came the awful reckoning: three or four *kasher* butchers came at night, always in a hurry. They headed straight for our backhouse. I'd try to hide on the rooftop, but I still heard the cry of the terrified sheep as it was readied for slaughter. Then came one loud snore, as it drew its last breath. Sickened, I'd look up at the sky, hoping to catch a glimpse of my little sheep's soul as it traveled up to heaven.

I didn't realize it then, but the seeds of my later becoming a vegetarian were sown as I watched for the soul of the sheep flying above the stars.

Rosh hashana falls at the beginning of *tashri* – the first month of the Jewish calendar. Beginning a month before that, we observed a forty-day period of soul-searching and reflection, and we recited daily *s'lihoth* -- special prayers of forgiveness and repentance. We started *s'lihoth* an hour before dawn. It was customary for the sexton to make the rounds among the faithful and knock on their doors to wake them up in time for *s'lihoth*. We could hear him knock on the door of our neighbors; at that time of the year we slept on the roof.

There was something unique about getting up in the wee hours of the night for *s'lihoth*, looking in silence at the star-studded sky above in the midst of total darkness, reflecting on the far reaches of the beyond, and pondering what God would want us to do to be better human beings.

I attended *s'lihoth* many times during my childhood. I remember throngs of people, too, walking hurriedly toward the synagogue for *s'lihoth*. Even some of those who did not regularly attend the Sabbath services often showed up for *s'lihoth*. Since so many attended *s'lihoth*, nobody walked alone to the synagogue. That was fortunate since it was not safe to walk the streets of Baghdad in the dark. There was safety in numbers. And there was faith that God Almighty would be our protector.

We sang most of the *s'lihoth* prayers in unison, and the melodies were gorgeous. There was something inspiring about those services, and we all joined in with vigor. I felt as if we were all traveling together, hand in hand, on the road of the faithful, that we were all bonded together in our bid for forgiveness for our misdeeds. We were humbled by our frailties but uplifted by our resolve to do better.

Many in our community made a point of taking a ritual bath, immersion in naturally flowing water, on the eve of *rosh hashana*, to reinforce their sense of purity. Many Jewish houses in Baghdad were fitted with artesian wells to serve as ritual baths for their residents. The house in which I was born had an artesian well. There were steps down to the well with rails to assist in making a steady descent to the running water deep below. During my earlier years of childhood both of my parents took their ritual bath in the well in our home.

The *kiddush* on *rosh hashana* was special. Several types of fruit and vegetables were brought to the table. We recited a special wish in Aramaic while eating each one. My father would lift up a piece of pomegranate and take the lead in reciting the "*yehi rasoan*" – "May it be

Your will, our God, that we be as full of good deeds in the coming year as there are seeds in this pomegranate." Then each one of us would take a turn, reciting the same wish over a piece of pomegranate. Following that there were some ten assortments of fruits and vegetables to go through, so it took quite awhile. In the meantime, we cracked jokes and made funny comments- all in high spirits. This was the time to be jolly, which would augur well for a happy and anger-free new year.

We avoided consuming sour, sharp, or salty food during *rosh hashana*. Sweet food augured a sweet year. We also avoided dark colors, and some wouldn't drink coffee because it was black. At morning services, we blew the *shofar*, or ram's horn. The short, curly horn used by the Babylonian Jews has a deep, resonant sound different from the longer *shofars* used in Ashkenazi services. The sound of the *shofar* penetrated to the depths of my soul, seeming to transport me across a boundless world. The experience always left me shaken but strangely uplifted. The sound of the Shofar echoes from my childhood through all the years that followed.

I never once failed to hear the *shofar* as far back as I can remember, although once I came within a hairsbreadth of not being there.

During the time when I taught at Stanford University, I developed chronic pain in both of my shoulders that made it difficult for me to raise my arm to write on the blackboard. X-rays showed the ligaments in both shoulders were badly torn, and surgery was required. The earliest the operation could be scheduled was the day before *rosh hashana*. The day before the operation, I presented myself at the hospital for preparatory tests. I was given a hospital gown and left in a room to wait, allowing me time to think.

I pondered how I'd never before missed the sacred sound of the *shofar*. "This year I'll be lying in bed under sedation or on the operating table, while Jews all over the world listen to the *shofar*," I thought. I'd be betraying something precious by missing that. "I can't do it," I decided. "I won't."

I dressed, told the attending nurse I was not going through with the operation and checked myself out of the hospital.

I was in agony during the two days of *rosh hashana*, but I did hear the sound of the *shofar* on both days of the holiday. I felt connected with my past, my ancestry, and with Jews all around the world who were celebrating as I was.

When the holiday was over I went to see my internist. An old-fashioned physician, he advised me to put heating pads on my shoulders when I went to bed. I followed his advice. After three weeks, the pain was gone.

When school started I could freely lift both arms and could use the blackboard without pain. Though I never rescheduled the surgery, my shoulders have not hurt since. What happened to those torn ligaments? They said they couldn't be repaired without surgery. Who did the repair work? Was it the heat? Or was it the *shofar?* Whatever it was, I'm glad I listened to that little voice inside that told me I should not miss the sound of the *shofar* on that memorable *rosh hashana* day.

Yom kippoor is the most solemn day in the Jewish calendar. We stuffed ourselves with watermelon and gulped water before beginning the twenty-five-hour fast. At the synagogue, chairs were shoved into the aisles to accommodate the overflow crowd, and the threat of fire and stampede was always present. We didn't wear leather shoes or belts on this day because they were seen as a sign of pride. But we did wear sneakers. My mother told me that when she was a girl, Jews walked to the synagogue on *yom kippoor* in their stocking feet. Arabs scattered broken glass in the streets around the synagogue while the services were in progress. The streets were not well lit, and it was dark by the time the services were over. Many worshippers returned home with bleeding feet.

My sneakers kept my feet safe, but the rigors of the day exhausted me, and though I knew how important it was, it was always a relief to know we wouldn't have to face *yom kippoor* for another full year.

Tish'a be'ab -- the day on which the Temple was torched, Jews were exiled -- had a special meaning for Babylonian Jews. The depth of feeling I experienced in Baghdad, as I listened to the haunting melody of the ode "By the rivers of Babylon, there we sat and wept as we remembered Zion" was greater than any I have felt since leaving Iraq.

I remember the last year I attended tish'a be'ab services in Baghdad. We were approaching the point in the services where the leader was to announce the number of years since the (second) destruction of the Jewish homeland. It was a tense moment. We stood in silence. Sorrow was reflected on every face in the congregation. The leader of the services, eyes closed, seemed to be struggling to speak. Then in a cracking voice, with moments of silence puncturing his words, he made the announcement.

"To day, we in the city of Baghdad, count one thousand eight hundred and eighty-two years since the torching of our holy Temple and the destruction of our homeland". People wrung their hands. A few clapped. Was it a mistake, or were they applauding because somehow we survived two millennia of persecution? Some men wept openly; women in the balcony wiped their tears. Would our Temple ever be rebuilt? A new Jewish state had just been established. Iraq's capricious laws governing the Jews' ability to leave the country had become progressively more restrictive. Would the Iraqis ever allow us to join our brethren in Israel? Would the exile of Babylonian Jewry ever come to an end?

At home we sat around my father and listened as he read the

story of Hannah and her seven children, how they were massacred one by one for refusing to abandon Judaism – an example of the tragedies that befell the Jewish people when they lost their homeland and were at the mercy of ruthless rulers. Hannah's was a moving story.

By mid-afternoon, the somber mood of the day in our home shifted to a lighter one, as we prepared for ice cream making and kite flying.

I remember running along the roof with the kite behind me to get it to fly. It did not always work smoothly. One time I backed up into one of the vats of tomatoes my mother had left to dry in the sun. My siblings laughed as I continued to run with my kite, covered though I was from top to bottom with tomato paste. I can still feel the joy of those times when the wind cooperated, and my kite took off. I watched it as it faded into a tiny speck in the distance and then tied its string to the railing surrounding the roof. Sometimes my kite's line became entangled with that of a neighbor's flying from an adjacent railing, and I watched in horror as the two tangled kites took a nosedive to the earth in a place where I could never reach them. But it was a delight when I got up the next day and found my little kite still flying, a shining star, way way up above, in the azure sky.

Festive *purim*, popularly known among Babylonian Jews as *m'djallah*, was my favorite holiday. It commemorates the deliverance of the Jews of Persia from destruction during the reign of Xerxes I. In Iraq we celebrated it for a full three weeks during the spring.

We children all looked forward to the special *m'djallah* gambling money our parents gave us weeks in advance. We played *dosa* and *naksh el'yihood*, (literally, "the embroidery of the Jews"), two games popular among Babylonian Jews. We played also bingo and other games of chance. Gambling was the order of the days, a way of thumbing our collective noses at Haman, the minister of Xerxes who, in the 5th Century BCE, tossed dice to determine which month to annihilate the Jews in the Persian Empire.

The games of chance brought us together with our parents and the extended family, who all gambled with us. Life was one big party: Gathered around the card table, we shared special *m'djallah* sweets and treats, told jokes and shared stories. Later, it felt good to share some of our gambling gains with the less fortunate in our community.

I loved the times when Baba served as the dealer for the *dosa* game. He was supposed to deal his card first and then everyone else's card. He had to pay those whose hand beat his and collect from those whose hand fell short of his. But Baba reversed the order to heighten the excitement. He dealt all the other cards first, slowly and with relish. Only then did he show his card.

"I am going to win this game," he would tease. "Get your money ready! My card is going to beat you all!"

"No it won't! No it won't!" we would scream, as some waved their hands dismissively and others bounced in their seats.

All our cards were on the table. Now it was time to show his. Tension mounted as Baba took his own good time. He would slowly look each one of us in the eye.

"What do you think?" he would ask.

"Come on. Show us. You are too scared to open your card. Show us," some of us would blurt out.

Baba accepted the challenge. Then the room was filled with cries of joy and groans of disappointment.

But it did not always end with that. Dad loved to cheat and get caught. He used to put on an innocent face when we caught him red-handed and ganged up on him demanding he pay a penalty.

Baba gave us our main allowance on the first day of the holiday. Then came our aunts and uncles, one by one, all of them adding to our *m'djallah*. The amount increased as we grew older. I got about 10 dinars (the equivalent of about $50) when I was ten.

Our *m'djallah* money had not been circulated before -- crisp, crackling currency and shiny, newly minted coins. The newness of the money added to the specialness and beauty of the holiday. I used to put the shining new *fils* (100th of dinar) under the electric light, turn it around, tilt it on its side, and marvel at its bright reflection of the light. For a long time, *purim* day was, for me, synonymous with shining new money. I assumed every Jewish child received shining new money on *m'djallah* day. I was surprised when one time I showed a fourth-grade classmate some of my *m'djallah* allowance and he told me he had never seen shining money before.

"Don't you get *m'djallah* money from your parents, aunts and uncles?" I asked.

"Yes, I do. But where can you get shining coins or crisp paper money?"

When I asked my father about it, I learned that we could thank *khalu* (maternal uncle) Guerji. *Khalu* Guerji was the Assistant Minister of Finance for Currency, the office that minted money, and so he was in a position to sell new money to my family.

A week or so before *m'djallah*, Mama, my siblings and I gathered around a large round table, with rolling pins in hand and a large bowl of dough in front of us to make *m'djallah* cookies. We made *b'abeu b'tamegh* - round cookies filled with dates and covered with sesame seeds; my favorite *simboosak b'shakar* –crisp turnovers filled with walnuts, sugar, cardamom and rosewater; and *simboosak b'jibin,* turnovers filled with Feta cheese and eggs. Wearing a thick head cover and with hands and arms covered, Jamila stood in front of our wood-burning clay and stuck our doughy cookies on the hot walls of the oven. Sometimes one or two of my aunts joined us on those afternoons. We took a tea break periodically and sat and chatted, all looking forward to the coming *m'djallah* day.

And on *m'djallah* day, it was Muzli's specialty to make us our crispy brown *zingoola*, the funnel cake that we adored. No one knew how to make those cakes as crisp as Muzli did.

I loved *simboosak b'shakar*. It was my favorite *purim* pastry. When I munched on their leftover in the days and weeks after *purim*, I felt they had a special taste. They carried memories from the beauty, liveliness and happiness of those marvelous *Purim* days.

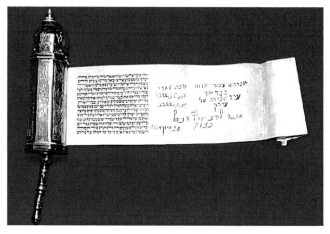

My father's m'ghellah
Baba dedicated the m'ghellah " to my son Joseph Daniel Khazzoom" on May 31, 1964. The
inscription shows also the date when he purchased it

Sometimes *m'djallahh* services in the jam-packed synagogue verged on pandemonium. We read the *m'ghellahh*, the scroll of Esther, four times during the two days of *m'djallah*. Every time the reader uttered the hated Haman's name, dozens of cap guns went off simultaneously. The poor walked the aisles of the synagogue asking for help, rolling coins in their hands. No one could be turned down. This was the day to be generous with the poor and to be generous with one another. *purim* was a time to visit friends (and be visited in turn) carrying gifts of *purim* sweets to share and to enjoy together. It was such a happy time, such a wonderful experience to be out and about in the balmy weather.

On *m'djallah* day a Jewish band roamed our neighborhood. I particularly remember the drummer, a short fellow, whose drum was almost as big as he was. We couldn't see his face, just his feet marching along, his hands swinging drumsticks in the air and crashing them with enormous force against the drum. The drumbeat rattled the surroundings, but was always out of synch with the music, adding to the general hilarity.

For a young boy, the *sukkoth* holiday was another exciting diversion. One of its highpoints was watching the workmen erect our traditional outdoor booth, or *sukkah*, where we visited with friends and family, took meals and sometimes even slept. My parents used a *sukkah* that my maternal grandparents had passed down to them. Supported by huge columns, it was so enormous it required a carpenter and three helpers to build and take down. Once, when I was four years old, I was watching, mesmerized, while a workman perched atop a ladder trying to bolt our *sukkah* to the second floor. Suddenly, the structure began to tilt. The three men standing on the first floor let out a horrified cry, and rushed to keep it from collapsing. I stood rooted to the ground in terror, while the structure tilted in my direction.

My parents were horrified at the near miss. At the end of the holiday, when the carpenter and his crew came to take down the *sukkah*, Baba told them to take it away. From that year on, Mama used the metallic frame and four poles of a huge custom-made bed as the supports for the *sukkah*.

The *sukkah* symbolizes the ramshackle dwellings that housed the Israelites during their 40 years in the wilderness after leaving Egypt. Ours had a ceiling loosely covered with palm fronds and was elaborately decorated with bundles of fruit and snow-white embroidered curtains. Silver bowls filled with sweetmeats and Camel cigarettes stood atop a table at the entrance. My father didn't smoke, but he enjoyed sitting next to a smoker and smelling the cigarette smoke.

Atop the bench facing the entrance to the *sukkah* stood the Chair of Elyahoo, or the Chair of Elijah, with silver finials adorning its four corners. The chair, holding a set of the five books of *torah*, predated my birth and perhaps the birth of my older siblings. But that relic is gone with the rest, as my parents had to leave most of their possessions behind when they left Iraq in 1958 and immigrated to Israel.

Sukkoth was a time of balmy weather and pleasant outdoor living, and we received our guests and visitors in the *sukkah*. One friend could always be counted on to show up on *sukkoth*, and that was the man we called "Ghahmeen *el Akhas*" – Ghahmeen the Mute. A handsome, thoughtful man in his fifties, Ghahmeen always came neatly dressed in suit and tie. I was fascinated by the thick tufts of hair sprouting from his ears, and had to stifle the urge to tug at them. Ghahmeen's vocal chords had never fully developed, but this infirmity didn't prevent him from being fully engaged in conversation.

My father and Uncle Moshe seemed to be able to decipher some of what he said, but what he lacked in vocal ability he made up for in body language. If you were to see him on a silent movie screen deep in conversation, if you were to watch his attentive expression, his emphatic gestures as he tried to reinforce a point, the puffing on his pipe as he listened raptly, you would never guess he was mute

Babylonian Chair of Elyahoo with the Pentateuch and embroidered cover.
The chair was smuggled out of Baghdad in the late nineties. I had it refurbished.

On one visit he made it known that he had forgotten his omnipresent pipe. Uncle Moshe offered him a cigarette. Ghahmeen signaled with raised eyebrows, a shake of his head and a wave of his hand that one cigarette was not enough. He motioned with a V sign that he wanted two. Uncle Moshe complied. If Ghahmeen's intention was to show off in front of us children, he succeeded. I still remember his look of contentment as he leaned back puffing on two cigarettes at once, while we watched in amazement.

Ghahmeen was a man devoid of self-pity, who appeared at peace with the hand fate had dealt him. I often wondered how he managed to take the bus, do his shopping, choose the cloth for his suits, and haggle with the tailor or shoemaker. No one knew where he worked or how he managed to pay his bills. No one knew what happened to him during the mass exodus from Iraq. He couldn't read newspapers. Did he know about the one-year window when the Jews were given the opportunity to file a petition to leave Iraq? Did he stay behind? If he did, did he know why his friends began to suddenly vanish?

NO WAY BACK
The Journey of a Jew from Baghdad

I absorbed Judaism like a sponge, as if it were the water of life—as, in fact, to me it was. This was one area in which my father and I did not conflict. On the night of *sh'buoth*, the anniversary of the giving of the *torah*, we gathered at Uncle Moshe's home and stayed up all night – young and old, men and women, pious and impious alike. We called this vigil *tikkun leil sh'buoth*. My Hebrew tutor explained that it was not enough to just observe the anniversary of the giving of the *torah*; one needed also to experience the receiving of the *torah* by spending the night studying sacred texts and focusing on the great wonder God brought to the world.

At midnight, we took a break. It was time for blessings, *z'man b'rakhoth*. Aunt Guerjiyi served fruits and cakes. Everyone recited aloud the blessing over the food, and all present responded enthusiastically as one chorus: Amen. But there was more to the break than the ritual blessing and eating. There was a sense of togetherness, a sense of pride and, in a country such as Iraq where life was precarious, there was a deep sense of gratitude we were alive to celebrate the occasion one more time.

We lit candles in memory of loved ones. Any one, young or old, man or woman could light as many candles as he or she wished. We whispered a short prayer from the heart. The candles stood in the far corner of the courtyard. I felt in tune with the mystery of life and death and a reverence for those who were no longer with us, as I watched the glittering flames.

One year, when I was eleven years old, I went up to the roof at Uncle Moshe's home, some fifteen minutes before dawn. The roof was one level above the courtyard. I sat on one of the beds on the roof. I could hear the participants singing the traditional closing hymn: "*yom yom odeh la el*" – "Day in day out, I thank God for giving us the *torah*." That song meant that the vigil had come to an end and that it was time to head for the synagogue for services. People sang with renewed vigor. There was a sense of relief, triumph, and pride. We had made it. We had followed in the footsteps of our ancestors, staying up all night engaged in *torah* study.

On the roof, the cool breeze blew gently. I looked at the sky and I thought to myself, "This is the moment when G-d appeared at Sinai. This was the day when G-d gave us the *torah*." I stared at the fading stars. It was a quiet, solemn moment. I felt the divine presence all around me, and I felt it in my bones. I stood motionless and let it wash over me. It was a moment of inspiration such as I had never experienced before. And for a fleeting moment, I felt as if I had melted away. I was no longer standing on this earth. I was way out there in the universe. I had merged with the cosmos.

It was awesome.

NO WAY BACK
The Journey of a Jew from Baghdad

I went downstairs. I was dazed. Nothing looked real. I saw my father and put my arms around him. I needed his reassurance. Baba took my hand. He gave me a long pensive look. It seemed as if I had managed to communicate to him what I had just experienced without uttering a word.

Slowly the two of us walked together and headed for the synagogue.

TRANQUIL INTERLUDES

My childhood in Baghdad, safe in the bosom of my family, was in many ways a wonderful life. It was the threat from outside that finally destroyed it. Those days are gone and I feel their loss. In the early days, we had no intimations of the terror and upheaval that the future held, and, for the most part, we enjoyed what life brought us. Some of my fondest memories are of our summertime swims in the Tigris River.

(Left) Floater for training beginners, carved out of the trunk of a palm tree (right).

When I was about ten, our father arranged for swimming lessons for Jacob and me. Our instructor swam in the river beside us with a huge inner tube around his waist. We could hold on to this tube any time we felt tired. We had an extra safeguard in our "floaters," pieces of the spiky bark of palm trees that were padded and attached to our bodies. I wore three of these floaters; Jacob—who was less enamored of the water than I-- wore four. Within three days, I had discarded one of my floaters and joined the group that swam all across the mile-wide Tigris and back. From then on, swimming became my summer passion

NO WAY BACK
The Journey of a Jew from Baghdad

Every morning during that summer, my father, Jacob and I made our way to the bridge in downtown Baghdad to meet our swimming instructors and about 50 other young Jewish boys who swam together. Often, we'd watch the young gymnast who dove from the top of one of the bridge's beams and did breathtaking acrobatics in midair before hitting the water.

Our swims took us to the opposite bank of the Tigris, a wild and green place where we were able to glimpse the strange practices of the tribal people who lived there. My father called them the "Sun Worshippers," and they immersed animals in the water before killing them for food. Women from the tribe stood in the water at the edge of the river, their black hair loose about their faces, their wet skirts flapping around their knees, their brawny arms holding a hen, a rooster or a sheep. They bent toward the water and muttered incantations, as they dunked the animals in the water. The shrill voices of the women mingled with the squawking of the hens, the crowing of the roosters, and the bleating of the sheep. All of the animals struggled to escape, the hens' wings flapping and churning up the water, the sheep's feet waving in the air, as they tried to find a footing in the riverbed. Sometimes the women ended up flat on their backs in the water, while an escaping hen or sheep flew or scurried toward the shore. There it was recaptured by other women waiting on the bank, guarding the animals next in line for immersion. The women took no notice of us as we stood in the water at a safe distance and watched wide-eyed.

During the summer, my father, Jacob and I would wake up before dawn and after our daily prayers, head for the river. I envied the boys who arrived early, for they got extra time in the water before the lessons began. One morning I decided to remedy that situation by turning the clocks in our home back so the alarm would ring early. Unfortunately I overdid it. The alarm sounded two hours earlier than usual. That puzzled my father and my brother. I kept mum. That morning we arrived at the bridge before anybody else and we had lots of time for swimming. If my father figured out what had happened to the clock, he never shared that information with me.

The freedom of the outdoors was a rare pleasure in my tightly sheltered world. As a small boy I had a tricycle that I wasn't allowed to ride in the street. We children were not allowed to venture beyond the walls of our home. As I grew older, bicycles were forbidden to me by my father—probably because there were so many collisions that left cyclists dead. I didn't listen. I had my own tutoring money, and I began riding a rented bicycle along the Tigris until I was alone in the wilderness. Cycling gave me an almost unheard of taste of freedom. One day, however, my exhilaration was interrupted when I fell off the bicycle and broke my wrist. I rode back to the rental shop in agony and went home to be comforted by my mother and roundly castigated by my father.

The matter of the bicycle was eventually resolved in my favor. My sister Jamila's husband, Ezra, worked for an agency that imported luxury bicycles from England, and he arranged for me to buy a shiny new BSA bicycle. Other members of the family sided with me against my father, and he was forced to give in. When I registered to leave Iraq and my possessions were confiscated, the only item that I missed was that beloved bicycle.

I never dreamed of owning a car. In Iraq cars were headaches. They broke down frequently and the few garages charged exorbitant sums for repairs. *ammu* Guerji, our family doctor, owned several cars to ensure that he always had one in working condition. He employed a chauffeur who doubled as a mechanic. When members of my immediate family wanted to get from one place to another, we took the bus, walked, or hired a taxicab or a hackney carriage.

The horse-driven hackneys were slower and more expensive than buses, but much more fun. Often we had an eccentric driver who flouted traffic rules and the police alike. He burst into full-throated song and danced while navigating the clogged streets. When the police signaled him to stop, he gave them a raspberry and kept going through an intersection, while cars swerved to avoid colliding with us. We children giggled with delight at his outrageous—and dangerous--antics. It was exciting to be the center of attention, and to see someone make fools of the police we dreaded but couldn't ourselves defy.

BAR MISWAH

In Iraq the coming of age for girls, *bath miswah*, and for boys, *bar miswah*, marked the time when a girl turned twelve-and-a-half and a boy thirteen years and five days. At that age, they were considered adults, subject to the privileges and obligations of a Jewish adult. A religious ceremony and festivities marked the *bar miswah* day. Nothing was done to celebrate a young woman's *bath miswah* day.

My *bar miswah* ceremony, on June 24, 1945, was held in my parents' home. As part of the ceremony, it was the custom to have the elder of the family demonstrate to the *bar miswah* boy how to put on the *tefilleen*, the phylacteries. Baba invited his close friend, Iraq's *hakham boshi* (Chief Rabbi) Sasson Kh'doury, to serve as the honored elder for my ceremony.

The house was in a hubbub hours before the celebration. A chef prepared special dishes; servants swept the floors, washed the courtyard and walkways, dusted the furniture, and polished the windows. Everyone in the family was busy doing something. A sense of urgency seemed to have gripped everyone - everyone, that is, except me.

NO WAY BACK
The Journey of a Jew from Baghdad

"What is the big deal?" I kept asking myself. The rabbi would show me how to put on the *tefilleen*. But I knew how to do that. I had watched my father put on the *tefilleen* many times. I would be reading from the *torah* for the assembled guests. But I read Hebrew well, and I was not worried that I might stumble. Why did people around me have to get so excited? Why was it necessary to wash all the walkways upstairs, shine the glass of every window?

On a sandbar in the Tigris near our home,
on my bar miswah day

Even now, as I look back, I am amazed at how nonchalant I was. But I realize I was the last in my family to become *bar miswah*, and my mother wanted it to be a big day. I remember her telling my father that she didn't want the day to slip by hardly noticed, as it had on Jacob's *bar miswah* day.

"I am not going to have another son. This is my last one," she told my father when he suggested we forgo a big celebration.

Early that afternoon, a friend and I sneaked out and walked the few yards from our home to the Tigris to take a swim. The sun shone brightly, the water sparkled and it felt wonderful to be away from the commotion at the house. I felt I was entitled to do what gave me most pleasure that day. It was fun to find a sandbar and lie on it in the middle of the river, surrounded by water.

The ceremony went without a hitch. Our home was filled to capacity with friends, family and neighbors. The most important guest for me was *ma demoiselle* Sim'ha, my favorite kindergarten teacher. Everyone seemed to have a good time. Mama radiated happiness, having gotten her wish.

On the following Sabbath, I was called to read my portion from the *torah* scroll. I went with the same self-confidence I'd felt on my *bar miswah* day. I knew that portion by heart. But as I stood face to face in front of the *torah* scroll, my self-assurance vanished. It was the first time I had seen the script of a *torah* scroll up close. Always before, I had practiced my portion using my printed *torah* book, which had all

On my *bar miswah* day, June 24, 1945

The hakham boshi, Sasson Kh'doury, shows me how to put on the tefilleen. I wore sesseed (prayer shawl) and sidara (Iraq's national hat). Hakham Sasson wore the Babylonian rabbinical vestment and amama, or head co

I sat in front of the hakham boshi, Sasson Kh'doury, and read the torah passages commanding the wearing of tefilleen, as my father (seated at the left end of the sofa with a sidara on his head) and guests listened.

Guests and family members
Maternal grandma Aziza (with the white head gear) seated in the center of front row.
Standing in the back, l to r: Mama, Reyna, Saleem (cousin), Helwa and Muzli. Latifa,
seated at the extreme left; Aunt Guerjiyi, seated 4ᵗʰ from the left, with white dress, facing to the right.

sentences and paragraphs marked. But the script in the *torah* scroll was one uninterrupted blur. I could have begun intoning my portion from memory, but somehow I was fixated on the script in front of me. Today *torah* readers practice from a *tikkun lakor'eem*, a book that replicates the *torah* script, and they are not taken by surprise when they come face to face with the script of the *torah* scroll.

The service leader must have sensed my bewilderment. Perhaps other *bar miswah* boys had had a similar experience. With his head lowered close to my ear, he began intoning my *torah* portion softly. That jump-started me. It took my mind off the bewildering scroll. I started reading, and it all came back.

When I finished, the service leader looked at me with a smile and intoned the traditional blessing "Hazak Obaroukh" – "May you be strong and blessed." I could never thank him enough.

In 1948 I passed the French Brevet –the equivalent of a high school graduation exam--and, with that, my *Alliance* days came to an end. I had yet to complete the ministry of education's Arabic program. So I transferred to Shamash School, where I prepared for the Iraqi secondary school test.

Shamash, a modern school operated by the Jewish community, was established in 1928. It was housed in an enormous structure donated by three Baghdadi brothers - Benjamin, Jacob, and Joseph Shamash. Shamash prepared its students to sit for the University of London's Matriculation. Like other *Alliance* graduates, I had limited training in

English. But when I took the Matriculation exam, I stuck to plain and simple writing. When the results were announced, and my name was among those who had passed, I felt emboldened.

There was talk in Shamash about an advanced test in English - English Proficiency. I was warned that nine out of ten Shamash veterans - those who had five years of high school English instruction - failed the test. Undeterred, I took time off from my regular study to prepare for the Proficiency.

I passed the written part of the test, but there was the oral part to contend with. The examiner gave me a text to read aloud and told me we would discuss it when I had finished reading it. Discuss it? Discussion in French or in Judeo-Arabic I could handle, but I couldn't speak two sentences in English without stumbling. Still, I had no choice. In for a penny, in for a pound, I said to myself, and began reading. It was difficult reading; there were many words I had not encountered before. Even now, when I see a word in English for the first time, my tendency is to pronounce it the French way. I did the same thing with that text. The examiner ended the session abruptly. "This is Chinese," he growled in disgust. I didn't need to tell him it was Chinese to me, too. Humbled, I went back to my regular class work.

Alliance graduates tended to stick together and didn't mix much with Shamash veterans. It was snobbishness on our part. But I thought highly of a number of my teachers. I remember my Shamash science teacher, the late Dr. Nissim Ezra Nissim, a graduate of the University of Michigan at Ann Arbor, a bright, lucid and dedicated teacher. Dr. Nissim was one of those needy students whose graduate work was fully paid for by our community.

Dr. Nissim reinforced what I'd learned first from my sister Jamila: that we couldn't know everything, that knowledge is too wide to be encompassed by any one person. When a student asked a question that he couldn't answer, Dr. Nissim readily confessed his ignorance, promising to research the question and get an answer. Another teacher might have dismissed the question or blustered his way through with a half-baked response. Not Dr. Nissim. He respected knowledge too much.

And there was Mr. Rogers, one of our English teachers. Mr. Rogers was a chubby, middle-aged Englishman, with blue eyes and thinning blonde hair. He had left his teaching position in England during the war years and joined the British military. After retiring from the military he joined Shamash's faculty. I remember him especially for his clarity and his sense of humor.

One day, when he was teaching in the classroom adjacent to ours, his students walked out of the classroom en masse. They were agitated, and they paced the hallway arguing among themselves. Clearly, something awful had happened.

It seems that during his lecture, Mr. Rogers had made a remark that the students understood to mean he concurred with Hitler's killing of the Jews of Europe. The story spread like a brushfire. World War II was still fresh in our minds. We were reeling from the horror of the extermination of European Jewry and were shocked to hear what the students next door relayed. My class had a lecture scheduled with Mr. Rogers right after the recess, but we decided to join the others in a boycott. We wanted the school principal to investigate the matter before deciding if we would continue the boycott.

The principal joined us in our classroom, and reported that Mr. Rogers had denied saying what was attributed to him. The principal told us he felt convinced of Mr. Rogers' sincerity; he thought we should hear him out.

We agreed to listen to his explanation.

Mr. Rogers looked tense, even frightened, when he walked in. He was stooped, his face was red, his hands were shaking, and he avoided eye contact with us. I felt sorry for him. I no longer remember the details of his explanation. But I remember feeling there had been a colossal misunderstanding and that the man might have been accused unjustly. Was I just trying to paper over an unpleasant incident I couldn't deal with? Was I concerned about what a prolonged boycott would do to our education? Or did I really believe him? I don't know. But the class finally agreed to accept Mr. Rogers' apology, and move on.

My high School class, 1949-50
Samra Shamash seated in front row, third from left; Daniel in back row,
sixth from left.

By June of 1950, my years of Arabic secondary schooling had come to an end. Two months later, the ministry of education announced that two *Alliance* graduates -- my classmate, Miss Samra Shamash, and I -- had scored the highest in the country in English composition.

Samra and I shared a five-dinar prize, which I accepted without much excitement. My mind was no longer on Iraq. I had already signed away my Iraqi citizenship in return for being allowed to emigrate, and was waiting for the day when I would leave the country.

That was also the time when *l'Alliance* was forced to shut down. From all I have been able to gather, to day *l'Alliance* lies in ruins, its doors broken, its windows shattered, its long beautiful walkways dilapidated. It saddens me to think of the fall of the giant. Sometimes I wonder about the portrait of Sir Albert, the nobleman who had made a gift of that building to my alma mater. What happened to that portrait? Is it still hanging proudly where it hung for generations? And the Sasson synagogue? It was opened for services on the Sabbath, kept always sparkling, and it had rolling steel doors to protect it from plunder. Does it, too, lie in ruins?

A HISTORY OF VIOLENCE

THE SWINGING PENDULUM

My parents lived through calm times in Baghdad and through times when Jews were persecuted. My father told me about the peaceful times, and though I drank in his stories, that is exactly what they were for me - stories.

In my experience, whatever peace we enjoyed in Baghdad during my years of growing up was shaky at best. Still, in the history of my community, there was no counterpart to the pogroms that took place against the Jews in Eastern Europe with the open support of those countries' governments. Our more fortunate history was due not so much to the tolerance of the local populace, as to the restraining influence of the Ottomans, who ruled Iraq for four centuries (1534-1918), a period of intermittent peace and persecution for the Jews. The Turks were protective of their Jewish subjects, and Jews were frequently appointed to high positions in the Ottoman Empire. Iraq's chief sarraf, or banker, was, as far as I know, always a Jew during the Ottoman period.

My father cherished his memories of the Turks from his law school days in Istanbul. He taught me Turkish when I was a boy, and shared with me much of what I know about the experiences of Iraq's Jews during his own lifetime at the turn of the century.

King Faisal I (in light coat) at the boys' Alliance Israelite in Baghdad, January 13, 1924.

In 1917 the British occupied Iraq and, in August 1921, invited Emir Faisal from Saudi Arabia to come to Iraq. In a national referendum held that year under British oversight, Emir Faisal, later King Faisal I, was elected king of an independent Iraq under British mandate. The

British mandate expired in 1932, at which time Iraq became an independent country and was admitted to the League of Nations.

Faisal I was supportive of the Jewish community, and the Jewish community loved him. His first Minister of Finance, Sir Sasson Haskell, was Jewish, a graduate of my alma mater - *l'Ecole de l'Alliance Israelite*. Some refer to Sir Sasson as the Alexander Hamilton of modern Iraq, for his genius in putting the newly independent nation's financial house in order. Faisal I was enamored of the educational accomplishments of the Jewish community, and often took dignitaries from abroad to visit the Jewish schools in Baghdad. I remember from my childhood when we spoke of Faisal I as *"mehasidei oummot haolam,"* or "Righteous among the Nations."

Faisal I died in 1933, a year after I was born, and his son Ghazi ascended the throne. That, my father told me, marked the beginning of the dark times of the mid thirties and forties for the Jews of Iraq, the years of my growing up in Baghdad. Ghazi surrounded himself with a group of extremists who were anti-British, anti-Jewish, and pro-Nazi. They were supported and financed by the German embassy in Baghdad and, according to my father, they circulated Hitler's *Mein Kampf,* the Protocols of the Elders of Zion, and other rabid anti-Jewish books. (I learned later that excerpts, rather than the full texts of *Mein Kampf* and the protocols, as my father told me, were translated by local newspapers). Even though I was only seven years old, I still remember how terrified we were when, in 1939, the Mufti of Jerusalem, *haj* Ameen al-Husseini, joined the group around Ghazi. The Mufti, interpreter of Islamic religious law, was a Nazi collaborator. In Iraq, he helped engineer the pro-Nazi coup, which culminated in the farhood, the massacre of the Jews of Baghdad in June 1941 that my family and I barely escaped.

Iraq's parliament might have had a mitigating influence, but it was a parliament without teeth - pretty much a rubber stamp for whomever happened to be in power. When I was eleven, one of the local papers asked a prominent member of the parliament which direction he thought Iraq should take in World War II. He responded: "Don't get me involved in politics." Even as a child, I was stunned to read his answer. But in time I came to realize that he knew his position was largely ceremonial, not one that could counterbalance or check the king and the prime minister. The most he could do was approve their policies and assist in their implementation.

The government set aside seats in the parliament for a number of non-elected individuals who were heads of tribes. A perhaps apocryphal story about one such member circulated in Baghdad when I was a teenager. When the roll was called in the Iraqi Parliament at the beginning of the session, one of the tribal heads was dozing when his name was called. The representative sitting next to him nudged him to respond. He opened his eyes and declared, "I vote in favor." His neighbor whispered that it was not a vote, just the roll call. The tribal chief opened his eyes and responded indignantly, "I vote in favor and I am also present." Then he went back to dozing.

The enforcement of law was at the whim of those in positions of power. A rule of men, not of law, prevailed. I grew up feeling there was practically nothing on which one could really depend. Everything was volatile and could explode into violence without warning. Rampant government corruption added to the instability and to my feelings of unease. The police, the body that should protect all members of the populace, operated under a system of bribery and payola, as did almost every other branch of the civil service.

Indeed, bribery permeated almost every government nook and cranny: issuance of passports, certification of documents, application for construction work or issuance of business permits. But perhaps the least visible was the annual income tax assessment. There was no estimated quarterly tax payment for business owners, independent professionals, and other self-employed people. Instead, the Tax Assessor calculated the amount owed and sent a tax bill annually to each individual. Those assessments were almost always exaggerated; the burden to show they were excessive was on the taxpayer. Usually this was accomplished with a bribe. The Treasury Department didn't entertain appeals, and taking the case to court was generally more costly than most people could afford. Bribing the Assessor was the path of least resistance.

Many Jews were businessmen and independent professionals, and they were hit hard by the corrupt tax system. One wealthy Jewish businessman enlisted my father to take his case to court. Baba took the case directly to the Appeals Court, where he asked that the Tax Assessor substantiates his assessment of the businessman's earnings. When it was plain the Assessor didn't have the flimsiest documentation, and the businessman had kept good records of his business transactions, the court ruled in favor of the businessman.

This tangled affair couldn't have been more different than my first experience as a U.S. taxpayer. When I filed my first tax return I didn't know I was expected to declare myself as a dependent and deduct a personal exemption from my income. The IRS corrected the mistake on my return and sent me a refund of $120. The government corrected a mistake I had made in its favor? I could hardly believe it. It wouldn't have happened in Iraq.

It was an open secret that the most lucrative government appointment in Iraq was that of the minister in charge of police. That minister appointed the district commanders and expected a monthly payment, which varied with the district, from every district commander. The district commanders in turn shook down the local station commanders, and those in wealthy neighborhoods had to come up with the largest sums. The station serving areas where wealthy Jews lived was one of those.

Accepting bribes was a favorite way to raise funds for the monthly payoffs. People were frequently arrested on trumped-up charges, which were dropped when the police were paid off. If the bribe was not immediately forthcoming, the detainees were tortured to extract confessions and to put pressure on families and communities to come up with the bribe. Since the payola came due every month, the last days of the month were the most dangerous days to walk the streets of Baghdad. Arrests would accelerate if a station commander had not yet raised enough money to meet his quota.

We collected money within the Jewish community in order to pay off the police and free the people who were wrongfully arrested. My father told me that no one liked to help perpetuate a corrupt system, but the Jewish community felt that it was important to save the lives of innocent people. When the arrested person was wealthy enough, he paid the "fine" himself, but there were many who could not afford the fine, and the community had to come to their rescue.

Those collections didn't always save people from torture. Sometimes not enough money was collected. Sometimes the collection didn't reach the police in time. And sometimes the police just enjoyed the sense of power torture gave them, even though they knew the money was on its way.

Many of the charges were preposterous. Two well-dressed Jews were picked up and accused of engaging in homosexual acts in the middle of the street. When they were brought in front of the station commander, he slapped their cheeks and spat in their faces. The arrested men knew exactly what was going on. This initial roughing-up was typical, and was meant to intimidate. It was a clear message hinting of worse things to follow, if the men didn't pay the expected bribe. And, of course, they did pay.

The police saw no need to cover up these activities. Corruption was built into the system, and inventing an original charge was something a police officer saw as an ingenious accomplishment. The station commander in charge of the "homosexual" case related his part in the story when he was a guest in the home of Jewish friends of ours. He bragged about his ingenuity in intimidating the two Jewish men. Our friends said he chuckled when he told them proudly, "You should have seen their faces when I slapped their cheeks and spat in their faces. They were even afraid to wipe the spittle off their faces."

It didn't matter to him that he was telling the story in a Jewish home. He knew the Jews couldn't do anything about the situation. He held the power and felt no need to conceal his contempt for the powerless Jews. He could visit in Jewish homes and eat Jewish food, and the very next day he could arrest those very same Jews on a trumped-up charge.

NO WAY BACK
The Journey of a Jew from Baghdad

NIGHT TERRORS

The local police station in our district was across the street from our home. Every sound from the station seemed to make its way into my bedroom at night, the time when the torture took place. I could hear the sharp sound of the bamboo rod as it hit human flesh.

This initial torture was often done on the ground floor. There was also a room in the basement, where the police would torture their victims to get them to concede or admit guilt. From there, the sounds of people in anguish rent the dark night. At first the victims cried and yelled. After a while, the cries turned to howling, just howling.

The worst time was summer, when we slept on the roof. The windows of the police station were open when the police started their lashings. The police didn't care what their neighbors might think; they knew that nobody would stop them.

I remained glued to my bed on the roof during those summer nights, as I heard the cries of pain coming from the victims and felt waves of helplessness wash over my body. The thought that a member of my family could be the next victim kept knocking at the doors of my mind. I held my hands over my face, trying to keep that horrible thought at bay. But I couldn't shut out the sounds of terror, the sounds that still invade my life.

For seven years—from the age of eleven until I escaped Baghdad—my dreams were haunted by these nightly sounds of human agony. I don't recall speaking with my parents about my fears. In those days, we didn't wear emotions on our sleeves, or talk much about feelings. If my parents sought to comfort me, it was usually with a touch or a hug. There was an unspoken understanding that we were highly vulnerable.

When I was in the transitional camp, *sha'ar aliyah*, immediately after my arrival in Israel from Baghdad, several times I awakened in the middle of the night screaming in fear. I was fortunate to be sharing the tent with a wonderful Kurdish family from Northern Iraq. When I woke up the first time, both parents were sitting at my bedside with their arms around me, gently telling me that it was OK, that we were no longer in Iraq. They told me I had been screaming that the police were coming.

Sometimes I still dream I am back in Baghdad sleeping in my bedroom. I hear the voices of the victims screaming in pain. I wake up terrified, look around and wonder, "Where am I?" It takes me a while to realize I am no longer in Baghdad across the street from the police station.

It has been difficult to shake loose from the terror. For years after I left Iraq, I remained conscious of fear sitting on my shoulder ready to spring from its perch, grow before my eyes into full-blown terror, and hold me frozen in its grip. To this day, I cannot bring myself to enter the Muslim quarter of any city. And late at night, an unexpected loud knock at the door or a sudden shout from the street is enough to leave me in a cold sweat and send shudders up and down my spine.

Probably the biggest legacy from my time in Iraq is this fear of torture. In 1956, when I was the sergeant of an Israeli combat unit on the Egyptian border, I worried that we might be taken captive while retreating. I preferred to fight until I was shot and killed in battle, if it came to that, rather than fall into the hands of Arabs who tortured their prisoners.

By law, I was supposed to reveal the line of retreat to the soldiers under my command. Instead, I kept the line of retreat to myself. Perhaps I should not have done so unilaterally, but at the time I felt I was probably the only person in the group who knew the awful consequences of possible capture by the Arabs. I felt protective of the soldiers under my command and couldn't bear to think of any one of them being tortured. I pictured their howls piercing the dark night, as did the howls of the people tortured by the police in Baghdad. I knew I could not let anyone, not just myself, go through that.

THE NAZI TAKEOVER

During World War II, all Arab countries had Nazi leanings, but Iraq was the only Arab country that invited the Nazis to come and make Iraq part of the Nazi axis. The fact that Iraq itself was a violent society only made the situation worse.

In 1941 the King of Iraq was six-year old King Faisal II. His father, the Nazi collaborator King Ghazi, had been killed in an automobile accident in 1939. At the time Faisal II's maternal uncle was appointed Regent until his nephew reached the age of 18. The Regent himself was only 18 years old, and a playboy to boot.

In April 1941, *rasheed* Ali alGaylani became Iraq's Prime Minister, backed by a junta of four pro-Nazi colonels, whose aim was to kick out the British and invite the Nazis to Iraq. The Regent, fearing for his safety, fled Baghdad. The city fell under the power of the colonels, and the British made a strategic retreat to Habbaniyeh, some 50 miles to the southwest. With neighboring Syria under Vichy control, the British likely calculated that the Nazis would be able to invade Baghdad from their nearby foothold in Damascus. Indeed, pilots dressed in Nazi uniform were observed in Baghdad not long after the coup was declared. Meanwhile, the pro-Nazi junta held Baghdad's Jewish community hostage. Cries of "Kill the Jews" were heard everywhere, and special youth paramilitary groups roamed the streets. Unarmed and unable to defend ourselves, we couldn't escape, as restrictions on leaving Iraq steadily tightened.

The arrival of other Arab nationalists from neighboring Syria and Palestine further fueled anti-Jewish sentiments. Swastikas were painted on the walls of shops on *rasheed* Street –Baghdad's main thoroughfare. During this period street attacks on Jews increased, and Jewish shops were often looted. These incidents often took place on Friday afternoons, when people filed out of the mosques. The mob would run in the streets, yelling and screaming, with bulging eyes that exuded hate. They screamed *"Allahu Akbar,"* "God is the greatest," with its implication that their violence was perpetrated on behalf of God. They attacked and beat Jewish people unlucky enough to be in their path.

I was nine years old when the 1941 coup took place. But I was overcome by feelings of isolation and despair when I began to realize what was happening to us. Only the fact that England was at war with Iraq gave us some hope.

The stakes were enormously high. We knew that if England fell to Hitler, we were lost. And our dread only intensified when we saw Iraqis jubilant and dancing in the streets, celebrating the imminent downfall of the British. At this low point, Winston Churchill's leadership lifted us from utter despair - he was our idol and inspiration. Uncle Guerji would listen to his speeches on the BBC in our home, and even though I couldn't understand a word, the defiance and resolve in Churchill's voice needed no translation.

Our father's unwavering faith in Churchill was palpable when he gathered us together and read us the British leader's speeches that he had clipped from the newspaper. We felt Baba's faith when he'd pause after reading a promise by Churchill that brighter days lay ahead, that England would win the war and punish Hitler for his crimes. Wide-eyed, he would silently look each one of us in the eye, as if to say, "Did you hear it? Did you get the message? We are going to win." With Churchill's words transmitted this way by our father and ultimate protector, the revered world leader might have been with us in the room. And his speeches from a faraway land became, thanks to Baba's intervention, intimate and profoundly reassuring sources of calm.

In May 1941, the British moved on Baghdad. During the British assault against the Iraqi military, British planes targeted military installations almost every night. One could expect them almost on the dot, at midnight. We waited for the raid to be over before we went to sleep. Bombs rattled our windows, our house shook and we quaked in our shoes. I went to sleep only to have nightmares about the bombs, and about the Iraqis who might break into our house at any time.

NO WAY BACK
The Journey of a Jew from Baghdad

The Jewish community's loyalties were with the British, though we could never openly say so. Indeed, the Iraqis coerced us into supporting their war effort against the British. Young paramilitary gangs, neighbors and all sorts of other groups came to our home to collect money for the fight against the British. My parents were afraid that rebuffing them would invite charges of treason and identify us as British sympathizers. My parents were giving money to support the Nazis who intended to kill us along with the British whom we saw as our friends. In effect, we were giving money to bring about our own demise. It was difficult to make sense of what we were going through.

Baghdad's Jews collected large sums of humanitarian aid for the Red Crescent, the Muslim counterpart of the Red Cross. Under Jewish law, Jews are expected to help the wounded and otherwise needy, regardless of religion or nationality. Even beyond that, we were shaken down regularly to help pay for the war against the British.

My family had its own private terror, too.

There was a huge lot for storing scrap metal behind our house. During the day, British planes circled above the lot, no doubt checking whether it was a military depot. The lot, the size of an entire city block, probably looked like military target from the air. The Iraqis often placed military depots in civilian areas to deter the conscientious enemy from dropping bombs on them and inflicting civilian casualties.

Every night we were overcome by anxiety. "Do you think they will bomb the yard tonight?" we would ask each other, our eyes wide as we stared out into the darkness. Nobody was brave enough to mention our worst fear. If a bomb was dropped on the lot, it could hit our home. Even the force of a near miss could destroy our home. We were terrified of being buried alive under the rubble—especially since we knew the authorities wouldn't spend time or effort in digging us out. And so every night we waited and, when the bombs fell on other parts of the city, heaved a sigh of relief and went to sleep when the raid was over. In the end the British never bombed the lot behind our house.

One night, a second cousin of mine who lived a block away from us tried to turn on the radio. The house was in total darkness, as decreed by martial law. Our windows were covered with dark curtains, but we were still not allowed to turn on lights. When my cousin couldn't find the station he wanted, he turned the lights on for a split second just to see the radio dial. The military happened to be in the area. They banged on his door with the butts of their rifles. When he opened the door they arrested him.

"We know you are trying to establish telegraphic contact with the British to direct their air raids," they told him, as they dragged him outside his home.

There was a stream flowing in front of my cousin's home, and the soldiers took him there to kill him. He struggled with them. His brother ran quickly to the police station on the other side of the street. The police had not noticed what was happening, and didn't even know the military were in the area because the night was dark as pitch. To my cousin's good fortune, the police and the military were on bad terms. The police came in force, not so much to rescue my cousin, but to object to the military's infringement on their turf. Under cover of the ensuing skirmish, my cousin escaped.

During the coup period, my brother, my two sisters, and I suffered from stress-related illnesses. My sisters Muzli and Reyna couldn't retain any food. My brother Jacob and I developed symptoms of urinary-tract blockages. Jacob's case was much worse than mine. Only at night, when my father got him out of bed half asleep, was he able to urinate.

It was not always possible to see our family physician because of the disruption. Many establishments were shut down. My father had a hard time practicing law during that period. When he left the house for his office, we never knew if he would return. Terror was palpable in the atmosphere at home. I could even feel my father's worry, though he tried so hard to hide it.

On the surface, my father comported himself as a non-Zionist, but I suspected his heart was with those of us supporting the struggle for a Jewish homeland in Israel. His pretense of non-Zionism seemed to be just that-- pretense. My father visited Palestine several times, a practice common among Zionists. In 1920 he bought a large lot on Mt. Scopus in Jerusalem. He held on to the deed until he arrived to Israel, even though it was extremely dangerous during the forties to keep such damning evidence of connection to "the Zionist entity".

I suppose my father reckoned he had much to lose antagonizing the Iraqis. In addition to being an independent lawyer, he was a member of the Governing Council that oversaw the six central--and most important--provinces of Iraq, including Baghdad. Because of his prominence and greater visibility, my father couldn't risk being perceived as an enemy of Iraq. As a leader of the Jewish community, it would also have further endangered our community.

FARHOOD

On the last day of May, 1941 rumor had it that the prime minister, Rasheed Ali alGaylani, and the Mufti of Jerusalem had escaped to Germany—rumor that later proved correct. That day, my brother and I felt cooped up, and prevailed on Baba to take us for a walk by the Tigris in the early evening.

NO WAY BACK
The Journey of a Jew from Baghdad

It was cool, and I was relieved to be out in the open. We drank in the scents of sweet grass and marigolds growing along the riverbank. Flocks of sparrows chirped above our heads. It was reassuring to see life around us, and it was soothing to stroll by the Tigris and watch its peaceful flow.

Then, without warning, a shot shattered the peace of the evening. I clutched my father's hand. His face mirrored the anxiety on mine. Jacob stood stock-still, and I could see that he, too, was alarmed. We didn't give voice to our anxiety, because that would mean admitting that something awful was happening or about to happen, something we didn't want to face. So we walked on, but our peaceful interlude was over. Jacob and I both walked as close to Baba as we could. It felt good to feel his hand enfold mine as we walked.

A few moments later, we heard the sound of a machine gun from close by. We could no longer ignore the potential danger. We turned in the direction of home and quickened our pace. I was terrified that somebody would kill my father. So many children had lost their parents. I didn't want to face my fear or think about what might be happening to cause it. Maybe it was the military causing the disturbance, but it could also be the mob. I didn't know which I feared most.

When we arrived home I could see the anxiety in my mother's eyes, and her relief that we were safe. Once we arrived there, we stayed at home. We didn't say much. We couldn't settle down to do anything. It was the eve of the Jewish holiday *sh'buoth*, but no one felt like celebrating. My father did recite the *kiddush* blessing and my mother and Jamila made half-hearted attempts to get us to eat.

We desperately wanted to believe that what we had heard was just one random shooting. We wanted to believe that with the removal of *rasheed* Ali alGaylani and his cohorts from power the worst was behind us. Yet the tension was thick in the very air we breathed. On the eve of *sh'buoth* we usually gathered at Uncle Moshe's home to study sacred texts all night. But on that *sh'buoth* night we were afraid to venture out.

The following morning, we didn't attend the synagogue. A close friend of the family, Shlomo Gah'tan--whom we reverently called *ammu* Shlomo, *ammu* meaning paternal uncle--dropped in to pay us the traditional holiday visit. *Ammu* Shlomo was a short, blond, blue-eyed man in his early sixties, a wealthy businessman who chose his words with great care. We children loved him like a grandfather. While *ammu* Shlomo sat and chatted with us, the telephone rang. It was his wife, *amma* Rahel – *amma*, meaning paternal aunt, being an honorary title. She had sent their car and driver to fetch *ammu* Shlomo and drive him home. Violence was rampant in the Jewish areas of downtown Baghdad, she said, and she wanted *ammu* Shlomo to come home.

NO WAY BACK
The Journey of a Jew from Baghdad

We were all plunged into deep anxiety. No more pretending, no more wishful thinking. The call from *amma* Rahel had said it all: The worst was not behind us; most likely it was ahead of us.

The government owned the radio station in Iraq, so we knew that nothing useful could be gleaned from the radio. The truth was never broadcast over the air. Even rumors, as uncertain as they were, tended to be more informative than the official broadcasts.

We lived in the modern part of Baghdad, where some streets were heavily Jewish, but where Muslims and Christians also lived. Downtown Baghdad, the old part of the city, was almost entirely Jewish. It was in that neighborhood that the massacre began. As the day wore on, we began to hear shots, but were still completely in the dark as to what was happening. We did know that when *rasheed* Ali alGaylani and his cronies escaped, they had left a vacuum in Baghdad. We had thought that the British had moved in to fill the vacuum. Instead, it now seemed that the mob was doing that.

We later learned that when the British had defeated the Iraqi army a few days before, they didn't return to Baghdad, but chose to stop at the outskirts of the city. The Muslim mob, joined by the Iraqi police and the military, seized this opportunity to vent their frustration on Baghdad's Jewish community. Because the Jews had quietly supported the British against the Nazis, we were cast as scapegoats. The British had dealt the Iraqis a humiliating defeat and now the Iraqis would settle that account vicariously--by slaughtering the Jews.

Ever since the pro-Nazi government in Iraq had come to power, hatred for the Jews had been simmering to a slow boil. Now it was boiling over. We, however, had no idea that the police, the military, and the mob had joined forces and that inside the city the mob ruled. Some of those who survived the attacks told us later that the police would come to a Jewish house with the mob and shoot out the lock. Then the mob would break in to loot and kill. They would drag children out of the house and force them to watch as they massacred their parents before their eyes.

We could hear the screams as the mob drew closer to our part of town. It was progressing from downtown Baghdad to our part of the city. We remained locked in our home. My father barricaded the house, but we knew the barricades would be useless against the mob.

In Baghdad, on that *sh'buoth* day, we couldn't flee. There was no place to go. But I could feel my young body poised, ready for flight.

The mob didn't reach our part of town that day. Night fell. The mob's noise subsided. It was especially dark because all the streetlights were turned off, as they had been during the entire period when Iraq was at war with the British. But we could see the pale moon in the sky. It was now the second night of *sh'buoth*. That was a dreadful night, and I don't think any one of us slept. We were cut off from any news of what was happening. We tried to act normally. Meals were prepared, but nobody ate much, and we children wandered about aimlessly.

Rumors flew among our Jewish neighbors the next day. The thrust of all we heard let us know that chaos reigned. The previous day the mob had attacked Jewish homes, and there had been enormous massacres of Jews in the older part of the city.

By midmorning the fearful noise resumed. It got louder as the day wore on. The mob was approaching our neighborhood.

Mama was overwhelmed. Her way of avoiding acknowledgment of the danger was to take a nap. When she woke up in the early afternoon, her cheeks were red, and she looked so innocent and beautiful. I didn't want her to be killed. She looked at me with sleep still clouding her eyes.

"Do we have any news, any news at all?" she asked.

I shook my head. But we both could hear the sounds of the mob and the whistle of the shots getting closer. They were probably no more than a block or two from our home, and we knew what that meant. Even then we didn't want to think about what was happening. My mother held out her arms and I fell into them.

My father had a book of Psalms open, silently reading from it, as he always did when he sought comfort. There was an overriding mood of helplessness. The mob could easily break the locks on our doors at any moment.

We waited and waited frozen in fear, and when the unexpected happened we couldn't at first take it in. We looked at each other in disbelief as we heard the shouts of the mob diminishing and falling silent. We heard horses outside and rushed to the windows to see mounted troops patrolling our street. We later learned these were military regiments loyal to the Regent, who had returned to Baghdad two days before. The British and the Regent had apparently decided that the massacre and chaos had gone far enough. The Regent had directed the units loyal to him to bring order, by whatever means necessary. The regiments had managed to stop the mob in its tracks.

It was late in the afternoon of the second day of *sh'buoth*, but it seemed as if centuries had passed since we had heard the sound of those first shots on the eve of the holiday. We thanked God for our deliverance, for the arrival of the troops.

Years later I read what actually transpired that day. Were it not for a fortunate convergence of circumstances, the Regent's troops wouldn't have made it to our part of town before the mob. Our home might have been invaded, and my family and I might have been massacred along with the rest.

The marauders didn't reach our home because they first spent time returning to their own homes to stash the loot stolen earlier from Jews. They wanted to secure their new riches, and the weight of the stolen goods slowed them down.

It took days before we felt safe enough to venture outside. Only then did we learn the extent of the death and destruction the mob had inflicted on the Jewish community of Baghdad.

Within the next few days we heard from other members of our extended family. My maternal Uncle Guerji had gone to work on the first day of the massacre, not knowing what was taking place downtown. We didn't know he had gone to his office and were too afraid to walk the two blocks to my grandmother's house to check on her and my uncle. Uncle Guerji told us he had left his office and headed home in the early afternoon of that day. The buses were not running, and the streets were chaotic, crowded with looters and gunmen. His office messenger, Mustafa, a Muslim, gave my uncle his uniform and turban, so that he would look like a Muslim. My uncle wore sunglasses to further disguise himself. The messenger escorted my uncle all the way from his downtown office to my grandmother's home.

"I was so grateful for his company," Uncle Guerji told us, "as we walked through *rasheed* Street and through the milling crowds. There were bullets flying all around. I shivered as I heard the bullets hiss through the air, but, thank God, no bullet hit either one of us."

He went on to tell how he had been stopped several times by hoodlums and looters, how he had responded to their queries in the Muslim dialect and how they had then allowed him to proceed unharmed, believing he was a Muslim.

"I am lucky to be alive," my uncle concluded as my mother sighed, and I knew she was thinking of the many others who had not been so lucky.

I remember thinking that my Uncle Guerji had served his country well as an honest civil servant. How could it be that his life was now in danger, just because he was Jewish? How could it be that we were all in danger of being killed, just because we were Jews?

Uncle Guerji's messenger was a reliable friend who saved his life. Not all of the Muslims who had professed to be our friends were as trustworthy.

Across the street from our home was a public school. A Muslim family who looked after the school lived there. They weren't rich, and we often shared our food with them and gave them clothing. Our home was open to them, and we thought of them as our friends.

In the afternoon of the second day of *sh'buoth*, when the mob was getting closer and we could hear their cries of triumph, the Muslim family washed the steps in front of the school and came out to sit there. Among themselves they talked loudly about the neighboring Jewish homes, including ours. They discussed which members of their family would go to which Jewish home with the mob and participate in the looting. They had assigned two members of their family to our house.

They saw us on our second floor balcony, where we had ventured out to try to see what was going on. They knew we could hear every word they said, but that didn't disturb them. They continued to talk openly about their plan to loot our home. To them we were as good as dead and no longer of any account. It still hurts me to remember how Mama used to call them "our good neighbors." I admired her for greeting them with a smile a few days later, when they knocked on our door asking for medicine for a sick baby.

I would like to think the British took back control of Iraq in order to prevent Jews from being massacred. But, if that were their aim, they would have moved on Baghdad sooner than they did. The fact is that the only sure way the British could count on access to Iraqi oil was to control Iraq. But, even though we knew the British acted out of self-interest, we still saw them as our rescuers.

Following their return to Baghdad after the Iraqi coup, the British kept a tight hold on Iraq. They pressured the Iraqis into declaring war against Nazi Germany. The Iraqis complied, but their hearts were not in it, and they cheered whenever the Nazis won a battle.

In our synagogue, I met Jews among the British airmen who moved into Baghdad. They were dressed in their military uniforms when they came to worship with us during the high holidays. They were treated with love and affection and given the seats of honor as treasured sons of the community. They were young and fresh and wholesome and sometimes a little awkward, but they were always respectful and polite.

There was an outpouring of love for the British. They were our friends; but the fact that there were Jews among them standing side by side with the rest of the British people made me very proud. This was a new experience for me—a realization that there were countries where Jews were treated as equal to other members of society. Seeing this first hand strengthened my resolve to leave Iraq one day.

I am not sure if the Jewish soldiers from England recognized how much our lives were circumscribed by living in predominantly Muslim Baghdad. But it was clear to me that their lives were not hindered by living in a Christian society. The seeds of my conviction that the majority in any society should respect minorities were sown, oddly, in Baghdad, a city in which that idea had no credence.

Order was restored as a result of the British presence in Baghdad, but we continued to live uneasily as a hated minority in a Muslim world.

Not long after the big massacre of *sh'buoth*, 1941, it was rumored there was going to be another one, even worse. Some Jews armed themselves. An older friend of mine bought a big handgun. He told me if the mob took over again, he was going into the street to shoot anyone who attacked Jewish homes.

Terrible fears returned. There were intermittent rumors that the mob was coming again. On one occasion, when the rumors held the ring of truth, and Jews wouldn't venture out of their homes, my brother and I started boiling water in the bedroom upstairs near the second-floor balcony, which overlooked the front entrance. We planned to toss bottles of boiling water on the mob when it came to attack our house. I remember the terror that rose in my throat, as we were boiling the water. We knew our tactic wouldn't stem the tide of violence; indeed it would probably further inflame the mob and result in our being tortured before being put to death. But we couldn't sit around feeling helpless; we had to do something to protect our home.

We felt safe pursuing our plan because Baba was downstairs reading the Psalms. We poured the first pan of boiling water into the bottles.

"This will teach them not to mess with the Jews," Jacob said bravely.

I nodded in agreement and began to refill the pan with fresh water.

"What are you boys doing?" I looked up and saw Baba standing in the doorway.

"When the mob gets to our home we're going to toss bottles of boiling water on them. That will stop them in their tracks."

A strange look passed over my father's face. I couldn't interpret it - maybe it reflected a mixture of pride and fear. But then his face settled into a look I more easily identified - one of sternness mingled with sadness.

"As I have told you, children, Jews don't kill."

"But it's self-defense," I protested. "The mob is coming to kill us."

"You can't be sure the mob will kill us. Unless you are one hundred percent sure, you can't attack."

It was a tortured argument, and I guess Baba knew it.

"So we have to wait until we are dead before we can fight back, do we?"

My father didn't reprove me.

"Empty the bottles, son."

I wanted to remind my father that the Maccabees fought back even on the Sabbath, but Jacob was already emptying the bottles.

Was it possible my father was wiping tears from his eyes as he turned to leave the room? No doubt it was heartbreaking to see his sons driven to violence by violence. It took me a while to realize that he was not so much worried about violating Jewish law; rather, he feared that an enflamed mob would torture brazen children who chose to fight back with boiling water—the same fear that tormented me.

NO WAY BACK
The Journey of a Jew from Baghdad

NARROW ESCAPE

As I look back, I realize the 1941 massacre was actually an intense manifestation of the terror that permeated our lives before and afterwards. We couldn't ignore the farhood. It was massive. But living in Baghdad, we tended to subconsciously bury—perhaps as a defense mechanism-- many of the specific incidents of violence and hatred toward us.

One such incident took place in the spring of 1940, one year before the farhood. I was eight and riding the bus home from school with Jacob, Helwa, and Latifa. It was a day when my father's messenger, Saleem, was not able to escort us for protection.

The bus made its way down *rasheed* Street, Baghdad's main thoroughfare, dropping off passengers every few minutes. Our stop was the one right after the bus turned left off *rasheed* Street, where *rasheed* Street met the Tigris boardwalk. On this particular day, we children and one tall Jewish man, perhaps in his early thirties, were the only people left on the bus by the time the bus reached the boardwalk. As the bus turned left, we made sure we had our belongings in hand, ready for our bent-over exit from the bus. We didn't want to get up until the last possible minute.

As the bus approached our stop, the driver braked and we got up to go. Suddenly we were thrown back on our seats as the driver sped up again.

"Stop! Stop!" we yelled in unison, but the driver ignored us. Instead, he went faster and faster. The bus headed toward the deserted section of a very long road past all of the unaware houses, including our maternal grandmother's house. I looked at Jacob in dismay. Where was the driver taking us? Jacob, thirteen years old at the time, looked pale and worried. What would our grandmother think, if she knew what was happening to us? What would our parents do, if we didn't arrive home ever again?

The bus sped past the long park on our left and then, beyond the park, into a deserted part of the road, so dangerous that we had never seen it before. Now we were too terrified to take note of it. I know there were tall trees and lots of undergrowth. We clung to each other, as the trees seemed to race past the bus.

I looked back at the conductor who was sitting on his special seat staring stone-faced ahead. He had to know what the driver's plan was. He held the door handle tightly, probably to make sure no one could open the door and jump out. My heart sank when I realized what was happening.

We were being kidnapped.

Jacob, Helwa, Latifa and I moved closer to each other as we hurtled into the unknown.

Suddenly a voice broke the silence.

"Stop this bus right now!"

It was the Jewish man who was sitting right behind the driver. But the driver didn't even slow down.

The man, who was probably a plumber, took a huge wrench out of a battered bag he had at his feet. He raised the wrench over the driver's head. His face was red and the veins stood out on his forehead, but to me he looked like a protecting angel.

"Stop now or I'll split your head open!" he yelled at the driver.

The bus screeched to a halt, and the man, still holding the wrench, ordered the conductor to unlock the door and get out of the bus. He then watched us get off the bus before he himself got off.

Shaken, we set out on foot, a three-mile walk we had not expected to take when we left home that morning. It was a walk that the bus driver had not expected us to take either.

I looked at my sisters. They were so beautiful. I didn't want to think about what could have happened to them. I glanced behind me. Our rescuer, carrying his heavy bag on his shoulder, was walking slowly a good distance behind us.

"That man was brave." I said.

Jacob nodded and I could tell he admired the man, too.

"He would have killed the driver and the conductor, both. The Jews from the poorer section of town are a lot bolder than we are."

Jacob's remark was borne out just a year later. During the farhood when the mob approached our prosperous neighborhood, we found ourselves totally unprepared. We had no idea how to defend ourselves. We were sitting ducks. In the poorer section of the city, however, the Jews fought back. My father's messenger, Saleem, a Jew who lived in that section, told us that when the mob came, he and his neighbors tore down a wall in his home. They carried the bricks from the wall up to their rooftop and threw them at the mob. They injured several of their attackers, including one policeman. The mob retreated.

World War II came to an end, the Nazis were defeated and the Jews in Europe who survived the concentration camps were liberated. The Arabs established the Arab League, a postwar pact between Arab nations whose battle cry was "Save Palestine," meaning from the Jews. The United Nations began considering the fate of the Jewish settlement in Palestine. Now, as we pinned our hopes on the establishment of a Jewish state in Palestine, the Hagganah, the Jewish underground that later became Israel Defense Force, took on new life.

The Hagganah broadcast underground news from Palestine in Arabic, but the Iraqis prohibited us from listening to it. We would hide with our radio in the far end of our basement, way in the back of the house, to listen to the news. We sat ever so close to the radio, so that the volume could be kept as low as possible. Those times with our Jewish brethren in Palestine were more important to us than our daily meals. We were filled with hope at the thought that the one thing we always prayed for would come to pass, and we would join our coreligionists on the other side of the divide in a Jewish state, all our own.

In Baghdad the government-orchestrated mistreatment of Jews reached new heights. Increasingly, we suffered the consequences of the conflict between the Jews and the Arabs in Palestine. The Iraqis were infuriated that the Jews dared to want a homeland of their own, and they organized demonstrations against Zionism. Each time a demonstration was held protesting the so-called Zionists in Palestine, Jewish shops in Baghdad were looted, Jewish gatherings were attacked, and individual Jews were beaten in the streets.

It was evident that it was not in Britain's interest that Israel be established as a state. Britain depended on Arab oil. It suited its purposes to appease the Arabs, and the Arabs were very much opposed to the founding of a Jewish state.

We no longer regarded the British as our saviors; for in the matter of Israel they were taking the side of the Arabs. In fact, when Israel became independent, the British Broadcasting Corporation took its cue from the Arab press and referred to Israel in their Arabic radio programs as "the supposed Israel." We couldn't trust the Arabic news broadcasts, and now we felt we couldn't trust the BBC, which regurgitated the news broadcast by the Arabs. It was a very lonely time.

After World War II, the Jewish community in Palestine had its own battle over British limitations on Jewish immigration into Palestine. The help the Jews in Palestine were receiving from people in the U.S. contrasted sharply with the active opposition of the British government. But would the American help be enough? Were the Jews in Palestine strong and determined? I, like my classmates, quietly contributed money, through the local Zionist underground, to help the Jewish community in Palestine. We wanted to go to Palestine and join our coreligionists in their struggle for independence. But we were not allowed to leave Iraq.

AL WATHBA

In the years following the farhood it seemed to me that everyone was more watchful and many doors that had been open to Jews were slammed shut. The screws were being tightened on the Jewish community. Jews were officially excluded from any college in the Royal School of Medicine, but through the intercession of the then minister of education, Jamal Baban, an old friend of my father's, my brother Jacob was admitted to the Royal College of Pharmacy in 1947, which was part of the Royal School of Medicine, in spite of the ban on the admission of Jews. Jacob wanted to become a doctor, but the minister of education's influence stretched only so far. As it was, Jacob was the only Jew in his college. People talked in whispers about getting out of Iraq if ever the opportunity arose. Some made their own opportunity and found ways to escape secretly.

Late in one afternoon of January 1948, Uncle Moshe walked into our home; he had some important news to impart.

"Did you hear anything about violent clashes between the police and demonstrators in downtown Baghdad?" he asked.

We shook our heads.

"Surely you heard about the demonstrations today."

"Demonstrations have been taking place for more than a week now," my father said. "What happened to-day?"

"College students have taken to the streets and the police shot straight into the crowd as it marched. At least that's what I heard. Several people were killed or injured, but nobody knows exactly how many."

"God help us," Mama exclaimed.

My mother's face was paper white.

"How can we find out what happened? Jacob!" she began, but couldn't continue.

The thought of Jacob being hurt or dead was too awful to contemplate. All of us heaved a sigh of relief and my mother's face regained its color when Jacob walked through the door an hour later.

I knew the background of the demonstrations. During the last few months of 1947, Iraq was in the process of renegotiating its 1930 treaty with England. Early in January 1948 demonstrations broke out daily in Baghdad in opposition to the new treaty. The demonstrations snowballed a few days later into violence apparently when news reached the demonstrators that, in spite of their opposition, the treaty had been finalized. It was signed in Portsmouth, England, the day before by Iraq's Prime Minister, Saleh Jabir, and the British government. The treaty came to be known as the Portsmouth Treaty.

What struck me most that day and what I still remember is the utter silence of the Iraqi Broadcasting Service on the happenings of that day. I can still picture our whole family gathered in the living room that evening, anxiously awaiting the broadcast of the evening news, hoping to hear the government report on the clashes Uncle Moshe had told us about. We were all disappointed. There was nothing in the newscast about any demonstration. Not a word. Could it be that the rumors about the injured and the dead were all baseless?

The following day's reports in the daily papers, divergent as they were, reminded us once again never to look to the Iraqi Broadcasting

Service for factual reporting. In the newspapers at least there were reports of demonstrations and casualties, although there was no agreement on the scope of the casualties or the causes of the demonstration.

The fateful day of the shootings was followed by several days of increasingly large demonstrations that swept through a wider number of colleges, and many segments of the population. Daily, throngs of demonstrators filled Baghdad's main thoroughfare, *rasheed* Street. As far as I can remember, they started their marches at *bab elmuatham*, gradually began to disperse when they reached central Baghdad, and totally disbanded once they reached the boundary of *bab elshargi*, the entrance to the modern residential section of Baghdad. The demonstrators slowly traversed a route that could probably be covered in about an hour or so of brisk walking.

Those demonstrations came to be popularly known as *alwathba*, an Arabic word meaning "the big leap".

The onset of the demonstration was a tense time for my family. My father worried that the unrest would turn into violence against the Jews. He knew the cauldron of Palestinian conflict was rapidly reaching the boiling point, and feared this might cause the demonstrations to morph into anti-Jewish riots, with the Palestinian conflict as an excuse.

Our schools, however, remained open during the weeks of demonstration. 1948 was also my last year in *l'Alliance*. We were preparing to take our French Brevet within four months, but during those *alwathba* weeks we spent little time doing serious work in school. Instead, we spent most of our class time discussing with our teachers the ins and outs of the demonstrations, never knowing where the discussion was drifting, never seeming to settle on anything substantive.

Jacob's predicament was different. The students' association in his college had decided to require all students in the college to march daily in the demonstrations. Jacob was not enamored of the idea. My brother felt there was nothing in it for us in the Jewish community, regardless of whether the treaty did or did not go through. He felt that the demonstrations were fomented by the *istiklal* party, an extreme Arab nationalist group that had no love for the Jews and that supported Rasheed Ali alGaylani's 1941 coup and resented bitterly his defeat at the hands of the British. My brother was also worried that the demonstration could get out of hand and degenerate into violence. But he had no choice. He marched daily with the rest of the College under a big banner "The Royal College of Pharmacy". One time he hid in the bathroom while his peers were getting ready to leave for the demonstration. When he left the bathroom some twenty minutes later, thinking all were gone, he was surprised to find two of his classmates sitting outside waiting for him. They dragged him with them to the demonstrations.

"I don't want to demonstrate, but I can't get out of it," he complained when he arrived home.

The Jewish community in Baghdad was presented with a dilemma when its leadership had to decide whether the students at the Jewish schools, the Jewish professionals, and the elders of the Jewish community should join in the demonstration. I do not know where the pressure to march came from. It may have come from the organizers, but, if it did, I don't know if it were presented as a suggestion or a threat. But I do remember my father and the rest of the leadership of the community agonizing over the issue. Most preferred that the community not take part, but worried that remaining neutral could put us in danger. In Iraq the concept of neutrality was not recognized -- if you are not with us, you are against us was the accepted credo. The Jewish community maintained good relations with the Regent, Abdul Ilah, and the Prime Minister, Saleh Jabir, the initiators of the negotiated treaty (although in the end, when the heat built up, Abdul Ilah wiggled his way out). Marching in a demonstration against the treaty risked antagonizing both – the Regent and the Prime Minister. On the other hand, sitting on the sidelines risked incurring the wrath of the extremist group, *istiklal*, and its supporters. That could turn the demonstration into violence against the Jewish community. The decision was finally made to demonstrate under the banner of *"alta'ifa al Israeliya"* – the Israelite group (or minority), as we were called in Iraq, and lay a wreath in memory of those who fell in the demonstrations. For me, that harked back to the times when we were coerced into contributing to the war effort against the British during the Rashid Ali alGaylani coup. My school, *l'Alliance*, took part in the demonstration under the banner of *alta'ifa allsraeliya*. I absented myself that day.

I have no recollection of violence directed at me or at the Jewish community during that period, something we feared at the onset of the demonstrations. Several times I ventured out of school to watch the demonstrations at *rasheed* Street. They were mostly orderly. I heard many slogans and saw many banners and I remember some to this day. One banner read, *"Ikhshoushanoo fa'inna eltaraf yazeel elnuam"*, which translates loosely as "choose the rougher way of life because a life of comfort destroys the goodness of life" – a worldview that one may agree or disagree with, but I was not sure how it related to the negotiated treaty, unless any connection with the more modern British was assumed to have a corrosive effect on Iraqi life. A slogan that I heard shouted repeatedly was "Nouri elSaeed *elkundara weSaleh Jabir guitan'ha*," meaning Nouri elSaeed (who served as prime minister many times and who was known for his friendly attitude toward the British) is nothing but a shoe and Saleh Jabir (the prime minister who negotiated the Portsmouth Treaty) is only its shoelace." Many danced and clapped their hands as they sang this slogan at the top of their lungs.

But as I watched the demonstrations and listened to the slogans, it all struck me as surreal. It had nothing to do with me, not really. I realized that to the outside world these demonstrations would be reported as demonstrations against the new treaty. Yet I wondered how many of these demonstrators knew or even cared about the terms of the treaty? Was this just a good opportunity to vent frustrations unrelated to the treaty? How many joined in simply because it was exciting? How many joined in voluntarily? How many were coerced like my brother?

The period of intense demonstrations ended in a bloody clash with the police in which scores of people were killed. That same day Saleh Jabir, who negotiated the treaty, resigned and with that the government fell. The treaty was rescinded not long after.

A few months after the treaty's rejection, opinions about the wisdom of *alwathba* appeared to be changing. Personally I did not care one way or another -- I wanted to leave Iraq. But I remember reading in *alsha'ab* newspaper, a moderate but bold daily, an article assessing the merits of *alwathba*. It had a title that said it all: "The leap that broke the leg of Iraq".

A BEACON OF FREEDOM

I am not sure if many people realize how devastating it is to be deprived of information about what is happening in the outside world.

The news blackout the Iraqis imposed after the establishment of the State of Israel was a dark time. We were deprived of access to papers other than those published in Arab countries. All radio broadcasts, other than those coming from Arab countries and the Arabic program on the BBC, were jammed. Looking back now, I liken the sense of utter isolation we felt then to slow strangulation.

When Iraq and the rest of the Arab countries went to war in 1948 to thwart the establishment of Israel, news came in on the Arab stations: "We have smashed the Jews here, and we have destroyed them there." On the first day of the Arab assault the Iraqi radio announced that the Iraqis had occupied a large part of what was to become Israel. On hearing this, my mother fell apart. She just sat and sobbed. The Arab radio stations reported one victory after another. The thrust of the news was that the Jewish settlement in Israel was being wiped out. We were doomed. The Jews would never have a homeland.

There were families among us who had sons and daughters in Israel serving in the *hagganah*, *irgun tsvaee leumi*, and the Stern underground groups. The news was so bad that those families prepared to sit *shib'a* for their loved ones in Israel.

Still, some lapses and inconsistencies in the Arab news reports began to make us wonder. One day the news reported that the Iraqi army had occupied *kokhav aveer*, a settlement in Israel. A day later came radio reports that the Iraqi artillery was shelling Kokhav Aveer. When I went to school, I asked my classmate Joshua Ezekiel if he had heard the same two reports as I had.

Joshua just grinned. He, too, had noticed the inconsistency. Why would they bomb *kokhav aveer* if it were in their hands, we wondered. They either never seized it, as they claimed, or lost it in the meantime, but wouldn't say so. We both shook our heads. Maybe the Iraqis weren't doing as well as they claimed.

We needed to know the facts and trusted the *Hagganah* radio to give them to us. But every time my siblings and I went to listen to the *Hagganah* station, we could hear only the first few opening sentences identifying the station. After that, there was nothing but static. We slapped the radio; we moved our heads closer; we changed the location of the radio. Nothing helped.

The Arab news media were telling lies, but we couldn't separate the falsehoods from the truth. Even the news from London was twisted. We wanted to know if our brethren in Israel were being decimated, as the Arab press had reported. We needed to look elsewhere for the truth.

Baghdad had three foreign centers of information: the French, the British, and the American. On orders of the Iraqi government, the British and the French centers shut down. The U.S. Information Center didn't comply with the order, and remained open. It maintained a large library and several reading rooms filled with current issues of American newspapers as well as weekly and monthly magazines. We turned there for honest reporting.

I don't know whether the American people were ever aware of the great service they rendered to humanity by establishing U.S. Information Centers around the world or how grateful we were for the unequivocal stand the center in Baghdad took by refusing to shut down. For people who live in open societies with a free press, our starvation for information must be difficult to grasp.

We knew agents of the Iraqi secret police were planted across the street from the Center, and we worried. If they caught us or took our pictures, that would be the end for us and for our families. We tried to sneak in without being noticed.

In the New York Times and other newspapers in the Center's reading room I read a completely different story from the one the Arab press had been feeding us. The Jews in Palestine were not being defeated. They were holding their own. In fact, they were winning. What a relief!

My friends and I had to be careful leaving the Center in order to avoid being noticed by the Iraqi secret service. Our strategy was to gather together inside the door and then burst through onto the street, running and fanning out in different directions. We felt this way the secret police would be taken by surprise and, before they could gather their wits, we would disappear. It was an adventure that could have had dire consequences. But we were desperate for truthful news.

EXECUTION OF SHAFEEK ADAS

On the day Israel was declared a state (May 14, 1948), Iraq declared martial law and set up military courts. A new government was formed, and Sadeq el Bassam was appointed Defense Minister in charge of martial law. My father was stunned at the news of Bassam's appointment. He told us that Bassam hated the Jews, and that he was known for his virulent anti-Jewish speeches. Under Bassam's leadership, the criminal code was revised, greatly stiffening penalties for those accused of Zionism. Sentences ranged from a minimum of seven years imprisonment to death. Since the military courts judged on the evidence of two witnesses, anyone who held a grudge against a Jew, or was inclined to take revenge on a Jew, could find a second witness to testify that the Jew in question was a Zionist. No appeal of military court decisions was allowed.

Martial law lasted nineteen months. During the intervening months, members of our community were arrested en masse and accused of being Zionist agents for the flimsiest of reasons: a prayer book printed in Jerusalem, a prayer shawl with a star of David sewn on it, or an amulet with Aramaic inscriptions. Arrested Jews were taken away and tortured. Some returned with broken bones. Some returned invalids for life. And some never returned.

Many Jews were sentenced to long-term imprisonment; others were required to pay enormous "fines" to avoid prison. Uncle Moshe was arrested and charged with distributing Zionist leaflets. He was to be tried and sentenced under martial law. My uncle was not involved in any Zionist activity, and no Zionist leaflets or any such evidence was seized or produced as evidence. Had it not been for the intervention of Supreme Court Justice Abdul Aziz alAaraj, at the behest of my father, Uncle Moshe would have suffered the same fate as others who were accused of Zionism. Justice Al Aaraj, who ordered Uncle Moshe's immediate release, was an old friend of my father.

The secret police raided Jewish homes in the early morning hours. The raids would begin with banging on the door with rifle butts. Sometimes the agents simply broke down the door. It was a favorite practice of the dreaded Criminal Investigation Department, or CID, to round up the Jewish children during those raids and force them to watch, as they bludgeoned their father or beat and kicked their mother. I spent sleepless nights worrying. I didn't know how I could stand to see my parents being violated. I dreaded the night for the raid it might bring; I was afraid to leave the house during the day for fear of being noticed by the police.

There was nothing we could do to stem the reign of terror that swept through the country. Every day we heard of new atrocities committed against members of our community. I remember in particular the hanging of a wealthy Jewish entrepreneur, Shafeek Adas, who lived in Basra. His death hit close to home, for he was a man I knew.

Adas was a multimillionaire businessman, the exclusive agent of the Ford Motor Company in Iraq and a partner in a closely held corporation that bought and sold surplus. I had met him a few years before his death at a lunch gathering in a Jewish club in Basra. I remember him as lively and personable; the gathering seemed alive and happy largely because of his presence. My father told me of the great sorrow Adas had in his life. His six-year old youngest son was retarded, but he loved that son as much as the child loved him.

Adas was arrested and accused of selling surplus goods to Israel – goods that he bought from the British and the American military, and sold to Italy for transshipment to Israel. Mutual friends, who could see the handwriting on the wall, later told my father they had urged Adas to call the Regent and ask for help. Adas was well connected, with powerful friends. But Adas didn't take their advice because, they said, he was unwilling to believe that he was really in trouble.

Fresh rumors began circulating not long after that: Now Adas was said to have sold Israel the tanks that it used to defeat the Iraqi army in 1948. I don't know if Israel possessed tanks during the 1948 war. But the rumor was a manifestation of something I noticed many times among Iraqis during my years growing up: the unwillingness to accept responsibility for failure and the fear of critical self-examination. The tendency was to find a scapegoat or search for a convenient excuse for the failure.

Now the Iraqi newspapers and radio latched onto the theme that Mr. Adas was the person who had caused Iraq to lose the war with Israel, and we repeatedly heard the radio commentators demand his head. Adas was tried and convicted of helping Israel win the war against Iraq. He was to be hung on gallows constructed in the front yard of a mansion he was in the process of building. He would never live in that house, and the authorities wanted him to see his unrealized dream house with his dying eyes.

My family and I listened, horrified, to the live broadcast of his execution in gory detail. The radio reported Mr. Adas was remarkably composed as he was led to the gallows, but collapsed when he saw his retarded son brought by the police to watch his hanging. The hanging was prolonged by the soldiers who, several times, pulled him back from the brink of death while the watching crowd screamed its delight

NO WAY BACK
The Journey of a Jew from Baghdad

Adas was hanged on August 23, 1948. All of his assets were confiscated, and his vaunted Ford agency was taken over by a Muslim. Adas owned only 15% of the shares of the surplus corporation accused of supplying tanks to Israel.

The entrepreneur Shafeek Adas
Hung by the Iraqis in 1948 on trumped-up charges.

In the fall of 1949, a Jewish high school student in Baghdad was arrested and accused of being a Zionist. He was tortured until he agreed to "co-operate" and name his collaborators. The police took him to Jewish schools and asked him to identify his "collaborators" from among the students. Many of those he singled out were known among their classmates to be apolitical. Some in the Jewish community felt he was pointing to people at random, just to save his skin, to avoid further torture. I dreaded the thought of that young man coming to our school. I never knew when he would be brought there and point to me as a collaborator. I don't think I worried so much about what that would do to my life, although I worried plenty about torture. I worried about what my arrest would do to my parents and the rest of my family.

The wave of arrests pushed thousands of terrorized families to seek to leave the country. Jews couldn't legally leave Iraq, so they turned to professional smugglers who specialized in getting criminals out of the country. Several of my classmates and a cousin of mine turned to the smugglers for help.

The escape routes were through Kurdistan in northern Iraq and then across the mountains to Iran. To conceal the Jewish identity of the escapees, smugglers had them wear turbans or Kurdish caps and Bedouin or Kurdish attire. The escapees either walked or rode on donkeys as they crossed through the mountains with the help of their handlers. This was how my two nephews, Rony and Emile, were smuggled out of Iraq. Among my memorabilia, I have a Kurdish cap that Rony's handlers had given him when he hid in the home of a Kurdish family in northern Iraq.

During the late forties, rumors circulated that the Iraqi government was considering an exchange of population - Jews going to Israel and Palestinians moving to Iraq to take their place. If it ever existed, the plan never came to fruition. However, five thousand Palestinian refugees came to Baghdad about the time of the mass exodus of Jews; Jewish dwellings and synagogues, including the synagogue I grew up in, were seized and turned over to them.

The Palestinians refugees were not allowed to work, perhaps out of fear they might compete with Iraqis. The Palestinians had a reputation of being more enterprising than the Iraqis. Somehow, one Palestinian family received permission to open an ice-cream parlor. It became so successful that it captured the clientele of all the ice-cream parlors in downtown Baghdad. Whenever I passed by the Palestinian parlor-- which I was actually afraid to visit--it was jammed with customers, while neighboring ice cream shops were deserted. Not long after, the government withdrew the license of the Palestinian parlor and shut it down for good.

PULLING TOGETHER

Through those days my parents showed no outward inclination to leave Iraq. My father, I know, kept hoping for the best, praying that better days lay ahead, with my mother, as always, supporting him. For better or worse, this was the hope that allowed my parents' generation, as well earlier generations, to survive the difficult spells they had lived through – the hope that the storm would pass and a more peaceful life would return. They focused on the good they could remember and tried hard to purge from their mind the harsh treatment they had encountered. It was as if they had been conditioned to see the violence against them as a normal part of life. Jews had to put up with episodes of violence, as if this was all that Jews could or should expect from life.

We could sense our parents' unease, mingled with the tenuous hope that the terror would end, that it would never touch our family. But every night I fell into an uneasy sleep, waiting for that battering knock on the door. The lot that my father owned on Mount Scopus in East Jerusalem was a source of worry. In the years following the death of King Faisal I in 1933, Jewish ownership of land in Palestine became grounds for arrest and imprisonment. My father's land had become a liability; there was no telling what would happen if someone were to unearth records of his lot in Jerusalem. I fervently wished my father would decide to leave. Anything was better than waiting for terror to arrive at our door.

NO WAY BACK
The Journey of a Jew from Baghdad

I don't know what instinctively drove me to resist the mistreatment we endured in Iraq—or why I didn't accept the situation, as my immediate family and ancestors always had. Accommodation was not my way. I simply couldn't be party to injustice, and couldn't push aside the horrors with vague hopes of better times ahead.

1948 faded into 1949, and Israel had been in existence for a whole year. On the eve of the first anniversary of the nation's birth, the Jewish underground distributed copies of the text of a new *kiddush* text written for the first *yom haatsmaout*, Israel's day of independence. The day of Israel's rebirth was now a holy day to be sanctified.

It was dangerous for a Jew in Iraq to be caught with any document about Israel, particularly one that sanctified the day of its creation. But I tucked my copy of the *kiddush* blessing carefully in my notebook, and prayed to make it home safely with it. Once at home, I set up the *mady*, laying out the customary loaves of Iraqi bread. I placed the saltcellar beside the bread, covering the bread with an embroidered cloth. Then I filled the *kiddush* cup with grape juice and set it on the table.

When my father came home that evening, he looked serious and was unusually silent. He looked at the table I had prepared and still didn't say a word. It was I who broke the silence.

"I have the *kiddush* ready, Baba," I said, as I handed him the text for the new *kiddush*, ending with the *shehehiyyanu* blessing that was recited on special occasions.

To my utter amazement, my ostensibly non-Zionist father took the *kiddush* cup in hand and recited the blessing as written in the text I had gotten from the underground. I looked at him with new understanding. He read the clandestine text in tones that told me he meant every word he uttered.

At the conclusion of the *kiddush* recitation, I went up to my father to give him the customary kiss on his hands before drinking from the *kiddush* cup. He looked at me, I felt, with pride. We didn't exchange words. But our silence spoke volumes. Now I knew. We were both pulling in the same direction. In spite of all appearances, Baba's heart was with our brethren in Israel.

EXODUS

On the eve of *purim*, March 9, 1950, at the peak of a stretch of relentless terror, the Iraqi Parliament decreed that Jews wishing to leave Iraq would be permitted to file an exit petition during the following year. The statute stipulated that those who filed a petition would forfeit their citizenship, but it was silent on other important questions. It didn't state, for example, whether the petitioner would for sure be allowed to leave Iraq. Prior to this, a public declaration by a Jew of the intention to leave Iraq was tantamount to treason, and the community worried that the new law might be a set-up. Could the statute be a ploy by the Iraqi authorities to flush out the "Zionists" for torture or execution?

The statute was also silent on what would happen to the petitioners' assets. Would they be forfeited along with citizenship, or could they be cashed in before departure? While many of us were troubled by what the statute left unsaid, none of us shed tears at the prospect of losing our Iraqi citizenship. But the leadership of the community worried about the legal implications of the loss of citizenship. According to international law, an individual stripped of his citizenship reverts automatically to the citizenship he had before, or to that of his ancestors. But it was a different story with us. We were there from time immemorial and had no other citizenship to fall back on. Without Iraqi citizenship, we became stateless. Where would we go? With the exception of Israel, no country accepted stateless people. Most of us wanted to go to Israel, but Iraq had declared war on our hoped-for homeland.

And so the leadership of the Jewish community agonized about the fate of those who would leave Iraq. The destruction of European Jewry during World War II was on everyone's mind. Did a similar fate await the Babylonian Jews?

The British government offered to permit the airplanes flying the Jewish émigrés to land in Cyprus, but wouldn't allow the émigrés to remain in Cyprus. We didn't know what would happen next.

About two and a half months after the enactment of the statute, I told my father I wanted to leave, but because I was under age I needed his signature on my petition.

"I absolutely will not sign," Baba said. "It's too early to tell whether this petition is a trap to flush out 'Treacherous Zionists' or if it is on the level. You don't want to get caught in the trap if it is one."

"Just by living here we are caught in a trap, Baba. I want to get out. You have to sign."

"Daniel, why don't you wait awhile? You'd be better off attending college in England. Maybe the door will open up one day for

Jews to travel to UK. Israel is a hard country to live in. I've been there and I know. Be patient, son."

"All my life you've been telling me to be patient. I don't want to be patient. I want to go. You have to sign for me. You just have to, Baba."

I would not retreat from my position, nor would he retreat from his. I asked, I demanded, I cajoled, I screamed. It was a tense standoff. My siblings supported me, told me their hearts were with me, even though they would miss me when I left. But I could also see they were beginning to get worried about our father as I ratcheted up the pressure. The constant badgering was beginning to take its toll. Baba looked haggard and was unusually quiet. He skipped dinner several times.

One morning I followed my father around as he was getting ready to go to work and implored him to sign my petition. He looked drained as he left for work without saying a word.

Bursting into tears, Muzli turned to me.

"Do you realize what this is doing to him? He looks dazed. He is walking like a zombie. I'm scared. What happens if he crosses the street and a car runs him over? We won't have a father."

It was a warm spring day, but I could not enjoy the sun and the gentle breezes. Helwa and Jacob stood by, looking worried, but not saying a word. Muzli wiped her tears as she looked intently at me. I could see the accusation in her eyes.

I was shook up. What if Muzli was right? I did not want my father to die. Should I let go? But I didn't want to give up. I wanted to leave Iraq.

I am not sure what transpired that day that made my father change his mind. Maybe my mother had a word with him. Maybe he felt too worn out to keep up his resistance. Whatever it was, he surprised me. That evening he told me he would sign for me. He looked peaceful for the first time in a good while. It was as if he had just shaken a heavy burden off his shoulders.

The following day Baba and I walked the three blocks to the registration center at Mis'ouda Shemtob Synagogue. I filled out the form. Baba signed on the dotted line as my guardian.

"May it be all for the good, my son," he said.

"Thank you, Baba."

We walked home together to wait for what would happen next.

Some three months after the passage of the exit statute, the first two British Airways planes carrying Jewish immigrants took off from Baghdad's airport and headed for Cyprus. From there, unbeknownst to the Iraqi government (and to any of us), the planes quietly continued on to Llyda airport in Israel. Later flights, although this was not publicized or officially sanctioned, went directly from Baghdad to Llyda airport.

NO WAY BACK
The Journey of a Jew from Baghdad

The sense that something was coming to an end permeated our lives. Our once-vibrant community was disappearing. The long lines that had always formed in front of the bakery on Friday mornings were dwindling. The streets and sidewalks were emptied of life. The light-hearted crowds that had always paraded along the Tigris riverbank on the Sabbath had by now thinned to almost nothing.

At Mis'ouda Shemtob Synagogue's Petition Center, Baghdad -
Jews wishing to file petitions to leave Iraq, waiting in courtyard for the petition office to open
This center is where my father and I filed my petition to leave Iraq

For those left behind in Iraq, there was great difficulty finding out whether their loved ones had in fact arrived in Israel. Letters couldn't be sent from Israel to Iraq; that would open the recipients to the charge of espionage by the Iraqi authorities. Moreover, since the Iraqis censored all letters addressed to Jews, no mention could be made in any letter about arrival in Israel. So simple codes were devised between those who flew out of Iraq and the families that stayed behind. An example might be the phrase, "I just bought a pair of shoes." People who arrived in Israel communicated with relatives or friends in Sydney, London, Paris, or New York. They in turn wrote to families in Iraq, including in their letter the innocuous sentence "I just bought a pair of shoes." In this way, the recipient in Baghdad got confirmation that their loved one had arrived safely in Israel.

In the fall of 1950, letters containing the prearranged codes began to trickle back to Iraq from France and other countries. At that point, the pace of registrations to leave Iraq accelerated. By March 9, 1951, the date on which the exit statute was due to expire, close to ninety percent of the 140,000 to 150,000 members of Iraq's Jewish community had filed an exit petition. My sisters Muzli, Reyna, Helwa and Latifa filed to leave a few months after I did. My parents stayed behind.

NO WAY BACK
The Journey of a Jew from Baghdad

Like several other leaders of the Jewish community, my father felt he could not turn his back and walk away. He felt he had a responsibility to stay as long as there were those who for one reason or another could not leave. There were also family reasons. Four of my sisters were not married. Marrying them off required large sums of money for their dowries. My father, who was 61 then, felt he couldn't take care of that in Israel, where he would not be able to practice his profession. He hoped that peace between Iraq and Israel might come one day at which time he could help with the dowries while still practicing in Baghdad. My parents, Valentine and Jacob left Baghdad in 1958.

Jews waiting outside Meir Twaig Synagogue Petition Center, Baghdad, 1950
Meir Twaig was the only standing synagogue found by US invading forces in 2003.

My sister Jamila and her husband hoped to be able to stay in Baghdad until their oldest son was educated. These were uncertain times and decisions were made in a vacuum. Jamila and her family were not able to leave until 1973. So my beloved, motherly sister and I had no face-to-face contact for 22 years.

During the one-year window for exit petitions, the Iraqi authorities allowed very few petitioners to leave the country. This first handful of émigrés was allowed to dispose of their assets before they left the country. Unfortunately, no one saw the trap being set by the Iraqi government, how this liberal policy was designed to lull the remaining Jews into complacency. Most Jews who signed the exit petition were left with the impression that they, too, would be allowed to liquidate their immovable assets and wind up their affairs before leaving. Practically no one disposed of his home or liquidated his business before signing the exit petition. People reckoned that, with the slow pace of flights out of Baghdad, it would take decades before their turn to leave the country would come.

And so it was a shock to all of us when, on the day the statute expired, the Iraqi authorities cut off all phone lines and closed all banks for three days. We didn't understand what was happening. Gradually the plot became clear. When the banks reopened and the telephones hummed again we discovered all assets of the Jews who had filed an exit petition had been seized.   Under a new "Decree for the Control and Management of Assets of Denaturalized Iraqis," Iraq's Custodian General was ordered "to lay hands" on all property belonging to anyone who had signed an exit petition and to "administer, dispose and liquidate it." Over one hundred and twenty thousand Jews were left without means. Overnight, millionaires became paupers.

Once they had seized the Jewish assets, the Iraqi authorities accelerated the pace of the flights. Now, instead of one plane leaving every two or three weeks, as has been the practice before the Iraqis seized our assets, twelve planes packed with Jewish immigrants left daily from Baghdad's airport. The flights came to an end in August 1951.

I was on one of those flights. My immigrant number was 14296. I left for Israel on April 1, 1951.

The period preceding my flight from Iraq was a time of enormous anxiety for me. How many more weeks or months would it take before I would reach safety? Would I ever really make it out? There was talk among Iraqis that by allowing the Jews to leave the country, Iraq was providing Israel's military with recruits that would turn their guns against Iraq. Might the government decide to call off the exodus? That was not unthinkable; in Iraq laws could be passed only to be ignored or even reversed without notice.

During the three-week period between the expropriation of Jewish assets and the day I flew out of Iraq, I mostly stayed at home to avoid being noticed. On the few occasions I went out, I walked the streets with trepidation. The "Jewish traitors" who had registered to leave Iraq gave the police and the mob an excuse, if any were needed, for a new type of harassment. Ordinary Muslims, not just the police, stopped Jewish men and women on the street, searched them and took what they found in their pockets, on the grounds that the government had seized the assets of those who had filed an exit petition. No one bothered to check whether the person being searched had indeed filed such a petition. And I doubt that anything seized from the pockets of the Jews on the street ever found its way to the government.

My own prize possession was the stamp collection that my father had given me. His collection included stamps from the time of the Ottoman period, as well as from the time when the British occupied Iraq in 1917. For a short while, the British had used the same postage stamps issued by the Ottoman Empire, printed with the added words "IRAQ in British Occupation," along with the new value of each stamp. In a few cases the word IRAQ was replaced by the word BAGHDAD. Those stamps were rare. Baba had a few in his collection, and I wanted to protect his valuable stamps in a safe place, away from our home.

One day, I put these stamps in my pockets and took the downtown bus to my father's office. He had not applied to leave Iraq, and I felt it would be safe to keep his collection in his office. I was relieved when the bus finally reached its destination. I had only a few yards to walk to the office. But my nervousness must have given me away. No sooner had I stepped off the bus than a tall, heavyset Muslim, who had just passed by me, turned and demanded to know what I had in my pockets. I froze, speechless. "My goose is cooked," I thought. The man was going to take the stamps, and then who knows what would happen next – perhaps he would turn me over to the police, and that would be the end of my dream of leaving Iraq.

Stamps issued by the British immediately after their occupation of Iraq in 1917.
(The "An" stands for Ana, an Ottoman currency unit, roughly equivalent to one penny)

The man frisked me, but never put his hands in my pockets to see what I had. He then asked if I had any money on me. I said I didn't. I had taken just enough change to pay for a one-way bus fare. I couldn't believe my eyes when he accepted my answer, turned around and walked away.

It was fortunate that the whole incident didn't last long enough for a crowd of curious spectators to gather around and attack me. In disbelief, I headed for my father's office, where he kept the stamps in his safe. He brought them with him when he, my mother and brother came to Israel seven years later and gave them back to me.

My lucky escape with the stamps didn't quiet my feelings of uneasiness. I had trouble sleeping during the weeks that preceded my flight from Baghdad. I dreamed of the police breaking into our home and throwing me in jail for declaring my desire to leave Iraq. I dreamed of being dragged out of the plane by CID agents, just as it was about to take off. My sleeplessness got worse as the immigrant numbers got closer to mine. My pain at leaving my family grew sharper. I wanted to leave, but knowing that I would be cut off from my parents weighed on my heart. I wouldn't be able to communicate with them once I got to Israel. Iraq was at war with Israel, and the Iraqis punished those who received communications from "the enemy" with long prison terms and torture. Sadly, in those times children were forced to choose between their parents and their desire to live as free human beings.

The March 9, 1950 law allowed denaturalized Iraqi Jews to take with them fifty dinars per person when they left the country. Rumor had it that some of the airport inspectors were regularly confiscating these funds before allowing Jewish immigrants to board the plane. That didn't bother me. I didn't care about money. I just wanted to leave the country alive. But it did bother my father; he worried that I might arrive penniless in Israel.

One morning, I was in his room, watching him get ready for work. He put his arm around my shoulder and told me he was worried that they might take my fifty dinars at the airport. I said I didn't care. Without waiting for my answer, Baba took off his wedding ring and asked me to wear it. He said there might be less chance losing the ring than cash. I was aghast. I burst into tears. "I can't take it," I told my father. He had not taken off that ring since his wedding day. I couldn't entertain the thought of ever taking it away from him. But I also understood his concern and what he was struggling with. Like the rest of us, my father felt helpless in dealing with the organized theft and the inspectors' lawlessness at Baghdad's airport.

I gave Baba a hug. He put his wedding ring back on. I never forgot the tenderness of that gesture.

The night before I left Baghdad, my aunt Rosa and her two daughters, Grace and Esperance, came to say goodbye. My two cousins and I were close. The thought that I might never see them again was painful. I sang to them as I swung gently in my hammock, *"Faut-il se quitter sans espoir, sans espoir de retour?"* ("Should we be parting with no hope of return?") As, if to reassure myself, I also sang the refrain, *"Ce n'est pas un adieu mes freres, ce n'est qu'un au revoir. Oui nous nous reverrons my freres, ce n'est qu'un au revoir."* ("This isn't an adieu, my friends, it is only an au revoir; yes, we surely will see each other again, this is only an au revoir.")

I wanted both worlds: I wanted to leave Iraq, and I wanted to stay in touch with my family. But in the tyrannical world of Iraq, my two wishes were incompatible.

The following day we called the registration center at the Shemtob synagogue. There was a good chance, they said, that my number would be reached within the day. That was it. This would be my last, bittersweet day in Baghdad. It was a relief to know that the suspense was almost over. I wanted to go. But this would probably be the last time I would ever see my parents. I cried, but I didn't want Mama to see my tears. I kept on my big sunglasses. Mama was composed at first, but by midmorning she broke down. She rushed toward me and hugged me tightly, as she broke into tears. "I will miss you, dear Dannu. Will I ever see you again? Why was it decreed that we have to suffer?" A gush of chest pain hit me. I couldn't breathe. The hardest part of my emigration was leaving my mother behind. I pushed her away. I don't know why, except that the pain was too much to bear. Perhaps I didn't want to see my mother in her moment of anguish. I went to my room and sobbed.

The registration center had promised to give us a call when my immigration number was reached. At dinnertime, we sat together to have our usual cup of tea with Feta cheese sandwiches. Nobody said much. I was composed throughout the evening. It didn't look as if I would be leaving that night. Still I felt a sense of inner peace. The wait was approaching its end.

At 10 p.m. the telephone rang. The plane could take one more passenger; I was next in line. Mama, had tears in her eyes. "Please stay one more night," she pleaded. But I was adamant. I wanted to go. I wanted to get it over with.

Latifa

Baba called a taxicab. Minutes later, Jacob announced the cab had arrived. My parents, siblings and Uncle Moshe stood in line in our courtyard to bid me goodbye. I hugged my mother first, then my siblings, then Uncle Moshe. Baba stood at the end of the line. His eyes glistened with tears. I had hardly ever seen him cry before. I gave him a big hug, and then turned toward the vestibule without looking back. I couldn't bear seeing Baba's tears.

Midway down the long vestibule on my way out, Latifa met me

as I passed by the dining room. She didn't say a word, but tears were streaming down her cheeks. She had been waiting in the dining room behind the door to be the last one to say good-bye. She took my right hand and kissed it. I hugged her and rushed out to the waiting taxicab.

Jacob, Baba and Uncle Moshe loaded my trunk on the back seat of the taxicab, and I headed for the airport alone.

The waiting lounge was brightly lit and full of emigrants—a sea of humanity. Some emigrants had been there since the afternoon. Some sat on their suitcases; others stood quietly or wandered around. I was rushed to a room, where I found myself alone with four inspectors and an armed policeman.

A kindly looking older inspector, probably the chief inspector, opened my trunk. He went lightly through my belongings, and seemed to be satisfied that I had nothing objectionable. He asked me to empty my pockets. I took out everything and put it on the table. He glanced at it, said it was fine and left the room.

I began to put things back in my pocket. The policeman stepped forward. My vision glasses and my sunglasses were in my hand ready to go back in my pocket.

"Why do you need two pairs of glasses?" the policeman asked. 'Give me one of them."

I put my expensive sunglasses in my pocket and handed him my vision pair. He put them on, shifted them up and down on his nose, and turned his head from one side to the other. Finally, he threw the glasses down on the table and walked away muttering to himself.

In the meantime the younger inspectors got busy working on the contents of my trunk. They went through item-by-item, and kept for themselves what they wanted. One paunchy inspector sized up one of my dress shirts. It was too small for him. He passed it on to the inspector next to him. It seemed to fit him; he kept it.

I felt detached, totally numb as I watched what was happening to my belongings. I didn't care. I felt as if I were perched high above, looking down with disinterest at what was happening to someone else's suitcase. All I wanted was to go. I was so close to freedom. But these inspectors seemed to take their good time – relishing every piece they kept for themselves. Would it ever be over? Why don't they keep my whole trunk and just let me go? Would I finally be allowed to leave Baghdad tonight? Would I really make it to freedom?

At that moment Israel seemed to be a million miles away.

PART TWO – ISRAEL

NO WAY BACK
The Journey of a Jew from Baghdad

OUT OF THE INFERNO, APRIL 1, 1951

When I got on the plane that was to take me out of Iraq, I knew only that I was leaving a country in which I had lived all of my life as a second-class citizen. Nobody on the plane knew our intended destination. We had heard some planes had flown directly to Israel. Other planes had landed in Cyprus. The uncertainty added to our anxiety.

I took my seat on the plane scarcely daring to believe that I was leaving. My fingernails dug into the palms of my hands as I waited for the plane to take off. I shrunk down into my seat. I didn't feel like talking to anybody, and I noticed the silence on the plane was almost unbroken.

I had never flown before, and it frightened me. But I was even more afraid that we would be dragged off the plane before it could take off. We had been stripped of our citizenship, but that wouldn't stop Iraqi officials from taking us into custody at the last moment.

The tension pervading the plane was palpable. Nobody dared to say we were glad to be leaving, not even in a whisper. Nobody dared to greet the sound of the closing doors with a cheer or even with a sigh of relief. When the plane raced down the runway and took off, the silence within the plane was still almost unbroken. As we ascended through the darkness into the night sky, I could see the lights of the airport below, but the only sound was the drone of the engines.

Then the woman behind me whispered to the plane "May God make you as strong as iron." Amen, I said in my heart. We, too, needed to be strong. We were leaving behind the only life that we had known, a life we certainly wanted to leave, but we faced the unknown.

No matter what lay ahead, I knew I didn't want to live in a non-Jewish society, not even in England where the standard of education was high and where some of our relatives lived. I wanted to avoid repeating our people's miserable experience in Iraq. In Israel, a land owned and governed by Jews, I would be in a country free of discrimination against Jews. There I knew I would be safe.

But my journey was tearing me away from my family, and there was no certainty we would ever be reunited. I blinked back tears. This was my choice. I couldn't live as a Jew among Muslims any longer.

The sleepless, tense nights I had spent anticipating my flight finally took their toll. I let go and, exhausted, fell asleep. When I awoke it seemed to me that the plane was no longer in the air.

"I think we have landed," the woman behind me said to her husband. "I see intermittent lights."

NO WAY BACK
The Journey of a Jew from Baghdad

We had indeed landed. The lights were on an airport runway. As we came to a halt the cabin buzzed with word that we had arrived in Israel. Was it really Israel?

I could hear the murmur of voices as I looked around the plane jammed with refugees from Baghdad. Someone was reciting the *shehehiyyanu*, a prayer of thanks. Many of the passengers just sat quietly, looking apprehensive.

I was dazed and disoriented when I staggered off the plane that early morning of April 1, 1951 at Llyda Airport (later renamed Ben Gurion Airport). I could hardly believe I was out of the inferno that people called Iraq.

I arrived ready to hug and embrace any and every one I encountered in my new homeland. I was in a country where every Jew belonged, where for the first time in my life I would be a part of the majority. In Israel I would be greeted with warmth and outstretched hands.

The other immigrants on the plane had come to this new life with their families. Staying with the family was the tradition among Babylonian Jews. I was eighteen years old, but I was the only one who had come alone.

In fact, this was my first venture on my own outside the boundaries of the sheltered environment in which I had grown up. And there was to be no going back. There would be no contact with my parents, perhaps forever. But the ramifications of my decision had yet to sink in. I could entertain only one idea: I was fortunate to be out of that Gehenna.

It was only later that afternoon when we were dropped off at *sha'ar aliyah*, a holding camp for incoming immigrants near Haifa, that I began to get a glimmer of the enormity of the step I had taken, and the radical way in which my life was about to change.

But now, waiting in the Llyda airport, I perceived only that it was overcast and cold outside, though I didn't feel cold. I was wearing several layers of clothing - my best suit, shirt and necktie; a blue sweater that Muzli had knitted for me; a leather jacket; an enormous overcoat, twice my size, that my father had had made especially for my flight to Israel. I wasn't wearing all these clothes for warmth; I was wearing them to make it harder for the Iraqi customs inspectors to commandeer them, to ensure they arrived with me in Israel. But even the clothes seemed unimportant now. Nothing seemed to matter except that I was in the Promised Land.

When we were led to Llyda's airport terminal, I followed as if I were a robot. Three hours ago I had been in Baghdad having my belongings pawed over by airport officials; now I was almost too numb to claim an Irish blanket somebody had found on the plane, a blanket I knew was mine. It was one my mother had packed for me, a prized possession she wanted me to have, and I could barely summon the energy to claim it. I walked when I was told to walk and stood when I was told to stand.

A burly sanitation worker with a spray gun in hand stood before me. Maybe because I was ready to embrace everybody I came across, I didn't regard him as hostile, in spite of his grim expression. He motioned for me to pull my pants down, and I complied.

Suddenly he aimed his spray gun at me and proceeded to spray my genitals with a powder that smelled like DDT. I recoiled and coughed. It was difficult to breathe. Why, I wondered, did he spray me with DDT? I thought DDT was used for killing bugs in agriculture. Even so I remained trusting. It couldn't hurt to breathe that stuff, I thought, because if it did, he wouldn't have done it. He was Jewish, like me, and would never hurt me. I was in a Jewish land with other Jews, and whatever was being done couldn't have been done with anything but the best of intentions.

Metallic trunk my father had commissioned for me -- airport inspectors often tore apart the cardboard suitcases of Jewish immigrants on the pretext that they needed to search for hidden valuables. The number 14296 is my immigrant number; a shipping clerk no doubt misspelled my last name; I is thinitial of my father's name, Ibrahim, as pronounced in Iraq.

The Hebrew I heard was spoken too fast for me to follow, but the main language spoken by those who met us at the airport was one I had never heard before. Later I learned it was Yiddish. But why I wondered - why none of the Jews from Iraq who had preceded us was asked to be here when we arrived. Didn't the authorities in Israel know that this was a life-transforming experience for us, that we needed someone to explain to us what was happening in a language we understood? I felt a mounting sense of frustration, but choked it down. I couldn't allow myself to feel. Maybe I wouldn't feel anything -- ever again.

Not one person who met us at the airport had smiled at us. Nobody seemed to understand that we were used to being welcomed by friends with smiles and steaming cups of hot tea. At that moment my family in Baghdad was probably gathered around our table drinking tea together, and here I was alone in a land where I didn't understand one word that was spoken. How could I have imagined Israel was my home? I quickly dismissed such doubts and allowed myself to sink deep into lethargy.

My fellow passengers were bursting with questions. How long were we going to be at the airport? Some people had arrived here almost a full day before me. They were weary and asking when they would be fed. Others asked about relatives who had left Baghdad a week or two before, how they could get in touch with them and where we ourselves were headed. All questions—in whatever language--were met with silence. People tried Judeo-Arabic, English, French - nobody in charge seemed to understand.

I didn't ask any questions. I sat quietly waiting for something to happen, but I had no idea what that something would be.

I felt my wrist and was relieved that my Omega watch was still there. That watch meant a lot to me. I had tutored students in math and physics when I was in high school, and my watch was the first thing I had bought with my own money. When I was being inspected at Baghdad's airport I had it pushed well above my wrist, hoping the customs inspectors wouldn't notice it and ask me to hand it over.

I couldn't tell how long we had been waiting outside the terminal. It had been just after dawn when we left the terminal. Now, it seemed the sun had been out for a good while. People were sitting on their luggage, and one man blurted out, "I knew it, I knew it. I knew this is how it was going to be. We will be left in the fields." Was this true, or had he gone off the deep end? Being left in suspense was beginning to gnaw at me.

Around noon a few open trucks arrived; we were to pile in. I had never ridden in a truck before, much less in the back of one. The journey to Sha'ar Aliyah took about two hours. The ride was windy and bouncy. It pained me to see the older people huddled together on the floor, some of them dressed in elegant suits. They looked worried and uncertain.

For me, however, the ride was a novelty. With the cool air on my face and the warm sun washing over me, I felt a new sense of freedom. This was my new country, my new homeland. I held the railings tightly and threw my head back. I felt alive, revived. We passed by orange groves, and the fragrance of orange blossoms triggered a memory of distillers coming to my parents' home to extract fresh rosewater and orange blossom water. Was this home? It smelled like my parents' home. Yes, it is home.

I was impressed and frightened as we turned onto the coastal highway along the Mediterranean on our way to Sha'ar Aliyah. I had never seen a sea before. The Tigris was wide, but it was nothing like this endless expanse of water. The waves were high and wild. I remembered Victor Hugo's poem, *"oceano nox,"* -- the treacherous waves, the drowning people, the wrecked boats. Here were those waves right before my eyes. They beat the shore mercilessly.

Finally we reached the Sha'ar Aliyah camp where we would stay until we were moved to semi-permanent quarters.

CHOOSING MY BIRTHDAY

After we climbed off the truck, we were herded to a barrack for processing. I took my place in a long line that snaked around the room. After a few minutes I pulled myself together as I realized I had moved to the head of the line and the official sitting at the table was addressing me.

Babylonian immigrants being processed in Sha'ar Aliyah

"What is the date of your birth?"

"1932," I told him.

"I need the day and month, too."

"I don't have that information."

The official's pen was poised over the paper on the table, but he set the pen down and stared at me.

"You don't?"

" I don't."

He shook his head and picked up his pen again.

"Well, I need it."

Nobody had ever needed it before. Not knowing my precise birthday hadn't posed any practical problem in dealings with officialdom in Iraq. There, it was the year of birth that was important - date and month were irrelevant on passports, school registration documents and the like. Though my father kept meticulous records of the birth dates of each of his ten children, he never shared them with us. Jewish tradition discouraged a preoccupation with birthdays, emphasizing instead one's good deeds and achievements throughout life.

There was little use in sharing all this with the official drumming his fingers on the table. What was I going to do? My father was far away in Baghdad, and in any case he kept our birth records locked in his cupboard. Whenever the subject had come up, he'd assured us he would give us our birth date when we married and left our parents' home—as he had when Jamila, my oldest sister, got married. He had expected to give me my own record before I left for Israel. But in the turbulent days that preceded my flight from Baghdad, my mind was on anything but my birth date. I suspect it was the same for my father.

But here I was. I needed to give *sha'ar aliyah's* bureaucrat a month and a day to jot on his form. There were three hundred and sixty five days to pick from. And I blurted out the first date that came to mind: January sixth. The die was cast. The harried Israeli official recorded the date and moved on to the next person in line.

I would later track down my actual birth date—June 14, 1932—from dates that my father inscribed on a picture of me on my *bar miswah* day.

It never crossed my mind that my phony birth date would stay with me for the rest of my life and would appear on every legal document I possess.

In many ways, however, my self-created birthday was fitting. On that first day in Israel I was embarking on a new life, bidding goodbye forever to the country of my birth and to a now-vanished way of life to which I would never return.

SHA'AR ALIYAH

Sha'ar Aliyah was a sprawling camp abandoned by the British military. To the east were the Carmel Mountains, majestic, beautiful against the sky. Baghdad is flat, and I had never before seen mountains. I felt a sense of peace as I drank in the beauty of the surroundings. But the camp itself was a dreadful place.

Sha'ar Aliyah lacked minimal hygienic amenities. The bathrooms were located at the far ends of the camp, and were not well kept. Nor were there enough of them. Even at night, there were long lines. Tempers flared. There were long lines for water, too. Only cold water was available, and people had to carry it in buckets for long distances. It was miserable when it rained, whether one was waiting for water, the bathroom, or the daily ration of food. The tents provided little comfort. They were poorly furnished, and most had gaping holes.

I didn't have to cook for myself, though I did have to do my own laundry. Fortunately, my mother had sent a large bar of soap with me to Israel. The first time I tried to wash my own shirt, I was sparing with the soap, because I had no idea how long it would have to last. I ran the soap lightly over the collar and rubbed it between my hands, but no matter how hard I rubbed, the dirt still clung stubbornly. I had seen the maids in my parents' home wash our clothes, and it hadn't looked difficult. I couldn't understand why the dirt wouldn't be moved.

Close to tears, I looked up and saw a young woman laughing at me. She had a round face and black curly hair. I thought she was beautiful, and, though her dark eyes reflected amusement, they also exuded compassion. She came over and put her arm around me.

"Here, let me do that for you. My name is Violette, by the way."

She not only took my shirt and washed it, but also invited me back to her family's tent. It was every bit as cold as my own, but it was filled with the warmth of love and caring.

When we arrived, Violette's father was sitting outside taking off his *tefilleen*. He reminded me of my father, whom I had so often watched performing the same ritual after morning prayers. Violette's father wore a head covering similar to that worn by the Kurdish Jews, and his accent was that of the Jews of Northern Iraq. I could tell that he was happy to be able to pray openly.

Violette introduced me to her family and then asked me to move into the tent with them. I accepted gladly, happy that I could help the family by carrying water for them. Her parents welcomed me. We were Jews helping one another, and it felt good.

As hard as I had tried to imagine harsh living conditions while leading my comfortable life in Iraq, I had never come close to imagining the hardships of Sha'ar Aliyah. Still, I put up with them without complaint. It was a small price to pay for freedom.

But those who had emigrated with young families in tow had it particularly hard. They were destined to struggle with inadequate water and poor hygienic conditions for some time, and were likely to spend years in tents or huts that offered poor protection from hot or cold weather. How and when would they fit into Israeli society? How would they educate their children? The uncertainty surrounding their lives weighed heavily on them. The Palestinians occupied our synagogues and houses in Baghdad. It would make such a difference to these families if they were given the assets left behind by the Palestinians in Israel, I thought.

I, however, didn't have a family to worry about. I planned to join the military immediately, and, even though an immigrant of military age was exempt from military service for the first year in Israel, I had no intention of spending a year in limbo. I would put my military service behind me and concentrate on continuing my education.

I decided to join the Air Force. I was determined to become a pilot for my own reasons. When I left Iraq I knew that, sooner or later, the Iraqi government would seize my parents' home in Baghdad. I had a deep attachment to my home and, as soon as my family was safely out of Iraq, I planned to fly my plane over Baghdad and bomb that house. The Iraqi government wouldn't be allowed to have it. I wasn't sure how I would locate the house or how I would persuade the other members of my crew to fly with me on such a mission. But, when the time came, I would find a way. Nothing would be allowed to deter me.

Something did.

"Your eyesight isn't perfect," the physician who tested me declared. "You can't be a pilot, but you could be a navigator."

Not be a pilot! My world was crumbling around me.

"I want to be a pilot, not a navigator," I stammered.

"But a navigator is also an officer," a member of the examining board explained.

An officer! Who cared about being an officer? I wanted to be a pilot, the one in charge of the plane. I wanted to be the one who ordered the bomb dropped on my home. But if I revealed that, I would kill my chances of joining the Air Force altogether. I looked into the puzzled and implacable faces of the board members and swallowed my dream.

Eventually it was decided I would be transferred to the Air Force ground crew, once I had finished three months of basic training.

Surprisingly, when my plans were thwarted it came as a relief, as if I had been released from a vow I didn't want to fulfill. I didn't want to spend the rest of my life hating the Arabs. I wanted to put the past behind me and concentrate on making a success of my life. The Arabs took our material possessions, I thought to myself. They can have them. I still have my life, and I am going to make a go of it. I would complete my military service and become a productive member of Israeli society.

And, though life was difficult in Sha'ar Aliyah, I was no longer totally alone. Violette and her family were my friends, and then I bumped into Nahoom, the receptionist at *ammu* Guerji's clinic. I hadn't known he was in Israel and it was wonderful to see him.

Ammu Guerji was a sought-after doctor, and it was Nahoom's job to see that patients saw him in the proper order. I often sat in *ammu* Guerji's waiting room and admired Nahoom's tact when he had to tell patients that they were not next in line as they claimed, but would get to see the doctor soon. Nahoom knew me. He knew my family. Here in Sha'ar Aliyah he was my family, my connection to home.

One day, an incident occurred at camp that left me shaken, but happy Nahoom was my friend. As I considered the camp's inhabitants and realized that many of them came from Baghdad's working class, I remarked to Nahoom: "Isn't it nice that we are all the same here?" Nahoom didn't get a chance to reply. On hearing my remark, a man twice my size stood up and bore down on me with a snarl. He probably would have made mincemeat of me if Nahoom had not held him at bay.

However, I didn't completely appreciate the depths of Nahoom's skill with people until I saw him strike up a friendship with one of the Hungarian women who served us our food at Sha'ar Aliyah's dining room. It was when I noticed I was being served large portions of food that I understood Nahoom's charm.

"It's not me. It's you," Nahoom explained.

He was friendly with the small dark server, but the tall fair one had told Nahoom that she fancied me. I couldn't quite believe Nahoom, but I appreciated the generous portions of food on my plate.

Later I discovered there might have been something to Nahoom's claim.

Every day the tall fair server smiled at me as she heaped food on my plate. Unfortunately, I couldn't eat much of it. It was not food that I or other Middle Easterners were used to, and I generally gave the extra to families with children. My big portions, however, vanished on the day this young woman discovered I was leaving shortly for military service. Then she didn't smile as she served me a miserly portion of food and pointedly requested that I leave the dining room and not linger over my food.

From that day on, my formerly friendly server wouldn't meet my eye as she slapped small portions of food on my plate. I found the situation disconcerting, but I put it out of my mind when I took my leave of Nahoom and of Violette and her family on April 17th 1951 and began my military service in Israel.

IN THE MILITARY

Nahoom didn't join me in the military, choosing instead to defer. I, however, was eager to join up. I wanted to serve my new homeland. I felt also the military would serve as a stepping-stone for entry into Israeli society. I would learn Hebrew, and perhaps a profession, both of which would prepare me to become a productive citizen.

But, though I didn't realize it when I signed up, I was not ready for the military. I needed time to mourn my uprooting and the loss of my family. I needed to allow my spirit to heal. During basic military training there was no time for any of that. It was go, go, go. For three months we trained almost non-stop. Emotionally, this total immersion was a difficult period for me, at least in the short run. In the long run, however, it was probably the best decision I could have made.

For basic training I was stationed in Saraphand, a major camp in Rishon leSion, a coastal town about ten miles southeast of Tel Aviv. I shared a large brick bungalow with some fifty other new recruits. Our beds consisted of mattresses on top of boards positioned over sawhorses. This made it easy for the beds to be overturned if we didn't leap out of bed when the wake-up whistle sounded. It seemed to me that I had barely gone to bed when that whistle sounded in the cold dark hours of the early morning. Almost as soon as our bare feet hit the floor, we were off for our jog at dawn. Dressed only in boots and khaki pants, I shivered as I ran.

Food, or the lack of it, was a problem. I often looked longingly at the fruit of the cactus growing all around us in the fields where we trained, but when I tried to eat it the thorns stuck in my mouth and I didn't know how to remove them. It seemed to me that all we ever got to eat was black bread, rock-hard frozen margarine, and salty, stinky herring, which I hated. The beverage of choice was weak tea, a far cry from the strong black tea with milk we drank in Baghdad.

I could have bought food to supplement my meal, as some did, but our allowance was the equivalent of about one dollar per month. Out of this I had to buy shoe polish, toothpaste and other personal supplies. To save on polish, I shined only the fronts of my boots. One day during inspection I got caught.

"I suppose this means you wash only your face and never your behind," my sergeant barked in biting tones.

We learned to crawl under two-foot-high barbed wire on our backs and on our bellies under a searing noonday sun. The fair-skinned among us often had blisters from the sun, which in this exercise were rubbed raw by the desert sand. Sometimes we were wakened at night to go out on maneuvers. Sleep deprivation was common, but it was never considered an excuse for underperformance. Sometimes we were up until after midnight cleaning our rifles, trying to rid them of sand particles.

Training in the field -. Daniel 2d row, 2d from the left

Daniel on guard duty

I remember the first time we trained at night using what we believed to be live *ammu*nition. It was frightening to crawl under barbed wire in the sand while bullets whistled over our heads. All hell broke loose that night. One soldier refused to take part in this exercise. He had a wife and children, and if he were to die fighting the enemy that was bad enough. He was terrified at the thought of facing Israeli fire. He sat on the ground and cried, begging to be excused while the trainers shot bullets over his head, insisting that he participate. I saw what was happening out of the corner of my eye, as I slid along the sand on my belly. Those bullets were scary, but we had to be ready for combat.

There was a two-week period when I had a respite. Those of us who had gone directly from Sha'ar Aliyah into the military were required to attend Hebrew classes for two hours every afternoon during that two-week period, so that we would at least understand some basic commands in our new language. Our Hebrew teacher was a young man who never woke us up if we fell asleep in his class; some afternoons I slept through the whole class. It felt so good to take a nap, and I was grateful to our easy-going teacher.

REUNIONS

Jews celebrate the giving of the Ten Commandments when the *sh'buoth* holiday arrives, and this year my joy in the holiday's arrival was doubled. A couple of weeks before I left Baghdad, *ammu* (paternal uncle) Silman, my father's younger brother, had left for Israel with his wife, *amma* Margo – *amma*, meaning paternal aunt, being an honorary title -- their daughter and two sons. I had finally found out where they were, and I was going to see them.

When I received my holiday pass at *sh'buoth*, I hitchhiked to the Khay'riya *ma'abara*, the tent city where my uncle had been assigned. It was night by the time I arrived, and there were no lights in the *ma'abara*. I wandered around, frightened and lonely. The scent of orange blossoms in the air only intensified my homesickness.

Slits of light gleamed from some of the tents, but it wasn't enough for me to find my way. I wished the moon were full, as I stumbled over the uneven ground and tripped over the ropes holding down the tents. I stopped to listen for a minute, as I heard the noise of a tattered tent blowing in the wind. I hoped my uncle and his wife weren't living in a tattered tent.

I stopped at tent after tent, but no one seemed to know my uncle. What would I do if I couldn't find my uncle and his family?

Finally, I found a man who was able to help. Following his directions, I made my way to my relatives' tent, and their welcoming cries drew me out of the darkness into a warm circle of light where we all kissed and embraced. They boiled the only egg they had and gave it to me. I agonized over eating it, knowing their food was severely rationed. But it was an offering of love, and could not be refused. I savored their love for me, even as I found it hard to swallow the egg.

Ammu Silman and I knew each other at some deep level, which we didn't need to talk about. We just felt it. I sat close to him in the tent and, for the first time since coming to Israel, basked in the warmth of family love. They, too, were displaced, but I envied the fact that at least they were together. *Ammu* Silman and *amma* Margo always lived in a rented house.

"Silman should buy a house," *ammu* Moshe would say. "There is security in owning one's home."

I thought of this as I looked around the shabby tent that *ammu* Silman and his family now called home. It seemed as though there was no semblance of security anywhere—not for a Jew in Baghdad, not for a displaced Jew living in a tent in Israel. I am sure that *ammu* Silman had felt some sense of security years ago, when he won the lottery and put the money in the bank, but that peace of mind had been fleeting. The day that *ammu* Silman had withdrawn the last two hundred dinars from his account, he was standing in the bank counting his money when a thief snatched it from his hands and ran away with it. The police just shrugged when my uncle reported the theft.

Ammu Silman's *ma'abara* was the usual tent city without proper sanitary facilities and almost impossible living conditions, especially for people accustomed to city life. Its one redeeming feature was that it was set in a field surrounded by orange groves. But even that had its drawbacks. Coyotes prowled the groves at night, keeping everybody in the *ma'abara* awake with their howling. As I lay in my bed during the two nights I spent with my uncle and his family, I was glad that I had decided to join the military instead of living in a *ma'abara*.

The uncertainties of hitchhiking worked against me on my way back to camp following the *sh'buoth* holiday. I was a few minutes late, and knew that returning through the main gate meant I would be reported for tardiness. I had, however, done my share of guard duty at night, so I knew the location of the holes in the fence that enclosed our camp. I had also learned to crawl on my belly and move silently when necessary. Basic training, I decided, could be used to benefit me as well as the army.

I sneaked into camp, moving silently through one of the fence's holes, afraid the guard outside would catch sight of me. I felt my heart pounding in my throat, even as I told myself the risk was worthwhile. I slipped into my bungalow minutes before roll call and wiped the sweat off my forehead, scarcely daring to believe in my own luck.

Though it was wonderful to see them, the visit with my uncle and his family intensified my longing to see other members of my family. And then the unexpected happened.

Across the road from our basic-training camp there was a *ma'abara* where new immigrants were placed. One day, about two months into my basic training, I heard that my maternal grandmother, *yemma* Aziza – *yemma*, meaning grandmother - had arrived in the camp with her sons, *khalu* (maternal uncle) Sion and *khalu* Guerji, her daughters *khala* (maternal aunt) Nazeema and *khala* Toya, and *khala*

Toya's family.

Khalu Guerji was the prominent member of that branch of my family. When he arrived in Israel, *khalu* Guerji was single and in his early forties. Until a few months before immigrating to Israel, he had served as Iraq's Assistant Minister of Finance for Currency. Traditionally, Jews had dominated the high positions in Iraq's Finance Ministry, a carryover from the time of King Faisal I, who was enamored of the Jewish community's commercial and banking know-how. It was also a carryover from the period of the Ottoman Empire, when the Empire's financiers were mostly Jewish.

With heightened Iraqi nationalism and increased hostility toward the Jews, more and more of the ministry's Jewish staff members were let go and replaced by Muslims. Uncle Guerji was one of the few members of the Jewish community left in a high position at the ministry. But life became increasingly difficult for him, too, in the late forties as hostilities against the Jews of Iraq gained momentum. At one point, *khalu* Guerji was threatened with court-martial for treason, when he opposed the hiring of someone, whose main qualification was that he was a Muslim and a relative of a cabinet member. In time, my uncle was eased out of the government. The ministry abrogated his pension contract and put him on notice that, if he chose to bring a civil suit against the ministry for breaking the contract, he would be charged as a supporter of the "Zionist Entity" and tried before a court martial.

I remember *khalu* Guerji as intense, energetic and hard working. In Baghdad he left home early in the morning to be at work before everyone else. He stayed behind long after everyone in his office had gone home. He was a meticulous, elegant man, dressed in the best of suits, his shoes always sparkling. In spite of his overwhelming commitment to his work, he maintained a great deal of interest in the world around. He followed the details of the war against the Nazis to the minutia. But, unlike my father, *khalu* Guerji never involved himself in the activities of the Jewish community or shared the burden of running its affairs.

By the time I reached the age of sixteen, I had attained the same height and build as *khalu* Guerji, and so inherited all his elegant castoff suits and neckties. To my delight, that meant that I became one of the most dapper young men around.

Khala Toya, whose name was a diminutive of Victoria, was my least favorite aunt, even though one day she would change my life with a single, highly uncharacteristic act of generosity. *Khala* Toya was one of my mother's younger sisters. She was a tall and imposing figure, and she carried herself as though she ruled the world. In fact, she was aptly named because she possessed Queen Victoria's regal, imperious air. Everything that pertained in any way to *khala* Toya was bigger, better or more desirable--at least according to *khala* Toya.

She was forever blowing her own horn and that of her immediate family. Her husband, Shafeek, who worked under *khalu* Guerji, never struck me as bright. But to hear *khala* Toya talk, the Ministry of Finance revolved around her husband.

"Everybody in the office comes to Shafeek with the difficult problems," she would boast.

Khala Toya filled any environment in which she moved with a deep sense of her own self-importance, and she never saw beyond that. Everybody else existed to do her bidding, in one way or another.

When they went out in public, many Jewish women wore a black silk cloak, called *abayi*, which covered them from head to toe. Not *khala* Toya -- she sallied forth into the streets carrying a large handbag and swishing her long skirts as she walked, her hard hazel eyes looking neither to the right nor to the left. Several of my siblings and I had no liking for her, particularly because she stole money from Jamila's trousseau budget, but I don't think she took much account of us. I wonder if she would have cared had she known that we privately called her *baghla*, or mule, because we thought she looked like one. She was not pretty, but she wore her high opinion of herself on her face for everyone to see.

My uncles Guerji and Sion, who worked hard to save for a dowry for their unmarried sister *khala* Nazeema, didn't have an easy time providing for the family, but *khala* Toya showed no consideration for either one. She, her husband and her three children showed up at my grandmother Aziza's house every night for dinner. *Khala* Toya never lifted a finger to put a plate on the table or wash a dish. She and her family sat at the table, expecting to be served by her sister, *khala* Nazeema, who was living at home with my grandmother and my two maternal uncles.

Worse yet, *khala* Toya helped to destroy Nazeema's first marriage. A dreadful marriage custom to which many families, including ours, subscribed played right into her hands.

This time, it involved the need to obtain proof of the bride's virginity and the groom's virility. After the marriage ceremony the bride and groom customarily retreated to a room where the woman was to be deflowered and the bloody sheet later produced as proof that she had been a virgin. After the proof was exhibited, friends and family who had waited outside the marriage bedroom rejoiced. This demeaning custom produced enormous anxiety in the man. Some men found themselves unable to rise to the occasion, and at times it took several days before the required proof could be produced. This is what happened to *khala* Nazeema, who married a shy and gentle young man.

When deflowering didn't happen on the wedding day, *khala* Toya made the situation her business. She advocated divorce, and in the end she prevailed: *khala* Nazeema divorced her husband. But when she returned to her mother Aziza's house, she cried for days and refused to be consoled. In time, she reverted to being the unhappy servant to *khala* Toya instead of being in charge of her own home.

I thought about all of this as I learned my grandmother had arrived. The separation and vicissitudes we all had endured had done much to soften my feelings toward *khala* Toya. After all, she was my mother's sister. I felt my love for my mother rise up to include *khala* Toya, and I looked forward to seeing her with the rest of my grandmother's family. I also thirsted for news of my parents and siblings who were still in Iraq. And so I was excited as I told myself I would soon see my grandmother.

But my initial excitement turned to frustration and disappointment. The *ma'abara* was just across the road, but I wouldn't get a pass to leave camp for another two whole weeks. I couldn't wait that long to see my grandmother. I made up my mind to sneak out of camp for a few hours on the coming Saturday to visit the *ma'abara*. Saturday, I decided, was the best day for my escape. The exact time, however, would have to be decided on the spur of the moment.

Saturday was a day of rest when we had no training. We could do as we pleased, short of leaving the camp without a pass, but had to be in our quarters when checks were made. At the conclusion of each check, the time of the next check was announced, and the interval between checks could vary anywhere from one to four hours. The trick was to leave during a longer interval and return in time for the next check, without my absence being noticed. This was not as easy as it sounds.

I picked the best time that I could to leave and removed my military hat so that I would be less easily identifiable as a soldier. Then I made my way down the hill and across the road to the *ma'abara*. I couldn't move too quickly lest I draw attention to myself, and I had to move confidently to give the impression that I was authorized to be out and about. My heart pounded. I ducked whenever I heard the sound of a vehicle on the road.

The welcome from my family when I found them was worth the risk I had taken.

"What has happened to your hair?" my grandmother asked, noticing that my thick curly hair had been reduced to a crew cut.

"You are so thin," my aunts clucked.

I had, indeed, lost weight. In basic training we used to joke that the army made us go for a run after lunch to be sure the mouthful we ate would be melted from our bodies.

But everybody kissed me and held me close. It was a joy to know that some of my family had made it to Israel, and that I had managed to spend a few stolen moments with them. But the joy was tempered with sadness. My grandmother shook her head and, with tears streaming down her cheeks, looked around the shabby tent, which was a far cry from her home in Baghdad.

"Look at what has happened to us."

Khalu Guerji sat quietly on his bed and didn't participate in the conversation. He looked worried, and seemed engrossed in his thoughts. Was he scared that he might be too old to find employment? Gone was the nattily dressed man who had given me the best suits I had ever worn; gone was the confident look and the enthusiasm of the hard-driving uncle I remembered from my younger years. He looked broken. He had suffered the biggest fall of them all, I said to myself. As I bade him goodbye, I wondered what the future held for him, for *khalu* Sion, and the rest of the family. They had to find work in order to survive. It was heartrending to see them uprooted in their middle years.

Grandma Aziza probably suffered the most. She was seventy when she arrived in Israel. She was the elder in the family. Everyone turned to her for reassurance and warmth at a time when she herself was overwhelmed with a sense of loss.

During our Baghdad days, Grandma Aziza had radiated serenity and composure. When we ate at her house she presided over a full table, urging all of us to have "just a little more." Now, the food rations were so small there was hardly anything to serve. Her eyes mourned the brimming bowls of food that had graced her table in Baghdad. In Israel that feeling of plenty and prosperity was gone. Here her face was set in worried lines. In Israel, her favorite son, Uncle Guerji, a former Assistant Minister of the Treasury, was just another unemployed person. In his early forties, Uncle Guerji couldn't hope to ever return to anything comparable to his former position. No one was sure, least of all Uncle Guerji, that he would ever be gainfully employed again. Younger men went begging for jobs. Uncle Sion, who was four years older than Uncle Guerji, was in an even worse position.

"How are we going to make it?" Grandma often asked. She was too proud to live on handouts, and there was precious little of that in any case.

And then there was Aunt Nazeema. She was the youngest in the family. Still, she was hitting forty. In Baghdad my two uncles had worked hard to save enough money to marry her off after her divorce and pay for her dowry. But all that was gone now. The Iraqis had seized everything they had.

"What hope is there for getting Nazeema married off when both Guerji and Sion are unemployed?" Grandma would ask. She knew all too well that there was nothing she could do to help. She had never held a job. She spent her younger years bringing up her children and was the rock on which the family leaned. And now at age seventy she was confronted with a grim and meager existence she could never have envisioned during her life in Baghdad.

Grandma never regained her sense of peace. She didn't live to see Aunt Nazeema and Uncle Guerji get married. She wore an expression of sadness and defeat until the day she died, six years after arriving in Israel.

AIR FORCE

When I completed my basic training I was transferred to the Air Force. During my remaining twenty-seven months of service, I was affiliated with Wing 4, the heavy and light bombers unit.

I was a member of a team in charge of technical supplies for the airplanes, mostly B-17s and Mosquitoes (two-propeller lighter bombers). It was a critical job. The planes, which flew mainly training and reconnaissance missions, were grounded for repairs as briefly as possible. Whenever we received a request for a part that contained the phrase "Airplane on the ground," the part necessary for the repair had to be available immediately. Somebody from our unit had to be on call twenty-four hours a day, and all airplane parts had to be in stock at all times. I had to be familiar with all the parts, and at times I had to travel from one base to another to pick up parts from warehouses.

The first few months I was with Wing 4 we were based at Tel Nof, a major airfield in South Central Israel, built by the British military prior to Israel's independence. We lived in big tents, four people to a tent. There was space to move around, store our belongings and create a semblance of order in our lives. It was the first time I began to feel I could be happy in a home other than the one I grew up in. But I was still delighted when Wing 4 moved to Has'sore, a few miles south of Tel Nof.

In Has'sore I shared a snug bungalow with two men from India, one from Iraq and an Israeli of Yemenite descent. We lived together in harmony. Soon I transferred my love of my Tel Nof tent to our new bungalow, and grew to think of it as home.

Soldiers who shared the bungalow with me
Daniel – front row in middle

Every morning when I woke up, I gazed at the land stretching out before my eyes in every direction. I could see kibbutz Has'sore up on a hill about a mile away, though its entrance cut through our camp. I could see its trees, lush grass and the red roofs of its houses in the distance.

Morning flag-raising ceremony in Wing 4 - Daniel on the right saluting the Israeli flag

At Has'sore there were movies, a library and weekly songfests. There was even a well-stocked store and snack bar. It was tempting to stop at the snack bar in the evening and have a cup of tea or enjoy a wafer or two. But the monthly allowance I received from the military was barely enough to pay for necessities. Those who could afford to patronize the store had family that supplemented their monthly allowance from the military. I didn't feel especially deprived, but when I learned that construction workers were well paid, I arranged to spend my next quarterly vacation -- five days every three months -- working in construction. I had no special skills in this field, for among Baghdad's Jews manual labor was scorned. So I was given the task of hauling bricks from ground level to the upper floor of a large apartment complex under construction. I spent my five days filling a large burlap bag with bricks, tying it to my shoulder and carrying it up to the top floors of the building. I had a weak back, and it hurt at night. But it felt good at the end of the day to receive my pay. The money I saved from those five days lasted me for months.

MORE REUNIONS

My older sister Muzli had married Naim Aslan in Baghdad two months before I left for Israel. They came to Israel a few weeks after my arrival.

During my childhood, my relationship with Muzli had been bumpy—I tried to stay out of her way, because she seemed to enjoy making life difficult for others. She changed for the better after her marriage to Naim.

Naim spent his younger years in Hilla, a town near old Babylon, some fifty miles southwest of Baghdad. He was outgoing, loved to host family and friends, and never failed to offer Turkish coffee with cardamom to anyone who dropped in for a visit.

One of Naim's entertaining talents was telling fortunes by reading the sediment of Turkish coffee. His readings were the highlight of any visit to their home. Sometimes it took Naim five minutes to "unlock the secrets" of the sediment and tell everything there was to tell. At other times, he would ponder a cup for as long as fifteen minutes.

He was such an accomplished storyteller that he swept his listeners along on the tide of his smooth and assured declarations. Everyone, believer and skeptic, listened attentively; you could hear a pin drop.

When Naim and Muzli came to Israel, they were assigned to *ma'abarat* Brenner in South Central Israel. The *ma'abara* was in an open field with tall eucalyptus trees and many cactus plants. Across the road there was a well-established kibbutz, Giv'at Brenner. The kibbutz hired *ma'abara* residents to help with work in the fields, and this was where Naim found work. About half a mile east of the *ma'abara* was an Arab village that had been largely destroyed during the 1948 war. New immigrants inhabited the village's tumbledown mud houses.

Like other *ma'abara*, *maabarat* Brenner lacked a sewage system. The pathway to the outhouses was lined with cactus plants. Walking at night to the outhouses was risky, particularly in the rain. There was no electricity, and flashlights were not available. Even with a kerosene lamp the path was hard to see. A misstep could end in a painful brush with a cactus plant. Cactus thorns, when lodged under the skin, were hard to dislodge. Tweezers were practically non-existent in the *ma'abara*, and medical help was not readily available. The thorns often resulted in swelling and infection.

Naim and Muzli were among the lucky ones who were allotted a canvas hut. The hut was no bigger than a tent, but it had a flat roof that made it possible to stand up straight inside. And, by contrast with the tents' dirt floors, huts had cement floors, which made it easier to keep clean. Naim and Muzli shared their hut with Naim's widowed mother, who had accompanied them on their flight to Israel.

NO WAY BACK
The Journey of a Jew from Baghdad

I hitchhiked to *maabarat* Brenner in search of Naim and Muzli, and it was a joyful reunion. Naim was a happy man by nature, and his temperament seemed to have rubbed off on Muzli. We hugged and kissed. There were lots of smiles and laughter. It was a beautiful, cool day. The *ma'abara* was bathed in sunshine and a sea breeze wafted over us, ruffling the eucalyptus leaves. We ate lunch together. There were no chairs or tables. We sat on the edges of the beds the Jewish Agency had provided. But no one seemed to mind. We were happy just to be back together under the same roof. Naim and Muzli had cooked a meal on their tiny kerosene stove. It was not the big Sabbath lunch we were accustomed to in the old country, but it felt festive nonetheless. Naim had bought the stove with money he had earned from his work. In a place where there were so few worldly possessions, it was a blessing to own a kerosene stove.

Muzli sitting in our home in Baghdad, April 22, 1949

I visited Naim and Muzli many times after that. Naim would come back tired at the end of his workday in the fields. His small physique was not that of a strong laborer, and he suffered from backaches. His fingers were calcified from working with the hoe and shovel, but he was thankful just to have a job.

Most of the time it was dark by the time I reached their *ma'abara*. Naim and Muzli had bought a small kerosene lamp, which hung on one of the posts in their hut. The lamp's faint light stood in marked contrast to the bright lights we were accustomed to in my parents' home. But we knew it was a luxury; many *ma'abara* residents spent the nights in darkness. We sat in the hut and talked, drinking hot tea. Sometimes Muzli sang Egyptian songs, and we all joined in. For a few moments, we seemed to forget our trials in Iraq and the difficulties of *ma'abara* living.

Naim, who felt honored to be a member of our family, couldn't do enough for me. Occasionally, he and I took a walk to the village east of the *ma'abara*, drawn by the bright light of the Aladdin lamps that the merchants had lit to sell their wares. One evening we walked through the village and admired the displays of artifacts and colorful fruits and vegetables. Gentle night breezes caressed our faces, as we walked under the star-studded sky. We were happy to be alive, happy to be together, happy that Naim's marriage to Muzli had made us brothers.

Naim, working now, though not making much money, knew that I had even less than he did.

"Let me buy you something Danny, something you would like – a peach maybe, or a pear."

I looked into Naim's eager eyes and saw how much he wanted to please me. I knew how hard he worked to support Muzli, his mother and himself and how important it was to him to make their home the hospitable place that it was. I remembered my parents' home in Baghdad. I could see it in my mind, ringing with life, a welcoming place filled with light.

Suddenly it struck me. What Naim's home lacked was bright light. Their single kerosene lamp was not enough. Naim and Muzli's home, one of the most welcoming places I knew, was dark, not a suitable atmosphere for Naim, not in the least bit reflective of him.

I looked at the shelves of the store in which we were standing and saw a single lamp there, waiting to be sold.

"Instead of buying me a peach or a pear, which I do appreciate, what I would really like, Naim, is for you to save your money and buy another lamp for your home. That's what I would like."

Naim's eyes shone, as he smiled his pleasure in realizing there was something he could do that would please me.

"I will do that, Danny."

A week later when I arrived there were two lamps hanging on opposite walls of the hut. Naim rubbed his hands together in glee as he noted my pleasure in the amount of light in the hut.

"You like it, Danny?"

"It's wonderful, Naim." Then, jokingly, I added, "But three would be better than two."

On my next visit there were three lamps hanging on the walls, and the light they cast into the room reflected not only Naim's happiness at my surprise and pleasure, but also seemed to be a symbol of the turn my sister's and her husband's lives were taking.

Naim saw his lamps as a way of pleasing me, bringing me happiness. Little by little, they were gaining a foothold in this land. We didn't have to live dreary and dingy lives. We could reclaim the kind of life we had enjoyed in our homes in Baghdad, a life filled with light and love.

On a Sabbath afternoon in a rowboat on the Yarkon River, Ramat Gan, 1955
L to R: Helwa, Naim, Muzli and Daniel

Ammu (paternal uncle) Moshe, his wife *khala* (maternal aunt) Guerjiyi and my sisters Reyna, Helwa, and Latifa arrived in Israel on June 16, 1951. They shared a tent in a *ma'abara* five miles south of Tel Aviv. Two months passed before I got to see them. I was overjoyed, but devastated when I saw their living conditions. When I was in Sha'ar Aliyah, the horrific conditions there didn't bother me as much. I knew my stay was temporary. But when I saw my uncle, aunt and three sisters living in a small tent in an open field, my heart turned over. I wanted to rush out, buy them a large house in the middle of a city and transport them there. But I knew my wish was idle fantasy.

Ammu Moshe and *khala* Guerjiyi were like second parents to us; they had no children, and they loved us as they would love their own children. After shopping for us every day in Baghdad, *ammu* Moshe came to visit us most evenings. He would tell us about his doings in the business world, share gossip about the commodities markets, and listen with us to the evening news.

Any time I stopped by at *khala* Guerjiyi's during my younger years there was something stashed away in the closet, waiting for me - a baklava, an almond bar, a quince *louzeena*, or a small bag of sunflower seeds. And on my way out, there were always a few *fils* that she would drop in my pocket for an ice cream cone. Now my beloved aunt and uncle looked frail and anxious. I could see the fear of the unknown in *khala* Guerjiyi's eyes. It was painful to see how they had fallen.

It was hot when I went to visit another evening that summer. Heat shimmered against the canvas of the tent and the air inside was stifling. Bugs came in and out at will. I remember walking into the tent and seeing Helwa—usually so calm-- shaking with fear at the sight of a centipede scurrying across the floor. She was crying and calling out for Mama, terrified.

In Baghdad, centipedes were believed to crawl in through a person's ear and make their way to the brain and destroy it. Our family didn't believe in such tales, but my sisters' lives had been turned upside down in a short period of time. It probably seemed to Helwa that anything and everything bad could happen in Israel in that open field.

I squashed the centipede with my big military boots. I put my arms around Helwa and held her until she calmed down. It was all I could do, and it wasn't enough. I couldn't protect my sisters, aunt and uncle adequately.

I couldn't protect them when they lay in bed and listened to the howling of the coyotes outside, fearful that one would barge into their tent, which had no doors that could be shut securely, no locks. I couldn't protect them from the daytime heat or from the snakes that lurked in their path when they visited the outhouse at night. They were suffering, and I couldn't do anything to help. It tore at my heart to see them living in the open, hostile countryside at the mercy of the elements.

The winter that followed, the worst on record in Israel, brought even more hardship. Heavy winds and rains swept across the land. The field in which my sisters' *ma'abara* was situated quickly turned into a sea of mud.

One winter evening I trudged through the mud to their tent. I was happy to arrive and to be out of the driving rain and the biting wind. Suddenly our exclamations of joy at seeing one another turned to cries of dismay, as the main tent pole lurched dangerously to one side. I could see that the tent was in imminent danger of falling.

"Mama! Mama!" Reyna cried, as she and Helwa sobbed. Latifa just stood there helplessly wringing her hands.

I ran outside and pulled on a slack rope to get the pole back into position, but the peg around which the rope was wound was coming out of the muddy ground and needed to be hammered back into place.

Ammu Moshe came outside.

"I need a hammer, a hammer," I told him.

The wind and rain pummeled me. I was crouched in the middle of a big puddle that filled my boots with water, as I desperately pulled the rope toward me to prevent the tent from collapsing. The raindrops came down diagonally. Driven by the wind, they lashed hard at my face like nails.

As I pulled the rope, I became aware of pandemonium all around me. Ours was not the only tent in danger of collapsing. The next-door neighbor's tent pole was tilting dangerously. There were small children in that tent. Terrified, they came out in their pajamas, crying.

Their parents held on to the ropes, as I did, calling for help. I was torn. I wanted to help. But I knew if I let go, the tent would fall on my sisters. I pulled tight. I waited for someone to hand me a hammer. The word came back: No hammer could be found.

A view of a ma'abara, one of many flooded during the heavy rain in winter 1951-52

I looked around and found a large stone. It would have to do. I used it to hammer the peg into the ground. I hammered and hammered. Was I trying to hammer my frustrations into the ground with that peg? My sisters were living under miserable conditions, and I couldn't do anything to improve their lot. Why did life have to be like this?

My intensity must have scared *ammu* Moshe. I heard him repeat over and over again:

"Stop, Daniel, stop!"

I paid no attention. As I kept on hammering, I heard the tent next-door fall to the ground. Next to the fallen tent stood an older woman with long black hair and an embroidered headband holding it in place. She held a kerosene lantern. I don't know why I noticed that the headband was missing the customary pearls. Did the customs inspectors at Baghdad's airport confiscate them? I wondered. Were we to be left with nothing? The few belongings that people had managed to bring with them out of their native Iraq were being destroyed in the rain in Israel as their tents were being knocked down. Would we ever see better days? I continued to hammer as these thoughts rushed through my head.

I could hear babies crying and people screaming all around. I wished I could help everybody, but all I could do was continue to hammer, until I got our tent secured.

We were city dwellers. We knew well-lit city streets and brick houses. We knew that danger lurked in the world outside in Baghdad, but being with the family gave us a feeling of security. Now I had the feeling that there was no safety, no security. Everything familiar had been ripped away, and we couldn't even keep inclement weather at bay.

Inside the tent, my sisters were shaken. It seemed as if every imaginable misery could happen here in Israel in the rain-swept muddy field. Conditions in Iraq had been bad, but on some level conditions in Israel were worse. Why did this country seem so inhospitable?

During the following months, Uncle Moshe managed to put together enough money to buy a 350-square-foot one-bedroom apartment in Ramat Gan, a suburb of Tel Aviv. My three sisters went to live with him and *khala* Guerjiyi in their apartment. It wasn't much, but it was better than living in a tent in a *ma'abara*.

Planting saplings at kibbutz Ein haShofet –
L to R: Helwa's friend, Daniel, Helwa's friend, Helwa

In Baghdad my sisters would have lived with our parents until marriages were arranged for them. In Israel they had to work at menial jobs to help support themselves. They were intelligent and found such work boring. There were so many inconveniences, each one perhaps unimportant in itself, but their cumulative effect weighed on my sisters' spirits.

Soon enough, Helwa and Latifa had to face the sticky matter of military service. Among Babylonian Jews it was unheard of for women to serve in the military. Here, everybody under a certain age was required to serve two years. Immigrants were given the choice of deferral for one year after their arrival. Married women or women who declared themselves to be religious were exempt from induction, provided they met standards of modesty in dress as well. But the definition of "religious" and "modest" in Israel differed from our Babylonian customs. In Israel, wearing sleeveless shirts and bare legs disqualified a woman from being classified as religious for the purpose of receiving a military exemption. No such strictures prevailed in Baghdad's hot climate.

Reyna, Helwa, and Latifa opted for the automatic one-year deferral. By the end of the year, Reyna was past the age for compulsory service. Helwa, by then twenty-three, and Latifa, twenty-one, had to report for service. They didn't. Neither felt they could in good conscience ask for an exemption from the military on the grounds of being religious in the sense accepted in Israel. Both wore sandals and dressed in sleeveless shirts, but they still believed, Helwa more so than Latifa, that it ran against our traditions to have women serve in the military. From the time they made that decision they became fugitives, just like undocumented aliens. Everyone in Israel carried an ID card showing current military status, and MPs, for security reasons, would often check ID's when people boarded buses. Helwa and Latifa lived in dread of being discovered. They avoided traveling by bus as much as possible. On the road they steered away from the vehicles of military police. Their undocumented status made them ripe for exploitation at work. They had to accept wages below those agreed upon with the labor unions, and which were barely enough for subsistence. There were times when they were cheated out of payment, but they couldn't complain for fear of blowing their cover. "How long should we have to take it?" Latifa would ask tearfully.

Latifa, in training overalls,
Heading for the mess hall Sep 3, 1953

Latifa, left, and two of her friends in
the antiaircraft artillery regimen

For Latifa, the answer was "not much longer." She went to the recruiting office and defiantly declared, "I am not religious." She was not penalized for not reporting at the end of her one-year exemption and served two years in the anti-aircraft artillery.

Helwa held on for four more years. Her trials came to an end when she got married.

A BOUT WITH PNEUMONIA

No doubt partly because of the foul weather during the winter of

1951-52, I became quite ill. I delayed seeing the camp doctor, hoping the sickness would pass of its own accord, until I could barely stand.

"Why did you wait so long?" the doctor asked me.

" I didn't want to open myself to the charge of malingering," I said.

The doctor shook his head incredulously.

"You have a bad case of pneumonia."

He ordered a vehicle to rush me to Tel Nof's hospital.

The trip to the hospital was not long, but it was excruciating. The motion of the vehicle rattled me. I coughed. I felt as if I were burning with fever, but at the same time I felt cold. My body shook, and I just wanted to lie down and close my eyes. The driver had all windows closed. He turned on the heater, but nothing seemed to help. Finally we reached the hospital, where I passed out.

When I finally opened my eyes, I was lying in bed in a room by myself. Several blankets covered me. My joints ached, and I couldn't move a limb. It was painful to breathe, and things looked blurry. Was I dying? What would happen if I were to die? Would my sisters find out? The military had no address for any of my relatives who had arrived recently in Israel. Would my parents be told?

When I joined the military, I was asked for the address of my next of kin. I gave my parents' address in Baghdad. But I worried how word would reach my parents if something happened to me. Iraq was still at war with Israel—it had never signed the armistice treaty after the 1948-49 war of independence. So I didn't expect the military to send my parents a notice of my death. But I wondered if anyone I cared about would be told if I died.

A nurse walked in. She had a needle in hand, ready to give me an injection. She smiled, patted my hair and asked me how I felt. I couldn't muster the energy to answer. I just nodded. I wanted to know how long I had been there, but I couldn't talk. She lifted the covers to expose my arm, and gave me the injection. It felt like an eternity before the needle finally came out of my arm. The nurse covered me and left. I lay in that room for two weeks. Eventually I gained strength and sat up in bed.

One bright morning, the nurse walked in with a smile.

"The doctor said we can wheel you out this morning, and you can have breakfast on the patio."

Outside, the sun shone brightly. It was a beautiful day. It felt so good to be out in the open. Other patients sat around the table and ate their breakfast. There were several food trays and bowls on the table. I was feeling disoriented, and was too weak to reach out for what I wanted. But I noticed a bowl of boiled eggs right in front of me. They reminded me of the brown eggs of the Sabbath days in Baghdad. I reached for an egg, peeled it and dropped the shells into a big metal bowl that contained what looked like garbage.

"What are you doing?" the young nurse asked, her eyes crinkling with laughter. "Why are you throwing eggshells into the bowl of herring?"

I explained that I hadn't done it intentionally.

"Now we know what you think of herring," she teased.

I could only smile weakly. I had given away my true feelings about herring, something I wouldn't have done normally. I made no distinction between garbage and herring.

Indeed, to me herring signified all that was wrong with the Israeli diet. In time I learned to tolerate East European foods like potatoes and black bread. But the one thing I never got used to was the dreadful, salty "*dag maloo'ah*," as herring was known in Israel. I still remember the barrel of herring wheeled around the mess hall during breakfast. The cook would move from table to table, stick his fat, filthy hands in the barrel and throw handfuls of herring into metal bowls, as the salty water from the barrel dripped from his hands all over the table. The herring smelled and looked repulsive.

"Eat it; dag *maloo'ah* is good for you," he would say.

The first time I witnessed this nauseating ritual I had to rush from the table and go outside to throw up.

After spending three weeks in the hospital, I was taken to a convalescent home in Mount Carmel. Most of the time I spent in bed, happy to sink into the peace and serenity surrounding me. Some of the patients had been wounded in training or in border skirmishes. Others had been seriously ill and needed, as I did, to regain their strength. But, as I recovered, I could finally notice my surroundings and reflect on all that had happened to me. I could mourn my separation from my parents and the dispersion of my family. I could drink in the beauty of the valley below and of the Mediterranean at the foot of the mountain. For the three weeks I was there I could be quiet and heal my spirit.

During that time, my thoughts seemed to flow constantly to my parents and the life I had left behind in Baghdad. My parents didn't know that I had made it safely to Israel. In the rush getting out of Baghdad, I didn't make arrangements to send them any coded message. But two months or so into my basic training I had written to them at our home in Baghdad. I must have written something innocuous, hoping that my parents would have no difficulty identifying who had written the letter. I knew it was risky, but I was desperate to communicate with them. But the military returned the letter to me with a note warning that the Iraqis opened letters sent to Jews and might harm them if they discovered the letter had come from Israel. I never tried to communicate with my parents again.

NO WAY BACK
The Journey of a Jew from Baghdad

I loved my parents, but I needed to face the fact that I might never see them again. I felt I had to sever my ties with the past to move forward into my new life in Israel. In order to become part of Israeli society, I felt I must adopt its values and customs as my own. At the time, I didn't foresee the devil's bargain I was striking: how much of my essential self I'd be giving up.

"STOP YOUR ARABIC!"

Hebrew was the official language of Israel, but many other languages that European immigrants brought with them were used and treated with respect. My native language, Judeo-Arabic, was not. The unmistakable message was that there was something intrinsically unacceptable about being a Jew from an Arab land. An older immigrant from Poland, who worked with me in Wing 4, invariably addressed me as "*attem hash'horim*", or "you the blacks," when referring to immigrants from Arab lands. Other soldiers would loudly mimic Arabic songs in a denigrating way as soon as they learned I was from Iraq. In the Wing 4 lounge, it was common for soldiers who were immigrants from Eastern Europe to shout back and forth to one another in Yiddish. But when Babylonian soldiers spoke Judeo-Arabic, there were usually cries of "Shut up!", "Stop your Arabic!" The pervasiveness of this prejudice was driven home to me during a planning meeting of Wing 4, which I attended.

A number of soldiers didn't understand much Hebrew and if they spoke Romanian, Polish or Yiddish, directives were readily given in those languages. This particular meeting was being run by a young second lieutenant called Battat who was Israeli-born, but whose family hailed from Iraq. Battat was the only soldier of officer rank on campus with a Middle Eastern background. I knew that he spoke and understood Judeo-Arabic. There were about a dozen soldiers at that meeting, and they were mostly from Iraq. It quickly became obvious to Battat that one young man wasn't following the discussion.

"What language do you speak?" Battat asked.

"Judeo-Arabic."

There was a long silence. Two European soldiers in the group were looking fixedly at Battat, who was clearly uneasy. Battat shifted in his seat and a flush rose from his neck to his forehead. The thoughts running through Battat's mind seemed to echo in mine, but I remained silent and looked away.

How could Battat admit to knowing Judeo-Arabic, a language deemed unacceptable in Israel? How could he associate himself with a despised minority? How could I? Even as the thought crossed my mind that Battat and I should be able to speak in any language we chose to, I pushed the thought away. In spite of myself, my mind strayed to the time I went to see the Muslim doctor when I was a boy and defiantly spoke to him in Judeo-Arabic, even though Muslims expected to be spoken to in their own dialect.

What had happened to me since then? Now I was careful to lower my voice when speaking Judeo-Arabic in public. Ours was a language that, in Israel, had been dubbed Arabic, the language of the enemy. And Battat obviously felt the same way. The fact that he was an officer who outranked the two Europeans in the group made no difference, just as it made no difference that the Jew in Baghdad was a professor and the Muslim he spoke with was a garbage collector. The Jew was expected to defer, to hide his Judeo-Arabic and speak in the Muslim dialect instead.

I wished that Battat would take a stand, but he couldn't bring himself to do it. He didn't translate his instructions into Judeo-Arabic. The young soldier from Iraq was on his own.

HELP! I DON'T WANT TO BE A PHYSICIAN!

My time in the military was drawing to an end, and I realized that I would need skills in order to survive. I enrolled in an evening accounting course in Tel Aviv. I had no clear direction yet, but I liked the subject and figured that if I were to make it to college, a job in accounting might pay my way.

At the same time I was preparing to take the entrance exam for Hebrew University Medical School. There were five physicians in my family, and becoming a physician was considered the height of accomplishment in my family.

I was not enamored of becoming a doctor. Unlike the rest of my family, I didn't hold physicians in awe and couldn't -- I still can't -- stand the sight of blood. One time my sister Latifa needed treatment for Leishmaniasis, a tropical disease common in Baghdad. I accompanied her to Uncle Guerji's clinic and stayed with her while he injected a needle into a painful boil on her finger. The sight of the bloody procedure and her writhing in pain was enough to make me pass out. When I opened my eyes, Latifa was standing next to me, holding a wet cloth to my forehead.

In spite of this phobia, I still felt I should apply to medical school. Though I was living far away from my parents and the community in which I grew up, I still felt their influence. Looking back, I can't imagine what I thought I was doing. Perhaps I was hoping that I would be turned down, so that I could say I had at least tried.

I hitchhiked to Jerusalem and took the medical school entrance exam. When I finished, I heaved a sigh of relief. I had done my duty, and now I could get on with my life.

Not long after, I received a letter from the admissions office saying that I should report to the university in Jerusalem for a preparatory meeting for entrance to the medical school.

I panicked.

"My God. This is getting serious. I don't want to be a physician!"

I wrote immediately to the admissions office saying that I didn't have money for the bus fare to Jerusalem, which was true, and as I expected I never heard from them again. If the school had offered to pay for my travel fare, I am not sure what I would have done. Whatever my future held, I knew it wouldn't involve medicine.

TWO CONSCRIPTS

As my discharge date approached, I began to feel regrets about leaving. I had gotten used to life in the Air Force, and had come to think of the conscripts in Wing 4 as my family. The camp at Has'sore had been my home for over two years, and during that time I rubbed shoulders with a number of memorable characters.

At Wing 4 we didn't have daily formation or inspection, as was the practice in the infantry or the artillery. The only exception was the sanitation crew. They mustered every morning, carrying their brooms, brushes, buckets, hoses, shovels, hoes, and rakes. Dressed in blue work overalls and berets, they stood in line for roll call and their assignments for the day.

Without fail, a spindly young conscript from Algiers stood at the head of the line. His name was Gilbert. He had dark skin, curly black hair, and the color of his eyes matched his blue overalls. He held his tall broom against his right shoulder, like a rifle. He beamed with pleasure, turning his face right and left as if to ask every passerby: Did you notice me? Can you see my enormous broom?

Gilbert spoke French. At times each word came out broken in pieces with quick breaths in between. At others, four or five words tumbled out at once. He spoke little Hebrew, and his speech all sounded like unintelligible French. But the broad smile of wonder and amazement never left his face even when he realized people couldn't understand what he was saying. On the contrary, he seemed exhilarated when people asked him to repeat what he said.

Gilbert loved to hear his name, particularly when it was pronounced the French way – Jilbegh, with the guttural French GH for

R. I used to call him "*Monsieur* Jilbegh," and that always elicited a bigger smile than usual, a straightened body, and an uplifted head.

Gilbert's favorite work assignment was cleaning the camp's bathrooms. Not surprisingly, he had no competition for this assignment.

When I was promoted to the rank of sergeant, I was moved to new, more spacious living quarters, closer to the Wing's entrance. Gilbert's face lit up when he saw my three stripes, and he pledged to come every day at the end of his shift, to sweep my bungalow. I declined the offer gently. I was not particularly thrilled at the prospect of having my bedroom swept with the same broom used to sweep the camp's toilets.

On the day of my discharge from the Air Force, I saw Gilbert and the rest of the sanitation crew for the last time. I yelled my usual, "Salut, *Monsieur* Jilbegh" and stepped forward to the parade and shook Gilbert's left hand, as he continued his march with the rest of the sanitation crew.

I often thought about Gilbert and wondered how he managed in society at large. Was he able to deal with the rough and tumble of civilian life? He seemed to be so innocent, so vulnerable. Did he continue in sanitation? Did he choose to return to Algiers to be with his family? Maybe his family too was displaced. Where could he have ended up? And to day, as I write my memoirs, I wonder about him, as I wonder about the rest of the conscripts of Wing 4 who made up my little family while I served in the military.

Zari Salloomee was quite a different character. Zari came from a poor Muslim village in Iraq. He was short and muscular, had black hair that stood up in spikes, a thick moustache, and dark skin. He was cross-eyed, adding to his fierce look and menacing appearance. Zari bore a close resemblance to a vulture, the type of person one would be terrified to bump against on a dark night.

Before coming to Israel, Zari had served two years in the Iraqi military. Jews in Iraq served at most three months in the Iraqi military; most were well-educated enough to qualify for shorter stints. Zari was the first Jew I ever met who had served the full tour of duty.

By all indications, Zari was a misfit. He didn't have the staying power to hold down a job, and there were few jobs for which he was qualified. Those who had dealings with him described him as unpredictable, driven by impulse. He would erupt at the slightest provocation. Some wondered if he was mentally stable. Others went so far as to say he was schizophrenic. But I had a hunch that Zari was a shrewd bully who knew exactly what he was doing. The reputation he had was precisely the one he had cultivated. He liked being able to behave exactly as he pleased and, because most people were afraid of his outbursts, he would do just that – blow up.

Whatever his personality disorders, the collective wisdom was that Zari was stupid. And Zari took full advantage of this perception. He was always ready to flex his muscles, and he got into fistfights frequently. He landed in the Wing's jail several times. Nothing seemed to help.

Zari treated me with deference, and would stop by my office to talk. I didn't particularly want to see him, but I never told him that. During our visits, he lashed out at Israel's military for what he sarcastically called the princely treatment of its soldiers. He maintained that the rough treatment he had received in the Iraqi army had enhanced his stamina.

"In the Iraqi military," Zari would tell me, "we all ate from the same big plate, and we felt we were sharing with our brothers. How do you create the sense of brotherhood when everyone has his own food domain?"

(I did know that conditions in the Iraqi military were deplorable: Cold showers, lice, floggings. Most Muslim conscripts were illiterate. It was said that because few of them could tell right from left, during training they were each given a tomato to hold in their right hand and an onion for the left hand. They were ordered to "turn tomato" or "turn onion" until they learned to tell left from right.)

The day arrived when Zari was talked into working in the officers' dining room as a server. After I was promoted to sergeant, I was entitled to eat in the officers' dining room. Zari was ecstatic when he saw me enter the officers' dining room for the first time.

"Welcome, *areef* Khazzoom," he said with a smile, using the Arabic word for sergeant.

He took my hand and seated me at one of the tables. I was flattered, but embarrassed by the special treatment. Still, who would dare question Zari's actions? He brought me a tray full of food. He had selected the kind of food that was closest to our daily diet in the old country.

At first I was very happy to get the kind of dishes I'd eaten in my parents' home. In time, however, my excitement gave way to discomfort. Zari brought me a lot more food than he brought the rest. I was embarrassed, and couldn't eat it all. Zari wouldn't listen to my pleas to bring smaller portions. Worse, he insisted that I eat everything he brought. I thought that he would be offended if I turned back the tray, and worried that he might turn on me.

I was beginning to feel helpless. And then it occurred to me that I was not obligated to eat in the officers' dining room. I could go back to the mess hall if I wanted to, and then I wouldn't have to deal with Zari. And so I did.

A couple of days later, there was a knock on my office door. It was Zari. He looked grim, and he had a forbidding look on his face. He didn't say a word. He closed the door slowly and sat on the floor with his back against the door, as if to make sure nobody could come in.

I felt a stab of fear. Why had he come?

Finally he broke the silence. Zari told me he was getting married the following week. He had applied for a wedding leave, but was granted only two days. He complained that it took him a whole day to hitchhike from Has'sore to his *ma'abara* in northern Israel. He was furious that he was not granted adequate time for his wedding celebration.

"So now I have decided to escape from the camp for my wedding. Would you, *areef* Khazzoom, look it up in your law books," he asked, "and tell me how long they would imprison me if I were to escape for, say, two weeks or three weeks?"

I checked the rules and gave him the answer. But it was not what he wanted. He hesitated a minute and came straight to the point.

"How many days of unauthorized absence would bring a maximum of three weeks in jail?"

"Eighteen days."

Zari's face lit up. There was a shrewd look in his eyes.

"That's good, *areef* Khazzoom. For the information, I thank you."

The rule was that when a soldier was imprisoned for up to three weeks, the days he spent in jail would count toward his military service. But if his imprisonment exceeded three weeks, his discharge would be delayed by the same number of days he sat in jail.

Now it was clear what Zari was after. He wanted to escape from the camp for a period of time that wouldn't extend his date of discharge. A week later Zari vanished from sight. He showed up exactly eighteen days later to turn himself in. The man was no fool, I thought to myself. He was a shrewd, calculating person who knew exactly what he was doing.

DAY OF DISCHARGE

October 2, 1953 was the day of my discharge from the military. Even though I had looked forward to it for a long time, I remember it as a bittersweet day. I felt sad, as though I were separating from a close friend.

I had grown a lot during the months I spent in the Air Force. I learned Hebrew, acquired new skills working in a large organization and received excellent care when I convalesced after my bout with pneumonia.

But there was a time to be weaned. And that time had come.

I rode down to the airfield where our shops were located to bid farewell to my coworkers. Hanan Landau came out of his office to greet me. Hanan, a major in the Air Force, was the head of our unit. I had worked with him during the last twenty-five months of my service.

Hanan was German-born, and had immigrated to Israel when Hitler took over. Prior to his arrival, a native of Israel had headed our unit.

I was still new to Israeli ways when Hanan arrived, and was not aware of the historical tensions between Jews of Eastern European background and Jews of German background. For weeks beforehand everybody talked about the misery of having this "*Yeke*" in our midst. When I asked friends in camp why a "*Yeke*" would be so bad to have around, I was told horror stories about how demanding, rigid, intolerant, and arrogant "*Yekes*" were. I took the stories seriously, and was terrified to think of what lay ahead, since I was supposed to work directly with the head of our unit.

But it was the surprise of my life when Hanan Landau came on board. Right from the outset, we had a close working relationship. We synchronized admirably. Hanan wanted everything above board, and so did I. He expected commitment, and so did I. He insisted on transparency and didn't tolerate fudging, and so did I. He abhorred favoritism - *protectsia*, as it was known in Israel- and so did I. In time, Hanan and I became good friends, and I learned to be wary of derogatory characterizations applied to entire groups.

I left Hanan's office and turned to what used to be my office. A coworker – my successor -- was already occupying it. We hugged warmly as I entered. I lingered for a moment taking in the scene. I ran my hand slowly over the top of what used to be my desk. I thought to myself I was so much more fortunate than those immigrants who had to live in a *ma'abara*.

Finally, I visited my bedroom, the most difficult place to part with. It was my refuge. I paused to take one last look through the window. There was the kibbutz that greeted me every morning when I woke up, as beautiful as ever. I said a prayer in my heart that the kibbutz and its members would never have to separate from each other. A separation from one's home was heart-rending. I had been through one myself.

I left my bedroom, kissed the Mezuzah at the doorpost, and closed the door behind me for the last time.

DETOUR IN THE NEGEV

I was discharged from the Air Force on October 2, 1953. The military gave me fifteen liras (about five dollars), a bus pass good for free travel and a voucher for dormitory-style lodging during the following two weeks.

I now had my sights set on attending college and majoring in science. In high school I was a top student in math, physics and chemistry, and math was my love. But courses in the sciences were offered only at Hebrew University in Jerusalem and at Israel's Institute of Technology (Technion) in Haifa, and I couldn't afford the tuition at either school. Reluctantly, I decided to postpone college. I would find a job and save money first.

I had two choices. I could stay in Ramat Gan with *ammu* (paternal uncle) Moshe and *khala* (maternal aunt) Guerjiyi and look for work in nearby Tel Aviv. My other choice was to go to Bersheba, an arid, sparsely populated Arab town in the heart of the Negev desert in Southern Israel. Most of the Arab population in that area was nomadic. Almost all the Jewish inhabitants were recent immigrants from the Middle East. I was not anxious to live in the desert, but I felt I owed it to my new country. Israel was striving to convert the Negev into productive farmland. But the Negev's arid climate and its distance from population centers discouraged people from moving to Bersheba. It was incumbent upon us, the younger generation, to do our share and help realize the dream of making the desert bloom.

I chose to go to Bersheba. The bus trip took five hours. As we pulled into town, we passed a few run down houses. One building stood out. It was Bank haPoaleem, the only bank and, as it turned out, the only solid building in town. A dilapidated hotel stood a few yards away from the bank. There was no bus station– only a bus stop. As far as I could see, Bersheba's sprawling *ma'abara* dominated the town.

I got off the bus with no idea of where to go or how to find a job. My voucher for lodging was good for twelve more days, so I knew I wouldn't be left out on the street. My aunt had packed food for me, and I had my fifteen liras in my pocket.

"Why put off the job search till to-morrow?" I figured. "Why not just go to the bank right now and inquire? What could I lose?"

The bank manager was a well-dressed, slim man in his late thirties with thinning hair. He had been born in Israel to parents who grew up in Iraq, I learned later. He had a poised manner and impressed me as a kind person, eager to help. He smiled and motioned to me to take a seat.

"My name is Daniel Khazzoom. I have just completed my military service, and I'm looking for work."

The words were out of my mouth before I knew it. I was terrified. "What have I done? Why so fast? I blew it!" But the manager seemed unruffled. He actually seemed to be pleased with my directness.

I told him I was a graduate of *l'Ecole de l'Alliance Israelite* in Baghdad, and briefly explained my work and responsibilities in the Air Force. But I dwelt mostly on the accounting course I had passed with distinction.

This seemed to interest the manager less than my earlier schooling.

NO WAY BACK
The Journey of a Jew from Baghdad

"You are a graduate of *l'Alliance* Israelite?" he said, beaming. "That is a top school. This is just wonderful. We need people like you."

Obviously delighted, he shook hands with me, and hustled me off to meet the assistant manager, who was also the bank's accountant. In glowing terms, the manager went on about my education at *l'Alliance*. The assistant manager, a Mr. BenBassat, suggested that we have a chat over tea.

A soft-spoken, stocky man in his early fifties, Mr. benBassat had been born in Sofia, Bulgaria. He had immigrated to Israel at the end of World War II, and joined the Hagganah. He walked with a limp, the result of an injury during the war of independence. Mr. benBassat had a fatherly look, and when he smiled, one scarcely noticed the lines deeply etched into his face or his thinning hair, which he smoothed down with his large hand.

I told him about wanting to help settle the desert and about my plans to go to college and make something of myself.

"It is so good to meet a young man with your sense of purpose."

When the manager returned, Mr. benBassat said he would like to have me work with him.

The manager motioned to an unoccupied desk next to Mr. benBassat's.

"Here is your desk. It is all yours. You can start working now, and I want to welcome you to our family."

I was on the verge of tears. I could scarcely believe I had landed a job.

That evening I found a bed in the hotel and settled in. I sat at the edge of my bed and looked around. I had nothing to eat since that morning. But I didn't feel hungry. I felt pumped up, exhilarated; I was on my way. The people I had met in the bank seemed like caring, warm human beings. It would be a pleasure to spend the next year or two working with them. Who knows, maybe by then a university would spring up here. Israel had grand plans for Bersheba.

That night I turned in early, but was awakened at midnight by loud voices in my room. A crowd of truck drivers had come in to occupy the other beds in my room, switched on all the lights, began smoking and sat discussing all that had happened to them that day. It was hours before they turned off the lights and settled down to sleep.

This became the pattern for my entire stay at the hotel. During the following few nights, I probably was more sleep-deprived than I had been in basic training.

"This can't go on much longer," I said to myself. I had to find a different place to stay. But where? There was no other hotel in town, and I couldn't afford to rent a private room. Sadly, I had to concede I was at a dead end. I realized I couldn't stay in Bersheba if I wanted to save money for college. I needed to go back to Ramat Gan and move in with my sisters and *ammu* Moshe.

It was a painful day when I told my colleagues at the bank what I needed to do. In the ten short days I had been with them, we'd grown quite close. The manager and Mr. benBassat didn't try to stop me from leaving, though I knew they didn't want me to go.

The manager accompanied me to the bus on my way back to Ramat Gan. He put his arm around my shoulder, as I was about to board.

"I wish you well, Danny. But remember, if ever you need a reference, you know where to come."

Bersheba is now a sprawling modern city; Bank haPoaleem is part of "Old Bersheba." Whenever I go there, I walk to "Old Bersheba" and spend a moment or two in front of the old building, remembering the first time I walked through its doors, suitcase in hand. Bersheba has many more bank buildings now, all modern and impressive. But this old building holds a special place in my heart.

I felt sad and discouraged as I rode the bus back to Ramat Gan. Would I ever find such marvelous working colleagues again? Would I ever be able to save enough money to cover the expenses of attending Hebrew University or Technion? Would I ever realize my dream of majoring in science? My short experience with living expenses in Bersheba had undermined my self-confidence. I was beginning to have doubts.

The salaries in Tel Aviv were higher than in Bersheba. I was beginning to wonder if I shouldn't postpone college until I had saved enough to live on my own in Jerusalem or Haifa. But by the time I managed to save enough, would I be too old for college? What other choice did I have?

I wanted to borrow money for college and pay off my debts after graduation. But in Israel, educational loans were out of the question. Banks wanted collateral, and I could offer none.

By the time the bus reached Tel Aviv, I had decided to compromise on my choice of major. Tel Aviv had an evening school, the School of Law and Economics, which offered degrees in economics, law, political science, and auditing. None of these fields was my calling. But whatever I would be doing in Tel Aviv would involve work with a business establishment. Studying economics or auditing while I was working might enhance my performance and earnings. If I managed to save enough in the meantime, I could then leave for Jerusalem or Haifa to major in science.

It was cold logic that led me to economics as a stopgap measure. Inertia and lack of adequate funds kept me permanently in a field that failed to ignite my imagination the way math and science always had. In Iraq, the social sciences were disparaged, and reserved for the least talented students. As a result, I lacked even the basic fundamentals of economics when I began studying it in college, and carried with me the tendency to look down on the field as well.

Today as I look back, I wish I had not been so cautious. I wish I had gone to Jerusalem or Haifa and taken the plunge. During my lifetime I took many gambles, and against all odds, things eventually fell into place. I wish I had adopted the same determined attitude toward my education.

In terms of accomplishments, I can't complain. I did well as an academic in quantitative economics, and my published research work has influenced thinking and policymaking in the U.S. and Canada. But in spite of all those achievements, my heart remains in the sciences.

COLLEGE YEARS

AN UNLIKELY BENEFACTOR

Tuition at the School of Law and Economics was one hundred and twenty liras, the equivalent of forty dollars. I had twenty liras, altogether – my original allowance from the military plus what I had managed to save from my work at Bank haPoaleem.

"May I give you the twenty liras I have and sign a promissory note for the balance?" I asked the school's Academic Secretary.

"No, I am sorry. The full tuition fee must be paid in advance."

"Is there a scholarship I can apply for?"

"No, there isn't."

"Could I borrow the money from a bank?"

"Banks don't lend money to pay tuition fees."

The Academic Secretary suggested that I send letters to several places, including the ministry of education and the office of the Prime Minister, inquiring about the availability of a scholarship or loan. No one responded.

The night before the start of the fall term, we had a family gathering at grandma Aziza's apartment. I told my relatives of my plight. Everyone sympathized, but it was *khala* Toya who took me by the hand and led me to the bedroom, where she took down a suitcase she had brought with her from Baghdad.

"What are you doing, *khala* Toya?"

She didn't answer. She opened the suitcase and tore between the two layers at the bottom, exposing to view a few banknotes she had hidden there before leaving Baghdad. I knew she had been holding on to the money for dear life, but she gave it to me to pay for my tuition. I was stunned, elated and grateful that this difficult woman, of all people, would be the one to rescue me at a time when she and her husband had such bleak prospects.

I wish I could say that *khala* Toya became a different person after she made this magnificent sacrifice on my behalf. She didn't. She still had nothing good to say about my father whom she had defrauded when she helped to buy Jamila's trousseau, and she constantly belittled others when they weren't present. But even *khala* Toya felt that family members should come to one another's aid in time of need.

I thought about that the next evening as I attended the first lecture of the semester.

To find a job, I registered with the Labor Exchange, an arm of the *histadroot*, the powerful labor union in Israel. The long arm of the *histadroot* reached into the government, healthcare, banking, industry, and the inner recesses of the private sector. Practically everybody who wanted work had to be a member of the *histadroot*. Every employer had to deal with the *histadroot*.

When I was not actively looking for work, I roamed the streets of Tel Aviv getting to know the city. I noticed how many middle-aged and older Jews from Iraq were sitting alone on the park benches along Rothschild Boulevard with a look of despair and resignation on their faces. Many of these men were entrepreneurs who had owned businesses in Iraq. They were used to being contributing members of society. Now they had nothing to look forward to. They were cast aside.

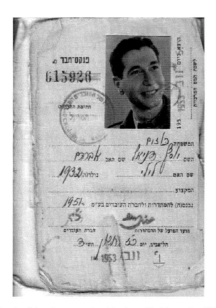

My book of histadroot membership, issued in November 1953

Among the faces, I saw one that I recognized: a French teacher from *l'Alliance* Israelite, *Monsieur Bonfils,* a stocky, gentle-looking man.

"*Monsieur Bonfils,* ," I called out.

I saw the familiar face light up.

"Joseph! Comment vas-tu mon *fils*?" he replied.

"I just came from the Labor Exchange. I am looking for work. How about you, *Monsieur Bonfils*? How are you doing? Are you working?"

The smile on my teacher's face faded into gloom as he shook his head in resignation.

"They have no work for me in this country. They say I am too old for what they have," he replied.

Monsieur Bonfils was not much older than fifty. He was not a wealthy man. He lived on a teacher's salary. He had a big house in Baghdad, but it was confiscated when the Iraqi government froze the assets of the Jews who left the country. How was he supporting himself and his wife?

*Monsieur Isaac Bonfils, my **Alliance** teacher*

What had happened to the members of the wonderful Jewish community from Baghdad? I wished we could have transported the community in its entirety to Israel. But things were different now. The community was scattered, and who knew what would happen to the people who had left or to those who remained behind? If my parents, my brother Jacob, my sister Valentine and my sister Jamila and her family ever managed to get out of Iraq and make it to Israel, I wondered if they too, would sit, despondent, on park benches. I remembered my old French teacher as a lion, exuding energy and a love of learning. He was a walking dictionary, and I looked up to him. It was shocking to see how fast and how far the mighty could fall.

My uncles were enduring similar humiliations.

A couple of years after our arrival in Israel, my maternal uncle Guerji received a small sum of money that he had stashed away in a Swiss bank years before he left Baghdad. He used it to buy the privilege of renting a small store in *sh'khounat hatikva*, a Tel Aviv slum, where he opened a restaurant. I stopped by the restaurant one evening. It startled me to see this once-elegant and powerful man wearing a white apron. Still, he seemed happy to have something that kept him busy. That evening, the restaurant was practically empty. Water was boiling in the pot for tea, but because of stringent rationing, he had run out of food. There was not even a piece of bread in the store. A tired-looking man in his sixties walked in and sat at one of the spotlessly clean tables. Uncle

Guerji set down a glass of water in front of the man, who ordered a plate of mashed eggplant. Uncle Guerji, inexperienced and apparently afraid of losing a potential customer, launched forth into a recitation in heavy, Babylonian-accented biblical Hebrew. He ticked off all the items on the menu: "And we had mashed eggplant, and we had fried eggplant, and we had Baba Gannoush, and we had crispy rice, and we had boiled eggs, and we had ..." The man's eyes bulged, as he grew increasingly impatient with this litany of "we had." He finally lifted the glass of water and brought it down hard on the table, shattering the glass. "Tell me what you have that I can eat," he howled. Poor Uncle Guerji sheepishly had to admit, "We don't have anything." With that, the irate customer stalked out of the restaurant. Sadly, Uncle Guerji took his chef's towel and swept the broken glass. A month later, he closed the restaurant.

I had great sympathy for displaced workers of my father's generation. But setting out on my life's journey was not all that easy either. I told my friend Yarmiyahoo Halperin of my frustrations landing a job. He was Russian-born, a former captain in the British navy and a staunch proponent of free enterprise. He told me that he had mentioned me to a Mr. Weinberg, the General Manager of Bank Leumi, Israel's largest bank.

"Mr. Weinberg told me the bank has open slots for young people like you, and would like you to apply," he told me. "Why don't you fill out an application?"

I presented myself to Bank Leumi's personnel manager, a man with gray curly hair, and glasses with metallic rims. I was struck by how small his eyes looked behind his thick lenses.

"No, no, young man. You can't come in here on your own looking for work," he said. "First you must go to the *histadroot* labor exchange. We hire all of our people from there."

I was puzzled. But I needed work, and if that was the accepted way of doing things, I wasn't going to point out that I was already registered with the *histadroot* labor exchange or that the bank's General Manager had said I should apply.

The man at the *histadroot* labor exchange was about as helpful as the bank official had been.

"What do you expect me to do?" he snapped. "We need a letter from the bank telling us there are open positions for someone with your background."

As the days went by, I wore a path between the bank and the *histadroot*. Each needed a letter from the other before anything could be done about employing me, but neither one was willing to make the first move.

The next time I visited the *histadroot* labor exchange, there was a kindly, soft-spoken Syrian gentleman behind the desk. I explained my problem to him.

"With your permission, I am going to go through our files and examine the record," he said.

"With your permission?" These were the first courteous words I'd heard in all my dealings with the Labor Exchange up to that point.

When he came back to his desk, he apologized profusely. It turned out that a letter from the bank had been languishing in their files for some time.

He wrote a letter of referral to the bank, shook my hands warmly, and apologized again for the runaround.

On my way to the bank, I stopped by Rothschild Boulevard to look for *ammu* Moshe. He had been worried about me and wanted to walk with me to the bank. Several of his friends, who were also anxiously following the saga, decided to join us in the march to the bank. I was touched. Perhaps they viewed my success as theirs, too. If they could no longer participate actively in life in Israel, as they had in Baghdad, perhaps they could do so vicariously through me.

Everyone waited outside the building, as I went up to the personnel office. I felt more confident this time; much of my anxiety was gone. I was surrounded by love, protected by the shield of caring that *ammu* Moshe and his friends had for me. My spirits were high.

This time, the meeting was brief. The personnel manager looked at the letter of referral, perused my school transcripts and declared:

"It is all go."

When I emerged from the meeting, *ammu* Moshe and his friends were all anxiously waiting for me.

"What happened? Did you get the job?"

Hearing my good news, they grinned and pumped my hand warmly.

"You're on your way, Danny. Congratulations!" a distant cousin in the crowd exclaimed.

My college career didn't run a straight course. It wasn't easy to work a full day and go to college at night, but it was especially difficult when my studies were disrupted by repeated calls for service in the reserves. Every year I was called up for four to six weeks, and the call could come in the summer, midwinter, or during final exams. No less problematic were the many shorter calls at odd times. My cell leader would show up at my office, or late at night at home, with orders to appear within hours at a certain camp. I, in turn, had to drop everything and notify the half-dozen members of my cell. Sometimes, the call was an exercise in preparedness, and we went back home once we all showed up. But sometimes the call was for real, and we ended up staying in camp a few days.

Without telephones or cars, these roundups were tiring. Some members of my cell lived miles away from my home. Running from one place to another to notify people was particularly difficult late at night when the buses were no longer running. Often I was too exhausted to attend classes the following day.

Daniel (r) training with bazooka, reserve service, October 27, 1955

And there was my problem with the professors.

Almost all our economics professors held high positions in government, *histadroot* or the private sector. Most viewed teaching as a sideline and dragged to class tired after a full day's work. Their lectures were stale, and some read verbatim from their notes of years before.

Our lectures were conducted in Hebrew, but only two or three members of the Faculty were native Israelis. Almost all the rest were Eastern Europeans, and their command of Hebrew varied widely. Generally the students were better versed in Hebrew than the professors. Sometimes this was a source of discord; at other times, it was a source of hilarity.

Most of our textbooks were in English, and they were expensive. The school had a library, but it rarely carried more than one copy of each textbook. We could not study in the library – it had no desks or chairs.

There was no place to study in my uncle and aunt's apartment, either. My sisters and I slept in the hall, and there was no space for a desk. The point was moot anyway. By the time I got home from school my sisters were in bed. I couldn't turn on the light to sit and study.

Sometimes I went to coffee shops to study after class. Occasionally I managed to do good work, but most of the time it was difficult to do serious thinking or concentrate on writing a paper in a coffee shop. On a few occasions I was kicked out for staying too long. To stay longer, I had to order more drinks. Sometimes I felt helpless. Where do I to turn?

Life consisted of non-stop work and study. More than once during my second year in college, I felt it was time to call it quits. I didn't get enough sleep. I was often hungry. I longed for free, unrestricted evenings.

At such times, visits with Naim and Muzli cheered me enormously. They lived in a cottage in Tel Aviv's Montefiore neighborhood, not far from school. On one visit I was feeling exhausted, dispirited, and unsure about continuing in college. I was not challenged, and I missed terribly my *Alliance* and Shamash days when I would be so engrossed in my physics, chemistry, and math classes that I didn't need to take notes. I was not getting much from college, felt I was a misfit in economics, and on top of that my instructors were mostly dull.

One of the many happy gatherings at Naim and Muzli's home in Tel Aviv
On the eve of the brith mila (circumcision) of Reuben, Naim and
Muzli's firstborn son. Seated, l to r: Albert benHayeem; Daniel; our cousin Sami; Helwa; (Reyna. Standing
in the back: Saleh (Naim's cousin); seated in the front Naim's grand cousin.

When I saw Naim's welcoming smile I knew that here I would be sheltered, if briefly, from the doubts that had been tormenting me. As usual, the aroma of the Turkish coffee brewing in the kitchen filled the air. We had our demitasse, and when Naim picked up my cup for prognostication I didn't resist.

Naim must have detected my sense of loss. He stared pensively at the grounds, turning the cup around.

"It looks confusing. I see something dark, heavy."

Naim paused a minute.

"These are clouds, gray clouds hanging over your head. But here—something very good, Danny. Very good."

I didn't believe in his prognostications, but Naim saw clouds hanging over my head. That was exactly how I felt. And then the good signs. Could something good lie ahead? Naim took his good time, peering into the cup.

"They are thick and gray," he said. "But they are moving. They are getting thinner. I see the sun at the other end. There is a boat, a big boat. It looks like you will be taking a long journey. Here are the stars."

I needed the stars. I needed the sun.

As it turned out, less than a year after that, I took the boat to France as an exchange student. But, whether Naim could see the future or not, just listening to him lifted my spirits. I walked away from his house with a lighter step. Naim had given me hope. I would continue on toward the stars.

I compared my situation with most of my Babylonian classmates, *ma'abarot* residents who, through no fault of their own, dropped out in their first semester of college. Their living conditions were not conducive to study, and, even worse, they had to miss the final two hours of classes every night in order to make the last bus to their *ma'abara*. The cumulative effect of missing so many lectures finally took its toll. They dropped out.

I recalled how my father had finished law school despite adversity. My life was certainly not as bad as his. I should expect no less from myself.

AFTER HOURS

My classmate Albert benHayeem and I studied together frequently. I admired Albert, who had escaped from Baghdad at the height of Jewish persecution in Iraq. We met on the first night of the school year and became friends for life.

One evening, after classes, Albert and I went for a walk on Allenby Street, Tel Aviv's main thoroughfare. We were both hungry. We passed by a small hall where a wedding was being celebrated, and stopped to watch. Wooden boards mounted on sawhorses served as tables, and people sat on benches around the tables. There was food on the tables. A small band played Israeli music. People sang, some clapped, others tapped their feet to the tune of the music. Not much pomp. But everyone seemed to be having a good time.

Albert suggested we move closer to the entrance to watch the goings on. He didn't stop at the door, but kept going. I followed him. A chubby middle-aged man, neatly dressed in a white open-collar shirt, stood at the other end of the vestibule. Albert extended his right hand and warmly shook the man's hand. He apologized profusely for arriving so late, and explained that it was all because of that darn professor who had a habit of going past class time. The man assured Albert not to worry, but Albert insisted that he still felt awful for barging into the celebration so late. And before I knew it, Albert had managed to engage his new friend in an animated conversation.

*Retreat for college students at Beit Berel, April 23, 1955.
Daniel seated, 2d row. Behind, Albert standing (bent)*

I stood at Albert's side, marveling at his ability to churn up so many subjects so effortlessly. From where did he unearth so many topics to talk about?

Then, Albert turned to me and with a big smile, introduced me, explaining that I was a classmate he had invited to attend the wedding. What chutzpah, I thought, squirming with embarrassment.

I doubt that the man believed a word of what Albert said. He must have known we were fakes. But it was a wedding, the atmosphere was jovial, and no one seemed to be in the mood to embarrass anyone else. And I guess Albert knew how to capitalize on that. We carried our books with us, and the man probably knew we were desperate college students looking for something to eat.

He took us to a table in the back, invited us to eat and wished us an enjoyable evening. Without hesitation, Albert turned to the food in front of us; I hesitated, but not for long. We ate our fill and joined in the celebration. We clapped and sang with the rest, and I felt invigorated to see happy faces around us. And for a few happy moments, I even lost sight of the fact that we were intruders.

Bank Leumi had a tradition of holding lavish *purim* parties for its employees. In 1956, the party was held in Bat Yam, a seaside town in central Israel, south of Tel Aviv. Today, Bat Yam is a resort town with 150,000 inhabitants, but in the mid-fifties, its population numbered ten thousand and it was notable for one thing: its large lunatic asylum. Among Israelis, the popular expression "Send him to Bat Yam" meant, "He is insane." On occasion, inmates escaped from the asylum and caused panic in nearby communities.

Because Bat Yam was isolated and somewhat inaccessible, the bank chartered buses to shuttle its employees to and from the party.

My date that evening happened to live in Bat Yam, not far from the hall where the party was held. We had a wonderful time. The food was good, the prizes fantastic, and the band outstanding. I danced till I was about to fall off my feet. Half an hour before midnight, the announcement came over the PA system that the last shuttle would leave in half an hour. We had time for one more dance, we decided. I didn't allow extra time to find my way back on dark, unfamiliar streets after escorting my date home.

We danced our last tango and left for her house, ten minutes away.

On the way back, I got lost and missed the bus.

I was tired and had no money for a taxicab. But it was moot anyway. There was nothing in sight, not a soul was around.

The hall was not far from the main road. If I stayed on the main road, I reasoned, I could walk to Jaffa, the next town. From Jaffa, I would do the same —stay on the main road until I reached Tel Aviv. From Tel Aviv I would head for Ramat Gan. How long would that take? Hours. But I had no other choice.

It was a moonless night, and the street lamps, few and far between, didn't do much to dispel the darkness. I began to worry. It was a period of incursions into Israel by *fedayeen*. These guerilla fighters, supported by Egypt, Jordan and other Arab states, could very well be in the vicinity. The road was dark and deserted - ideal for infiltrators. My head was heavy and my feet were getting sore, but I trudged along.

A police car whizzed by. Suddenly it stopped, turned around and directed its spotlight on me. Two policemen got out of the car and approached me carefully.

"What is your name?"

"Daniel Khazzoom." The name meant nothing to them, and why should it?

"Where are you coming from?"

"Bat Yam."

"Bat Yam!" The two policemen glanced at each other quizzically.

"And where are you going?"

"To Ramat Gan."

"Hum, you are walking from Bat Yam all the way to Ramat Gan, right?"

"Yes."

"What were you doing in Bat Yam?"

"I was at a party."

"At a party! And what did you do at the party? Were you dancing?"

"Yes, I was."

"You were, were you? You like to dance?"

"Yes, I do."

I remember one of the policemen raising his bushy eyebrows and the other shaking his head, as they looked at each other, as if to ask, "What do we do with this lunatic?" And then, all of a sudden, it hit me,

"Bat Yam's lunatic asylum! These policemen must be thinking I am an escapee." It was too late. I was too slow to grasp what was happening. But I was so exhausted I couldn't begin to explain what had happened with the shuttle. I remember thinking maybe it was all for the good. Maybe they would decide to take me to city jail. I wanted to lie down. A night in jail would bring welcome relief.

But the law didn't cooperate. The two policemen checked my ID card and verified my address. Then they turned their backs and drove away, taking with them my chance of spending a restful night in jail.

I didn't arrive in Ramat Gan until early morning, when the city had come awake and the buses were rumbling through the streets. I found my sisters, my uncle, and my aunt up, worried and waiting for me.

"Where have you been, Danny?"

Seeing how exhausted I was and the way I tumbled into bed, my sisters didn't find it hard to believe I had walked the twelve long miles from Bat Yam to Ramat Gan. And they didn't let me forget the night I was taken for a lunatic.

DEFENDING ISRAEL

In 1956, infiltration from Egypt into Israel intensified, and the *fedayeen's* sneak attacks on border communities grew in ferocity. Kibbutzim and *moshavim* -- agricultural co-operatives -- along Israel's borders were forced to divert most of their residents to guard against attacks, leaving practically no one to attend to farming or the daily needs of the community. There was an urgent need to shore up those communities and prevent their collapse.

A volunteer program was put in to help these communities. I volunteered to work for Kibbutz Sa'ad.

Sa'ad was a modern Orthodox kibbutz founded in 1947 by Jews from Germany and Austria. It was a green oasis surrounded by desert stretching as far as the eye could see. Not long ago, this oasis was a desert like the rest, nothing but sand.

During my stay, I helped build a fence around the kibbutz, and dug ditches around the fence. At night, I did guard duty.

I spent much of my spare time around the kibbutz' livestock enclosures. I loved to watch the cows showering their calves with affection. As a child, I had watched cows being milked, and I remember how touched I was to see how cows stood motionless when the calf drank its milk.

But perhaps the most rewarding part of my volunteer work was watching Sa'ad's community--men, women, and children--as they sat in their dining room and ate peacefully. It was gratifying to think that I might have had something to do with restoring a sense of peace to that embattled community.

Volunteers to help kibbutz Sa'ad, May 1956. Daniel seated first row second from left

Daniel erecting a barbed wire fence ...   digging a ditch around outer fence

*Hammering with a post hole-digger before installing a barbed wire fence,
Kibbutz Sa'ad, May 1956*

NO WAY BACK
The Journey of a Jew from Baghdad

A few days after my return from Sa'ad, I received a notice for my annual service with the reserves, and was stationed on a small hilltop on the border with Egypt. The Egyptian military was stationed across from us on three hilltops in a horseshoe formation, and a narrow valley separated us. Occasionally, when the wind blew in our direction, I could hear the Egyptian soldiers talking to each other.

Bolstered by a flow of new Czech ordnance, the Egyptian soldiers rarely missed an opportunity to flex their newly armed muscles.

At night our group descended into the valley and lay on the ground to intercept infiltrators and thwart beachhead advances by the Egyptians. Our location changed every night. We returned to our position atop the hill just before dawn.

One night, a shot came flying from one of the Egyptian positions. Soon more shots began to fly in all directions, echoing in a frightening cacophony. The shooting could have been a ploy to discover our location, and I worried that someone in our group might be tempted to return fire and reveal our location.

That did not happen, and soon the shooting died out. An Egyptian informer we were expecting to cross to our side that night never showed up. Was he captured or killed by the Egyptians? Could that have caused the commotion? I never found out.

Then there was the chain smoker under my command, a feisty man in his early forties. We were past midway in our service. By then, the long days of sitting guard and the sleepless nights spent lying on rocky terrain down the valley had taken their toll. Nerves were taut and tempers flared. The group grew increasingly edgy.

One night while we were down in the valley, the chain smoker covered himself with a blanket and lit up. The blanket was thin, and, although he was a good distance from me, I could clearly see the light.

"I sympathize with your need to smoke, and I wish I could help," I told him the following day. "But there isn't much I can do, given that we are where we are. I must ask you to refrain from smoking when we are in the valley."

Grabbing his rifle and pointing it at me, he yelled,

"You better lay off, if you want to return alive to your family."

I reiterated that I expected him to obey the rules.

I was anxious when we went down to the valley that night. If he lit up, I would have to initiate a disciplinary action against him. He would be prosecuted and probably jailed. Nonetheless, he seemed hotheaded enough to carry out his threat. But I couldn't give in.

He surprised me.

He didn't light up – neither that night, nor the following nights, and all was quiet on the Egyptian border.

NEW VISTAS IN EUROPE

In the spring of 1956, I was among a group of Israeli economics students chosen to travel to France on a student-exchange program. The purpose was to give us exposure to the management of major business establishments in France. I was paired with a brick factory, les Tuileries de Marseille, and a bank in Marseilles and received a stipend from both institutions.

At sunset, Daniel standing on the deck of boat, on the way to Marseilles

I left by boat for Marseilles that July. The trip took seven days. During that time the tensions that had built up during my time on the Egyptian border dissolved. In the daytime I stood at the deck's railing, watched the wake, felt the breeze on my face, and let my eyes roam over the endless expanse.

At night, as total darkness surrounded the boat, I lifted my eyes to the stars and was reminded of the summer nights in Baghdad when I had slept on the rooftop.

On the first night of our trip, I met Nissim Tal, a student at Hebrew University who was part of the exchange program and was also being sponsored by the brick factory. Born in Jerusalem, Nissim was of Babylonian descent, and could speak a few words of Judeo-Arabic.

Nissim told me about his family's struggle during the long siege of Jerusalem by the Jordanian army in 1948, before independence. No food or medical supplies could get through during the six-month ordeal. People tried to manage on whatever they had and shared with their neighbors as much as they could. Nissim's father, a grocer, had his storage room filled with cans of sardines, which sustained the family and their neighbors throughout the siege. Nissim told me that he could no longer stand the sight or smell of sardines, and had not touched them since.

I spent four weeks at les Tuileries de Marseilles, rotating through several departments. It was a big company, with shipments all over France. On my first day, I was invited to meet Les Tuileries' chairman. He was awe-inspiring, correct, but very human. He said he was happy to have his organization sponsor students from Israel. "*Nous sommes des amis,*" "we are friends," were his words.

We worked long days with a three-hour siesta break. Every time we came to work, morning and afternoon, and every time we left work, we made the rounds and shook hands with everyone in the department. This was a ritual I had never seen before, but in time I came to see that it injected a human dimension into the workday, allowing me to meet and get to know my coworkers.

At the end of four weeks at Les Tuileries, I transfered to my second sponsor, a bank in Marseilles's financial district. In the bank, as in the Tuileries before, I was rotated through different departments. Those rotations gave me a panoramic view of the bank's workings, and I appreciated that a lot.

Nissim (left) and Daniel on their way to Les Tuileries de Marseilles

I was surprised to discover how much hostility my coworkers at the bank felt toward Germans and Germany. The memories of the Nazi occupation of France were still fresh, and my coworkers seemed to be resolute in their rejection of any reconciliation with Germany. In Israel I had met survivors of the concentration camps and so tended to see the bitterness toward the Nazis primarily through the Jewish experience. Yet none of my French coworkers were Jewish. Their bitterness and aversion to anything German surpassed much of what I had heard from Jewish survivors of the concentration camps.

One of my newly made friends in Marseilles took me one evening for a walk to show me around. We passed by seafood restaurants at the beach. There, for the first time in my life, I saw people gulping down clams and eating crabs. I had seen crabs only in pictures before. To me they looked like big scorpions, and I never thought people would want to eat them. My friend took me inside one of those restaurants. There I saw a lobster being taken from the midst of ice cubes and thrown into a large pot of boiling water. The lobster was alive when it was thrown in the boiling water. I was aghast. I never saw a lobster before, and did not like the looks of what I saw. But I could not get over the fact that it was being boiled while still alive. This is inhumane, I screamed. My friend did not seem to think much of it. The sight of a live lobster being dropped in boiling water plays back in my mind to this day.

Marseilles boasted one synagogue, founded by Jews from Tunisia.

Nissim and I went there for services on a Sabbath day. A few minutes into the services, I heard organ music and noticed a large organ high above the sanctuary entrance. I wondered if we had stumbled into a church by mistake.

A congregant seated next to me explained that the membership felt that the organ music helped them focus and communicate their prayers to God. But since observant Jews were not allowed to play a musical instrument on the Sabbath, the synagogue engaged the services of a young Catholic musician to play. That confused me too: If music was intended to help communicate our Jewish prayer to God, why did it need the intercession of a Catholic to help it reach its destination?

Nissim and I walked out to the courtyard. We noticed a small gathering in a chapel at the far end of the courtyard. The synagogue made the chapel available every Sabbath day to a group of postwar immigrants from Central and Eastern Europe, who followed the Ashkenazi rite. We joined in. The services were traditional, but I couldn't understand a word. Even so, it was a relief to be in a traditional milieu.

During my sojourn in Marseilles, I vacillated between the Sephardi and the Ashkenazi congregations. Neither was satisfactory. The hardest day was *yom kippoor*. I struggled the whole day as the organ blared, at times drowning out the cantor and everyone else. When the day came to an end, and people began to disperse, I stepped up to the hekhal, put my hands on the sefer *torah* and recited quietly my own prayer of atonement. I asked God for forgiveness and prayed for my parents' welfare in Iraq. I remembered the days of *yom kippoor* in my parents' home when we lived under the same roof, and I intoned quietly the beautiful poem of *yom kippoor*, one we sang in unison in our synagogue, "Hatanoo lefaneikha, rahem aleinoo," or "we transgressed, dear God, have mercy on us."

I hugged the *sefer torah* and headed home to break the fast.

My work at the bank in Marseilles was drawing to a close, and my thoughts began to turn towards Paris. During my time in *l'Alliance*, I had heard a lot about Paris, and now I was going to see it with my own eyes. Nissim had already left for the French capital and I planned to meet him there.

I would journey to Paris by truck, a mode of travel that was commonly used by French students at the time. By custom, the students paid for the trucker's meals and, in theory at least, provided him with company on a boring ride.

When I first met with my trucker to arrange for the ride he seemed to be a pleasant fellow, dressed neatly in a suit and tie. It was a shock to see him wearing baggy overalls on the evening we left Marseilles. His stomach stuck out, and his bald head glistened in the fading daylight, giving him a sinister look. He was short and swarthy, and looked ready for anything. I marveled at how clothes can make the man.

I climbed into my seat beside the driver and we were off. Before long, night fell, and all I could see were lights shining here and there through the darkness. I put my head back on the seat and dozed off.

I was jolted awake by the sound of tires squealing and the truck rocking dangerously from side to side. I saved myself from going through the windshield by slamming my hands against the dashboard. A small red car was stopped at the side of the road in front of us. The truck driver got out to confront the tall, thin well-dressed young man getting out of the car. By the time I joined them, two young women in dresses were standing behind the driver of the car. They looked as if they had just come from a party.

"I must insist that I see your driver's license," the tall man said. "You should not be allowed on the road. We were almost killed."

The young women were silent, as indeed I was. I surmised that someone had gone through a stop sign, and from what I could gather, it probably was the truck driver. The trucker's face was red, his eyes almost closed, and the words sputtered from his lips.

"Just because you decided to have fun, does that mean you should deprive me of my livelihood?"

The trucker turned around and climbed back into the cabin. I did too. The young man's face darkened.

"Your license, if you please."

The trucker shook his fist at the young man.

"Do you want me to cut off your head? Just say the word. I would do it whenever you want me to."

The young man hesitated for a moment. Then he turned and got into his car, followed by the two young women who scurried across the road and almost tumbled over one another in their haste to get away.

I watched the taillights of the red car disappear into the darkness.

"Insolent young puppy," the trucker said.

I was silent, not wanting to have anything more to do with him. I had seen too much violence in the streets of Baghdad, where every argument and disagreement seemed to be settled with physical combat. I didn't like the violence on the French country road any more than I had liked it on the streets of Baghdad. From that moment on I didn't allow myself to doze off.

Shortly after this encounter, the trucker abruptly pulled off the road and climbed into the bed behind his seat. I sat in the darkness nervously playing with my fingers, listening to his snores, afraid to fall asleep. I longed for the bright lights of the restaurant where we had stopped earlier and I had bought the trucker coffee and a sandwich. I wanted people around me talking and laughing. I didn't want to be sitting in the truck alone with a violent man. I wondered if saving the cost of a bus ride to Paris was worth it, if it meant driving all night with a man who couldn't control his temper.

In Paris, I was able to make the first contact since leaving home with a member of my family still living in Baghdad. While in Marseilles, I had learned, through relatives in Liverpool, England, that my brother Jacob was in Turkey on a short trip. I had written to him, asking for news of home, and his reply arrived when I was in Paris. I opened the envelope with trembling fingers.

I learned that both my parents were still alive, but that *ammu* Shlomo, the beloved family friend who had paid us a visit during the farhood, had recently died. The loss hit me hard; Shlomo had been our surrogate grandfather. My cheeks were wet as I read Jacob's letter and saw the travelers' check he had sent me. What money he had remaining before heading back to Baghdad he had sent to me. I decided to spend it on what became a six-week trip to England.

Nissim and I got to see many shows in Paris. We had student ID's that allowed us to buy tickets to performances at very cheap prices. Of course the seats were not the best. Once I remember sitting on the side in the front row of a theater where the lights from the stage shone straight into my eyes obscuring my vision of what was happening on the stage. But it was wonderful to be able to go to the theater, as it was wonderful to walk through the streets of Paris at all hours of the day and night. At every hour the streets pulsated with life, with the music of human voices, with the sound of guitars playing in coffee houses, with the swirling crowds and the sounds of happy laughter.

One night as we were wandering through Paris we stopped in a coffee shop where a crowd of young people was singing and playing instruments. It was there that I met Christine from Vienna. Christine was a medium built woman in her early twenties. She wore a colorful Slavic apron, which stood her out in the crowd, and she seemed to exude a sense of tranquility and composure. I felt a sense of peace just looking at her clear, unaffected gaze and beauty. Christine was not a student, but a tourist who had hooked up with a group of students. I introduced myself to her and we went out for a walk along the Seine River that night. Christine and I began to hang out together, enjoying our walks, our visits to the theaters, and each other's company. We both knew our relationship had no future.

One night as we held hands and watched the glittering reflections of the moon on the Seine, Christine turned to me and her blue eyes looked sadly into my brown ones. "I am Catholic. You are Jewish."

There was nothing to add. We were as deeply committed to our religions as we might have been to each other if things were different. But it wasn't to be and we knew it.

VENICE'S JEWISH GHETTO

Before we parted ways—Nissim back to Israel and me to England—we decided to visit Rome and Venice. I admired the historical sites in Rome, but I fell in love with Venice at first sight.

Nissim and I wandered through the alleys of Venice and took the ferries from place to place. But the area that tugged at my heart was the Jewish ghetto. The ghetto square had five synagogues, but they were now all museums. I walked toward the Spanish and Portuguese synagogue. It looked beautiful from the outside, but it was closed. I managed to get into the Oriental Synagogue, a gorgeous building with stained glass windows. Alone inside, I touched the *hekhal's* velvet curtain and ran my hand over the seats. If that synagogue could talk, what stories would it tell? In the eyes of my mind I saw congregants flock in for the Friday night services, a *bar miswah* being called to the *torah*, a young couple standing under their wedding canopy. What had happened to all those people? Where were they now? How did this synagogue feel with its children all gone?

When I left the synagogue I paused again in the silent ghetto square. I closed my eyes and pictured a Sabbath morning in Venice before the war, before the Nazis steamrolled through, flattening the Jewish community. I could see people, old and young, streaming out of the synagogues and filling the square. I could hear the laughter of children, see youngsters running and chasing each other, and I could hear the cries of babies and the greetings of "*shabbat shalom*" filling the air. The savory smells of Sabbath lunches wafted through open windows, carried on the summer breezes. I reveled in the scene for a few moments and then I opened my eyes. Only stones and silence and empty houses remained.

I went to visit with the rabbi of Venice. He was a soft-spoken older man who spoke Hebrew fluently. He told me about the history of the community and its tribulation during the war years. When the Nazis occupied Venice, they called in the head of the Jewish community and ordered him to submit a list of the names and addresses of all the Jews in town. Knowing this would consign them to deportation to death camps, he refused to do so, and chose death over cooperating with the Nazis. He went home and committed suicide. The rabbi's sadness at the decimation of his community was palpable.

"Still I am glad there is a country like Israel where people can go," he said.

Venice was a beautiful city, but its Jewish community had been destroyed, just as our community in Baghdad had been destroyed. A cloud of mourning seemed to hang over the Jewish Ghetto, as the few families that were still there sat on their suitcases poised for flight to the Promised Land. I wondered what awaited them there. I wondered what memories they would carry with them.

In 1998 I revisited Venice and found a burgeoning Jewish community in what used to be the Jewish Ghetto. I looked at the Jewish bakery and stores and at the Jewish children playing in the alleyways. It was late Friday afternoon. I stopped first at Habbad House to light the Friday night candles with the community, and then headed for the Spanish and Portuguese synagogue to attend services. I was overcome with emotion when I lifted up my eyes and, for the first time in more than four decades, saw the Spanish and Portuguese synagogue before me. Its door was now open, and worshippers were streaming in. I couldn't contain my emotions. I broke down and wept.

MY LESSON IN DEMOCRACY

Back in France, I crossed the Channel to Dover from Calais. It was a rough voyage, and my stomach felt it. There were, however, some quiet moments during which I thankfully turned to my book, which was written in Hebrew. As I turned the pages from right to left, I glanced up occasionally to meet the puzzled eyes of an older man sitting opposite me. Several times he seemed on the verge of speaking to me, but sighed and leaned back in his chair when my eyes returned to my book.

Finally he leaned forward and tapped me on my shoulder.

"Young man, what are you reading?"

"A book in Hebrew."

"Do all Hebrew books start from the end?"

"No. We read Hebrew from right to left, unlike English, which is read from left to right."

His mouth dropped open, but he continued to sit and stare as I continued to sit and read. It was my first encounter with an American in Europe. I wondered if he were astonished to discover that things were done differently in different parts of the world. It was a lesson that was to be brought home to me in spades when I met the English in their own country.

At the University of London's Hillel House, where I stayed, it cost one shilling a night for bed and breakfast. I guarded my little store of wealth carefully, making my pennies last. Breakfast was a substantial meal, and it became my main meal. For the rest of the day I subsisted on bread and the strong, sweet English tea, similar to what we always drank in Baghdad.

The London underground was a great novelty, just as it had been in Paris. Riding the subway, I'd daydream about the streets opening up so the pedestrians would see us riding below them. That was pure fantasy, of course. But I had not counted on my entire life opening up in London. Yet open up it did.

My stay in London coincided with the Suez Canal crisis. Many of the English felt their country had no business being in the Suez; others supported their country's involvement. We had many discussions on the topic at Hillel, and a student there suggested that I visit Hyde Park to hear more.

When I got to the park there were knots of people gathered here and there around men who stood on low boxes or stepladders, which raised them above the crowd. Everyone was engaged in debate. I stopped at a gathering where the speaker spoke in favor of the British involvement in the Suez campaign. The debate with the crowd heated up, and tempers began to flare. I watched the speaker's face grow red and spittle begin to form at the edges of his mouth. A man from the crowd with whom he was arguing was equally involved. I held my breath as the man stepped forward toward the box. He shook his clenched fist as his voice went up and his face turned purple. "My God, someone is going to be killed; someone is about to be stabbed," I thought. That was what happened on the streets in Baghdad when people disagreed. I turned my back on the scene. I didn't want to see blood. I couldn't bear to look over my shoulder, but I was waiting to hear the first scream of pain. It never came. Sheepishly I turned back to look. The speaker was still there. The man who had moved forward to the speaker's box was walking calmly away.

Amazing! I couldn't believe my eyes.

The same scene repeated itself later with another member of the crowd. And still nothing happened. There was no gunfire, no exchange of blows. People seemed to agree to disagree and walk away from one another without laying as much as a finger on one another. What was going on?

I stood in silence drinking in the scene. It was drizzling, but I scarcely felt the rain on my face. I remembered the American on the ferry who was puzzled watching me read from right to left. I could explain to him that Hebrew was read that way, but who would explain to me what was happening in Hyde Park? I didn't even know what questions to ask. Suddenly it hit me. "This is democracy."

The following Sunday I went to Hyde Park again, this time at dawn. I was there as the speakers were setting up their platforms and launching their speeches. There were debates and sharp exchanges. But again, there was no violence.

During my remaining two weeks in London, I went faithfully every Sunday to Hyde Park and stayed there until almost everyone had left. Those visits to Hyde Park were a turning point in my life. For the first time I began to realize that there was more to democracy than voting for a parliament. Not every place in the world was like Iraq. I could turn the pages of my life from left to right or from right to left. It was up to me, and nobody would deny me my right to do so. Better still, in a democracy nobody would want to.

I wanted to run though the streets shouting "Eureka! Eureka! I have discovered democracy in Hyde Park in London."

THE REMARKABLE PENNY

I knew my time in London was running short, and that I'd soon have to return to Israel, for my carefully hoarded funds were running low. And then fortune smiled on me.

I used the public telephone in Hillel House to make local calls, which then cost three pence. One day my third penny, a well-worn coin, didn't make the required ping, and I didn't get a dial tone. I pressed the coin-return button, but nothing happened. In frustration, I slapped the telephone box hard. Six pence fell out of the telephone. I repeated the operation using my lucky penny and slapping the phone box. This time it spat out five pence. Now I almost had the twelve pence I needed to pay for another night at Hillel.

In the following days, I used my private system to fund a longer stay in London. Each morning, the lucky penny and a firm slap to the telephone box would produce the necessary change. I was careful not to take more than my required twelve pence. Then I went downstairs to the dining room, paid for another breakfast and one more night's lodging. My luck held out for about ten days. Finally one morning my treasured penny remained within the telephone and I knew it was time to leave London.

In the scheme of things, that telephone windfall was modest, just as my stay in England was relatively brief. But the benefits were enormous. I returned to Israel a much different and more perceptive young man than the one who had sailed for France several months before.

MY EUROPEAN EPIPHANY

LIVING IN DENIAL

My sojourn in France and England was the period of my awakening to the cold truth about my place in Israel as a Jew from an Arab land. I had closed my eyes and made myself accept or overlook the fact that my people were second-class citizens in Israel. I had ignored the situation because this truth was so difficult to accept—and I had so much wanted it to be otherwise. During my stay in Europe I gathered the strength to acknowledge that I had been leading a double life.

Outwardly I was a normal, perhaps ambitious, young man forging ahead, fitting into Israeli society. I served in the military, attended college while working to support myself, voted in elections, and did many of the things a civic-minded young man would do.

But there was another side – a subterranean side, a life parallel to my outward life. It was the life of a Jew from an Arab land - a life of pain and confusion; a life in denial; a life of struggle with identity, disappointment, and shattered dreams. I managed to contain that life during most of the time I lived in Israel. It bubbled to the surface and took over following my trip to France and England.

In Iraq we had never talked about German Jews, Polish Jews, or Russian Jews, but rather about Jews from Germany, Jews from Poland, Jews from Russia or Jews from Iraq. The distinction is a fine one, but we believed that Jews were first and foremost Jews. That they happened to be born in one country or another was incidental. Our real homeland was the land to which Moses led our ancestors when they left Egypt, and all Jews, no matter where they were born or where they lived, belonged there equally.

I was a Jew who grew up in Iraq and I viewed myself as a human being, entitled to live in peace. As far as I was concerned, all peoples including Arabs and Jews should be treated with dignity. But though Jews had lived in what is now Iraq for centuries before Islam came into being, the Jews of Iraq were branded as the enemy and singled out for mistreatment by the Muslim majority.

I chose to leave Baghdad because I was no longer willing to subject myself to persecution. Nor did I want to live as a tenth class citizen with far fewer rights than the Muslim majority. Leaving my parents' home before marriage was a wrenching break with Babylonian Jewish tradition and a traumatic change in my own life, but I was completely clear about my desire to live as a Jew among Jews. Nothing was more important than that.

NO WAY BACK
The Journey of a Jew from Baghdad

When I got off the plane at Llyda airport I was euphoric to at last be in a place where everyone else was Jewish. No more would I be a member of an ethnically despised minority. No more would I be pushed around. And no more would I endure discrimination.

But the reality didn't match my dream.

Jews from Arab lands faced hostility and discrimination in Israel, where the dominant attitude was that Europeans had built the country, entitling them to priority treatment.

It was not easy living in this climate and enduring derogatory stereotyping. When a Jew from Iraq, Egypt, Morocco or other Arab land committed an offense, the newspapers were sure to print the criminal's country of origin. This reinforced the perception of rowdy, uneducated, and violent Jews from Arab lands. It was the opposite when one of those Jews had an achievement to his credit. When I became the first graduate of a college in Israel to be admitted to Harvard, the haArets newspaper headline read: "A Young Israeli Broke the Barrier to Harvard." Nowhere did it mention that I was an immigrant from Iraq, as it probably would have had I robbed a bank.

At first I brushed off the hostile attitudes, believing that an integral part of assimilating was to go along with the majority opinion. At the time, I didn't realize how much I was hurting myself by living in denial.

I even accepted the argument that blamed immigrants from Arab lands for their own problems. Conventional wisdom had it that the problem was a conflict of cultures: the western culture of the Europeans living in Israel versus the primitive culture of those of us who came from Arab lands. Moreover, this conflict was said to reflect differences in education, between those who were educated and had a tradition of education on one hand, and immigrants from Arab lands who were uneducated and lacked a tradition of education, on the other. Nothing could have been further from the truth, but I refused to let myself acknowledge that.

I didn't allow myself to dwell on the fact that all of my sisters, all of my cousins, three of my four aunts and I were all educated in French schools in Baghdad, that French culture, literature and poetry were ingrained in us, that we treasured educational achievements. Nor did I boast, even to myself, that in my immediate family we had five physicians, one nuclear physicist, two pharmaceutical chemists, or that my father was a distinguished lawyer. Instead, I conceded that there were Babylonian Jews who were ignorant and uneducated. In doing so, I failed to acknowledge a critical cause of the educational disparities: Palestinians who came to Iraq were given Jewish homes and synagogues, while their vacated properties were nationalized by Israel. Israel refused to process Middle Eastern Jews' claims against those Palestinian assets. Had we received compensation for assets seized when we fled our homelands, Jews from Arab lands would have had the means to start anew in Israel and educate their children. Any compensation for our seized assets, no matter how small, would have given the Jews from Arab lands a boost to restart life and give their children a better education. In my case, for example, even the relatively small sum of a hundred and twenty liras I received from my aunt made such a big difference in my life. Without it I might have missed out on higher education. The decision of the government of Israel to nationalize the Palestinian assets instead of processing the claims of Jews from Arab lands against them took a toll on the lives and particularly the educational achievements of the children of these Jews.

Jews from Arab lands ended up living in housing one and a half times as crowded as the average for their European counterpart. Not many in Israel seemed to grasp the connection between crowded housing conditions and inability to prepare homework, truancy, school dropouts, vagabondism, juvenile delinquency, and criminal record.

The sweeping nature of the stereotype, and the derogatory way in which it was almost always expressed, was distressing. No less troubling was the flip side of the dictum, which left the impression that there was a college on every street corner in Eastern Europe. Still, I swallowed it whole, because I didn't want to shatter my long-held illusion of Jews living together in harmony in Israel.

But even in those days when I was so eager to accommodate, I had great difficulty dealing with the epithet that was often hurled at us: "Attem Aravim" – "You are Arabs." In Iraq we had been persecuted by Arabs for being Jewish. In Israel, all of a sudden we became Arabs. That hurt.

True, we were not the same as European Jews, but we were Jews nonetheless, with a proud history of maintaining our identity in the face of adversity. Although we didn't live in ghettoes and no brick walls separated us from our Arab neighbors, we did maintain our distinct Jewish life. We lived by Jewish Law, and had our own governing institutions, schools, hospitals, and courts.

But it was also true that my people had lived in an Arab milieu for generations, and there was a lot of Arab in us – cuisine, music, dress, hospitality, holiday practices, gift giving, etc. It would be silly to say Jews in America are not American, just as it would be silly to say that the Jews of Iraq had not picked up traits of the Arab culture. But in Israel, when they said, "You are Arabs" they were calling us the enemy.

As a case in point, our native tongue, Judeo-Arabic, was mimicked as the language of the Arab enemy.

Judeo-Arabic, one of many Jewish languages, is a mixture of medieval Arabic, Hebrew and Aramaic with a smattering of Turkish and Persian. It is an outgrowth of Aramaic, the language my ancestors spoke and used to write the Talmud. Yiddish, or Judeo-German, as it is known linguistically, is the native tongue of most East European Jews. It is medieval German with a mixture of Hebrew and other local European languages. Like Judeo-Arabic, it is written in Hebrew characters, though the characters are different from the Hebrew characters used in Judeo-Arabic.

In short, linguistically both Judeo-Arabic and Yiddish are Jewish languages. Deriding Judeo-Arabic as the language of the Arab enemy is no less absurd than the corollary, which would equate Yiddish with German, the language of the Nazi enemy. And while Judeo-Arabic was ridiculed as Arabic, Yiddish was exalted as the epitome of Jewish; Judeo-Arabic was derided as cacophonous, Yiddish was hailed as music to the ear.

In many ways this was an ironic turn of events, given that the Zionist pioneers of the late nineteenth and early twentieth century were unwavering opponents of Yiddish; they were committed to the revival of Hebrew as a living language. Eliezer ben Yehuda (1858-1922) refused to speak to his neighbor, and asked his children to do the same, unless she spoke in Hebrew. The arrivals from Eastern Europe during the nineteen forties, mostly refugees, were very different – they were not driven by the same ideals that brought the pioneers from Eastern and Central Europe to Palestine. And they were mostly the ones we came in day-to-day contact with.

Our difficulties were not limited to our native tongue. Any differences with the East European outlook, practices, and traditions were treated as inherently inferior.

Unlike observant East European Jews, Babylonian Jews didn't wear skullcaps all the time. We were viewed as lax for that and, like our level of education, our level of religious observance was seen as needing to be "elevated."

In Israel's religious-school system, which is part of Israel's public school system, every teacher had to be observant according to the tenet of East European Jewry. When a woman who taught in the religious school system married an observant Jew from an Arab land who didn't wear a skull cap all the time, she was fired on the grounds she had married a non-observant Jew. Such dismissals, over differences in ancestral religious practices, were still occurring a few years ago, according to my friend, the late Abraham ben Yaacob, a noted author and historian of Babylonian Jewry.

A rabbi from an Arab land who sought to serve in a religious capacity in government had to abandon his own traditional rabbinical robe and don the black hat and long black coat of the East Europeans – otherwise he would be denied a rabbinical position. It was troubling to see the venerable Rabbi Silman Hougy, an old family friend from Baghdad, dressed in the East European attire. The religious practices of

NO WAY BACK
The Journey of a Jew from Baghdad

Jews from Arab lands are being swallowed up bit by bit, I thought to myself.

When my sister Latifa married Felix Aknin, his father, a learned Jew from Cairo, wanted to officiate at the wedding ceremony. But he was not allowed to do so. An official from the Ministry of Religion had to officiate or the marriage wouldn't be recognized as legal. The official came dressed in long coat, black hat, and long forelocks −anathema to our practices. None of us could relate to the ceremony he conducted. When he left, Latifa's father-in-law, with a shaven face and wearing white, repeated the ceremony in the way it would have been conducted in Egypt.

Living in Baghdad, I found it relatively easy to recognize that Arabs hated me just because I was a Jew. It was unjust, but frankly I didn't care what the Arabs thought of us. It was much more difficult to face discrimination by fellow Jews.

Celebrating Latifa and Felix's wedding
L to r: Latifa, Albert benHayeem, Daniel, Muzli

I had not expected my chosen country to be a place where "All Jews are equal, but some are more equal than others," as Levi Eshkol, a former prime minister of Israel, once put it. I was wearing rose-colored glasses, glasses I had designed for myself that clouded my vision. I was unable to see clearly that the difficulties we were experiencing in Israel were not isolated incidents, but part of a pattern.

When I first arrived in Israel it was extremely disheartening that no one assigned to help us settle in spoke our language. There was no welcome awaiting us, no hugs, no smiles, and no handshakes to ease the impact of the sudden change in our lives.

Instead we were greeted by stone-faced sanitation workers armed with spray guns.

Later I learned that many immigrants from East European countries were greeted upon arrival in Israel by bands and delegations of dignitaries. It was then that I began to view our experience at the airport through a different lens. Every refugee had suffered irreparable losses; all immigrants had difficulties in adjusting to a new environment. But just a simple handshake or a welcoming smile on our arrival would have eased the transition and helped alleviate the pain. This Jews from Arab lands did not experience, and it would have made a difference. The discriminatory practices that followed made the lack of a welcome even more stark.

GOVERNMENT COMPLICITY

What was particularly insidious about the discriminatory practices was that they were not so evident to people of goodwill and to Jews in the Diaspora, particularly America. I believe American Jewry wouldn't have stood idly by had they known what was truly going on. But the problem was well hidden under a veneer of institutional authority.

The price of rice was one example.

The staple of the European diet was potato, while rice was the staple in the diet of Jews from Arab lands. The government subsidized potatoes heavily but did not subsidize rice. The result was that potatoes were dirt cheap, while the price of rice skyrocketed. Because the immigrants from Arab lands had a higher unemployment rate, earned less than their European counterparts, and had larger families than the Europeans, the escalating price of rice hit hardest those who could least afford it.

The same was true of other food items. For a long time, the government subsidized only the black bread "*lehem shahor*" favored by East European Jews. The price of pita bread, which was part of the diet of Jews from Arab lands, was a multiple of the price of black bread, pound for pound.

I puzzled over these price disparities during my stay in London. It was only after returning to Israel later that year that I realized the invisible hand of a culturally insensitive government had been responsible.

DUSTY BYROADS OF JEWISH HISTORY

My sudden loss of social standing hampered my adjustment to Israel. Within the Jewish community in Iraq I had been admired for my distinguished family and my own intellectual abilities. Now, in Israel, I was lumped in with the uneducated and the ignorant. In my eagerness to shake off this stigma, I intentionally distanced myself from my heritage.

In my heart I knew my heritage was important and respected within the wider Jewish community. I was proud that Babylonian Jews had written the Talmud, the cornerstone of Jewish life and learning. But in Israel, I pushed these facts to the back of my brain. I couldn't let myself admit that the accepted Israeli view of Jews from Arab lands sprang solely from prejudice.

The notion that my people belonged to the dusty byroads of Jewish history and civilization permeated every aspect of Israeli society, including universities.

The obligatory course on the Economic History of the Jewish People, which I took in my junior year in college, was typical. As the semester wore on, it became clear that that course was limited to the economic history of the Jews of Central and Eastern Europe. It had nothing to say about Jews from Arab lands, or the Sephardim in general: Nothing about the contributions of the Cochin Jews of India or the international business and philanthropic empires of the Babylonian Sasson, Kh'doury or Hardoon dynasties. Nothing about the Pereira brothers, who were instrumental in propelling the industrial revolution in France but whose risky lending practices ultimately led to their downfall. Nothing about the sixteenth century international banker and businesswoman Dona Gracia Nasi, who also rescued thousands of Jews from the Inquisition. I was flabbergasted that such a big chunk of Jewish history was being ignored.

I considered trying to set matters straight by writing my term paper on the economic contribution of Babylonian Jewry. But my background and heritage had already been called into question too many times. I couldn't muster the courage to invite another rebuff.

Instead, I wrote a paper about the Jews of England. I now know that my conflicted feelings about this course were part of my journey toward reclaiming myself. My hunch is that if I had taken that course after my visit to France and England, I would have written the paper about my own people.

THE AWAKENING

It had been enlightening to realize how much more comfortable I felt while traveling in Europe. Away from Israel, I saw that I'd been walking on eggshells. In France I could relax and be myself for the first time since leaving Baghdad. But then I wondered: Could that be because I was educated in French schools and was fluent in the language?

NO WAY BACK
The Journey of a Jew from Baghdad

The real breakthrough came during my stay in England. It was then, standing away from the dazzling influence of Israel, in a totally unfamiliar foreign culture, that I had the courage to confront the question directly: Could it be Israel's problem rather than ours?

At the University of London's Hillel House I met several Jewish and non-Jewish families, Jewish leaders, and community activists. And I felt at home, no less than I did in France. Here, too, I found that I didn't have to guard my tongue. I could express myself freely without fear of ridicule. It was a heady experience.

I talked with the English about controversial subjects, but the conversations never degenerated into personal controversies or name-calling, as had happened so many times in Israel. At no time during my six weeks in England was I cut down or derided for my ethnic background, dress habits, skin color, or political views. It was refreshing to be treated with courtesy.

Walking through the streets of London, I asked myself, how much more western could one be than being British? Or French? In western cultures I seemed to have no difficulty. Indeed, I had the time of my life. Why was it not so in Israel? Could it be that what Israelis called the clash of western versus "primitive" cultures was just a smokescreen for a need to dominate, to put us down?

I found it striking that most European Israelis knew very little, nor cared to know, about the history, culture, living conditions, and aspirations of Babylonian Jewry. Many refused even to entertain the notion that we had a culture or decent living conditions in the countries from which we came.

In fact, I had enjoyed a life of physical comfort in Baghdad. Yet because people in Israel considered Levantine the equivalent of backward, they scoffed at my story about being called from the Baghdad airport at midnight to get the last seat on the plane to Israel. They simply didn't believe my family had a telephone.

The Israeli establishment openly expressed eagerness to keep the State of Israel from being afflicted by "Levantinization." More than once, I was told, "Don't be a Levantine." What else was I supposed to be? What is a Jew supposed to be when he is told, "Don't be a kike"? When the legendary Ben Gurion warned that Israel was running the risk of Levantinization, he was, in effect, ratifying the notion of European superiority. And when the same Ben Gurion said, "We got rid of some good Arabs and got bad Jews in their place," he was talking about me and other Jews from Arab lands. Had Ben Gurion made that statement in the U.S., there would have been an outcry from American Jewry. But he made the statement in Israel, where it was accepted as true.

In England, I saw for the first time the similarity between those slurs and other ethnic-based prejudices, and it was cold comfort that

Jews had voiced them. Most distressing of all was the realization that we, Jews of Arab lands, had internalized them.

I recalled how contemptuous I had become of the elders in our community, whom I saw as the epitome of "Levantines." Not even our family elder, Uncle Moshe, was spared: I was impatient with his opinions and ideas, which I saw as springing from an inferior way of thinking and viewing the world. I was deeply chagrined to realize how unwittingly I had absorbed the supremacist attitudes surrounding me.

I thought about the time Uncle Moshe had approached me to write a letter of recommendation for a middle-aged immigrant from Iraq who had applied for a managerial position at Bank Leumi. The man had been a manager at a bank in Baghdad, but because of his age had not been able to find a comparable job in Israel. Uncle Moshe felt that because I had established myself at Bank Leumi, a letter of support from me would be helpful. I didn't know the man, but Uncle Moshe swore by him, saying that he would attest to the man's competence and declaring that, if hired, he would put to shame many managers at Bank Leumi. What I remember is my utter disdain for Uncle Moshe's judgment. How could someone from the backward Iraqis surpass a manager of the big Bank Leumi? What did they know about banking in Iraq? Yet the truth was that while Iraq had an underdeveloped economy, it had a highly developed commercial banking system. The scorn I felt for my uncle, and for his high opinion of another immigrant from Iraq, was symptomatic of the problem.

I chided myself for what I now saw as self-destructive efforts to merge into Israeli society. I had socialized mostly with young Ashkenazis from Eastern Europe. I was drawn to them even though I knew I was not fully accepted by them. One afternoon as my friends and I sat together and shared stories from our past, I was telling about the time I had gone to an upscale shop in Baghdad to buy a velvet jacket. The store was on the first floor of the Semiramis Hotel, a three-story luxury building on the banks of the Tigris.

As I described the building I overheard one member of my group mutter, "As if there are any three-story buildings in Baghdad."

My pleasure in reliving a happy experience vanished. I didn't respond to the comment. I lapsed into silence and didn't finish my story.

Such incidents were disturbingly common. Yet, if I took exception to a derogatory comment, I was chastised for being too sensitive, and asked why I couldn't take a joke. Now, from the vantage point of England, I saw that those frequent jabs at my culture were, indeed, no joke. Each incident in itself didn't amount to much, but the constant barrage had worn me down and made me feel less than acceptable.

I longed to share my new insights with some of the other students living in Hillel House. Undoubtedly, many of them had encountered anti-Semitism, but did they know much about the plight of Israeli Jews from Arab lands? Yet I kept mum, out of loyalty to Israel. If British Jews learned about our situation, I was afraid they might not support Israel.

Nonetheless, in my own mind I was no longer sweeping the problems under the rug. I couldn't change the way Jews from Arab lands were regarded in Israel. But I could see it for what it was and stop identifying with it.

CHANGING DIRECTION

By the time I returned to Israel, I had decided that I needed to find a home elsewhere. As a college senior, the end was in sight. Graduate study abroad seemed to offer a solution.

In the short term, meanwhile, my work at Bank Leumi in Tel Aviv had become unsatisfying. I was doing repetitive work in the Foreign Exchange department that offered few professional challenges while cutting into the time I could devote to study.

When I decided to leave the bank, its workers' union negotiated an agreement with management that allowed me to receive in one lump sum my three-year accumulated pension. These funds helped greatly with living expenses. At last I could concentrate exclusively on my studies and attend classes feeling fresh and rested. There was a new spring in my step.

Less than three months after quitting the bank, opportunity knocked again.

Yits'hak Guelfat, one of my economics instructors, was on the board of directors of a nonprofit organization, the Consumers' Cooperative Society, Israel's largest retailer. Now the Society was recruiting an economist, and Professor Guelfat recommended me for the job.

During my interview with the Society's president, Yisrael Sh'pan, I could feel his hesitancy to hire a Middle Easterner battling with his respect for Professor Guelfat's opinion. But as our discussion continued, he grew increasingly interested in my background. In the end, he hired me. I was elated.

The job at the Society gave me the practical experience I wanted in applied economics, but my commute to work in Tel Aviv from Ramat Gan cut into my study time and the cramped family apartment was no place to study. Because I could now afford it, I rented a room in an apartment house in North Tel Aviv. It contained only a bed, a folding table and a folding chair, but I could close the door and concentrate.

As time went by at my new job, I felt Yisrael Sh'pan's respect for me grow. He trusted the reports I wrote and appreciated my analytical ability. The other members of the Society also respected me, though some appeared to do so grudgingly. The only other Middle Eastern employee was our middle-aged elevator operator. As I rode the elevator every day up to my office, I could feel the operator's pride in me—a situation that was as sad as it was heartwarming.

Instead of slavishly attempting to assimilate into Israeli society, I was finally becoming comfortable with my identity as a Jew from an Arab land. It was good to realize that at least some of my coworkers at the Society saw me for who I really was, and also as a person worthy of their respect.

Of course it wasn't as simple as all of that. When I was in the military I was also respected by my fellow soldiers and officers for the person that I was, for my skills and for my abilities. But there were civilians who worked on the military base who treated me as if I were the lowest of the low and did not hide their disdain for me. I tried to ignore their slurs and their jibes about "the dark skinned people", and "You the blacks", but it wasn't always easy. And now, though I was respected at work, I still had to deal with put-downs on the street and in fleeting encounters. To the casual observer in Israel I was the black one who did not belong in Israel. The people who hurled insults at me did not know me, but that did not make the insults easier to handle. Couldn't they see that I was a person, albeit different from them in lots of ways, but deep down basically the same?

I had a good relationship with my landlords, Joseph and Miriam Schlezinger. I believe Joseph in particular was interested in all Jews coming together from all over the world and forming one society. I remember one evening in particular when he came home from a meeting very upbeat and excited. His eyes danced and his arms flailed the air as he tried to tell Miriam about the meeting. I thought at first that he had discovered some wonderful new knowledge at the meeting. However, when I could cut through the excitement that laced his words to discover its source, I found that what he was excited about was the fact that the attendees at the meeting were "*amkha*" - Jews from many, many countries. He had loved being with them all, feeling that all of these Jews were part of his people.

I grew fond of my landlords, Joseph and Miriam, but they, too, had their prejudices. They despised Romanians. I never told them that I had dated a Romanian-born woman.

Every Friday night during my senior year, as well as the following year I spent in Israel, I attended the lectures and discussions that were held in the building of the Zionist Organization of America. Those discussions were informative. They opened my world to wider horizons and broadened my views. People from other countries, members of the *k'neset*, members of the Cabinet and others lectured there and discussed topics of interest. I remembered one program in particular, a round table discussion.

The topic under discussion was the election of members of the *k'neset* by the varying parties instead of directly by the people. Direct election, of which I am in favor, still does not happen in elections to the *k'neset*, though the Mappai party, the party in power at the time, was in favor of it at that discussion in the mid 1950's. People who spoke in favor of the concept were listened to, but the speaker who got the loudest round of applause spoke against direct election by the people.

"If I am elected by the people in a district," the speaker declared, "my view of Israel would be a narrow one, focused on the people in that particular district. If, on the other hand, a party selects me, I have a more national perspective and am focused on the good of the whole country. Would the Negev desert ever have blossomed if we had direct election by the people in Israel?"

His words and the ensuing applause disheartened me. In focusing on what the parties saw as the whole country, whole segments of that country were overlooked or deliberately ignored. Jews from Arab lands were very easily lost in the shuffle even while the desert bloomed.

Still I remained determined. I would rise above whatever biases that existed and make my way in the world.

Receiving my hard-won college diploma from the school's dean

I graduated from college in November 1957. The commencement ceremony was utterly lacking in pomp and splendor: no caps and gowns, no stately procession of graduates and faculty, no outdoor reception on a campus lawn. We assembled in a drab lecture hall at night -- everyone had already put in a full working day.

Still, spirits were high. Every one seemed relaxed and in a good mood. Graduates were called to the podium, one by one, to receive their diplomas

It took a good while before it was my turn. I didn't think I would feel excited to receive my diploma. It was only a formality, I felt. Yet when I stepped up to the podium, I was elated when I held that document in my hand.

I missed my parents' presence that evening. I remembered how my father had sat me down not long before I left Baghdad, and told me that I should not think of college as the be-all and end-all, that it would be all right if I didn't attend college. Baba's observation puzzled me. It ran counter to my entire upbringing—and to my father's own history of going to law school despite his poverty. Could it be that he was worried I might fall into despair if I couldn't make it to college in my new homeland? I was not sure how to react. But on the night of my graduation, all that had faded away. I only wished my mother and father could have been there. I felt they would have been proud to see their son among the graduates.

During my senior year, the School of Law and Economics joined with other academic departments that had sprouted in Tel Aviv, to form a new university, Tel Aviv University, which has since rivaled Hebrew University. My class was the first to receive diplomas with the new insignia - Tel Aviv University – School of Law and Economics.

I graduated with a Bachelor of Science in Economics. But I always regretted my lack of a liberal-arts education. In Israel people attended college in order to acquire a profession, to learn a trade. Attending college to acquire knowledge for its own sake was unheard of. The dominant attitude was that there was insufficient time or money to spend on discovering oneself or learning about the finer things in life, which might not have immediate applications or contribute directly to one's ability to make a living. Viewed through that prism, accounting was considered fine; economics was acceptable; philosophy was a waste of time!

A LONG SHOT

FLOODING THE MARKET

Even if I had wanted to stay in Israel, Hebrew University was not a viable option for graduate work. To protect its hegemony, Hebrew University had practically declared war on Tel Aviv's School of Law and Economics. It didn't recognize the Tel Aviv diploma and expected Tel Aviv University graduates to start from scratch as candidates for a bachelor's degree at Hebrew University before applying for graduate school. The antagonism extended to job openings. Hebrew University graduates dominated the top echelons of the Central Bank and the Ministry of Finance, Israel's two leading economic institutions, and they effectively blocked the appointment of Tel Aviv graduates as economists at both.

I decided to focus primarily on the U.S. in my search for a graduate school. I had a great admiration for the US, its democratic institutions, and its freedom of the press. And I remembered with gratitude the courageous stand of the US Information Center in Baghdad when it defied the Iraqi government's order to shut down.

At the U.S. embassy's library in Tel Aviv I unearthed a goldmine: Voluminous guidebooks to American graduate schools and financial aid.

Every day after work I combed those guidebooks for schools offering programs in my field, scholarships and loans. I rented an Underwood typewriter, and every evening I sat at my folding table and typed letters to graduate schools and financial-aid organizations. I flooded the market. I wrote to top schools and to schools I had never heard of. Sometimes I was drawn to a marginal school simply because it was located in a region with a balmy climate.

The workload mounted as the responses began to come in. Sometimes I stayed up until two o'clock in the morning and got up at seven to go to work. The number of letters of reference that my former college instructors had to send on my behalf mounted too. Some accepted the burden cheerfully; others were not so happy about it.

I remember that period as one of utter exhaustion, mixed with a sense of determination. On the Sabbath I would stay in bed all day to catch up on my sleep. The mounting pressure energized me. Giving up never crossed my mind.

Some of the responses were disappointing. One financial-aid institution advertised that it specialized in scholarships for first-year graduate students indigenous to the Middle East. I was thrilled; I was as indigenous to the Middle East as they come. This was one application that would bring sure-fire results, or so I thought. But the response to my application made it clear that only Arabs were eligible; Jews were not.

All the other financial-aid institutions I contacted turned me down.

But there were pleasant surprises, as well. While I was turned down by several lesser schools, such as Alabama State University, I was admitted to a number of elite schools. I held off responding to any offer until I heard from the prize I sought: Harvard.

A DREAMER?

When I told friends I had applied to Harvard, they thought I'd taken leave of my senses.

"No graduate, even from Hebrew University or Technion, is known to have made it to Harvard. You graduated from a dinky little school that no one ever heard of. You are setting yourself up for disappointment," my friends told me, sometimes gently and sometimes disparagingly.

Others pointed out that Harvard was expensive. The annual tuition fee for the Graduate School of Arts and Sciences was $1,000 - among the highest in the U.S. It was a staggering sum by comparison with the annual per-capita income in Israel at the time, which was around $500, as I recall.

"Are you out of your mind? How are you going to pay for it?" people asked.

I didn't have an answer. But I was not deterred. I clung to my longstanding conviction that lack of money need not be--and should not be--an obstacle to education. But I had no idea how was I going to implement that lofty principle. I would cross that bridge when I came to it.

Each of my university applications involved a series of hurdles in the admission process. I never allowed myself to become overwhelmed by the mounds of difficulties that lay ahead. Instead, I focused on one hurdle at a time, the one that lay immediately at hand. Only when I got over that hurdle did I turn my attention to the next.

I departed only once from that rule, with near-disastrous results.

When I began applying to graduate schools in July 1957, I had also set in motion an inquiry about getting a visa to the U.S. Obtaining a sponsor's affidavit for a visa was likely to take time, I figured, and it would be wise to have that out of the way in case I was admitted to a school.

I wrote to David Bassoon, asking for his help getting the necessary affidavit. David was the manager of the Baghdad branch of Shasha Trading Company, an international company headquartered in

New York and owned by the Shashas, a Baghdadian Jewish family. David and his wife, my cousin Grace, had joined my brother Jacob on the trip to Turkey when I was in Marseilles. I had reestablished contact with them at that time, before they had all returned to Baghdad.

I had to be discreet to evade the censors in Iraq. In my letter to David, I was careful not to reveal my identity—while providing enough hints to let him know who the letter was from and what I was asking.

I sent my letter to the Liverpool branch of the Shasha Trading Company, with instructions to enclose it in one of the company's official envelopes and mail it on to David in Baghdad. It never occurred to me to ask the company's secretary to discard my envelope—carrying Israeli stamps and my return address-- before forwarding my letter. I assumed everyone in the Liverpool office knew it was dangerous for Jews living in Iraq to receive correspondence from Israel. I should not have taken anything for granted.

The secretary in Liverpool tucked my envelope and letter into one of the company's envelopes and mailed it to David. Like all mail addressed to Jewish residents of Baghdad, the letter from Liverpool went first to the censor's office. Something fortunate happened this time. The censor stamped the envelope "Approved for Delivery" without ever opening it.

When David opened the envelope he was terrified to find inside the incriminating envelope from Tel Aviv. He couldn't destroy the evidence without being noticed at the office, or without leaving traces that his Arab employees would discover. So he put the letter in his pocket, walked matter-of-factly out of his office, and headed home. There he burned the envelope.

Everyone in the family was shaken when they heard the story. My parents, too, would have been implicated had the censor opened the letter.

David was magnanimous about that awful incident. Though I had put him at great risk, he went immediately to work on my request. Less than six months later, I received an affidavit for a U.S. visa from the company's headquarters in New York. The company's president, Maurice Shasha, had pledged his company's assets as a collateral. This gesture moved me to tears. I had never met Maurice Shasha, yet he was willing to go to such lengths on my behalf.

When I received the affidavit, I was so moved I cried. I had never met Maurice Shasha, yet he was willing to go to such lengths on my behalf.

The last step in my Harvard application was the requirement that I write an economic analysis on a subject of my choice. Of all the universities to which I had applied, only Harvard had such a requirement. I knew a lot rode on that paper, and I gave it all I had.

Now there was nothing to do but wait.

Harvard's answer came a few weeks later. Academically I was qualified to enroll in the PhD program, without going through the Masters program.

But there was one big hitch. Before granting me admission, Harvard needed evidence that I had at my disposal $4,800 to cover my first two year's tuition and living expenses. I barely had the equivalent of $30 in my bank account. How was I going to come up with the rest?

Israel's foreign exchange controls made matters worse. Even if I had had the money in Israeli liras, I couldn't just walk into a bank and buy dollars. I needed to apply first to Israel's Treasury for permission to purchase dollars. That involved extensive paperwork, and it took weeks and months before the Treasury rendered a decision. The Treasury was particularly tight-fisted with hard currency -- dollars and pounds sterling -- and it was guided by a list of priorities, in which graduate work abroad in the social sciences was at the lowest rung.

Everything seemed to militate against meeting Harvard's $4,800 requirement.

A BIT OF SUBTERFUGE

While working for Bank Leumi, I had learned the intricacies of foreign- exchange controls, the mechanics of applying to the Treasury, and the Treasury's approval process. I also became familiar with how the bank processed foreign-exchange applications once the Treasury had approved them. All this came in handy when I needed to show Harvard evidence of financial responsibility. But, even today, I feel uncomfortable about the devious way I put that knowledge to use.

This is how it worked.

When the Treasury approved an application for foreign exchange, it sent a notice to Bank Leumi, authorizing the bank to sell, say, $5,000 dollars to the applicant. The notice didn't obligate the applicant to buy all or part of the $5,000. It merely approved her right to do so.

Upon receipt of the Treasury's approval, Bank Leumi mailed a one-liner to the applicant, addressed to " To Whom It May Concern," stating, "This is to certify that the Treasury has allotted to so and so the sum of $5,000."

That one-liner might work for me if and when I could convince the Treasury to approve my application for $4,800, I figured. Reading the one-liner, Harvard might conclude that the "allotted" dollars were actually sitting in my bank account, and accept the bank's letter as evidence of financial responsibility.

It was worth a try. If it worked, it would give me breathing time until I had to face paying my tuition and living expenses. Maybe I could borrow money from an American bank. What basis did I have for expecting that to happen? None, really. The truth is that I had no idea how to finance graduate school, any more than I knew how to pay for my airfare to the U.S.

Harvard had given me only five weeks to give my answer. I appealed to the Treasury committee for urgent consideration, and asked to be present when it took up my application. With trepidation, I traveled to Jerusalem and hand-delivered my application.

The committee called a few days later to say that they expected to consider my application on the following Friday afternoon, and that I would be allowed to attend.

I was tense the day I received the call. I continued to fret about how to anticipate questions, stay alert, be at my best while I awaited that all-important interview. What if some committee members were graduates of Hebrew University? How would they react to the application of a graduate of Tel Aviv University? There were civil servants prejudiced against Middle Eastern Jews. What if one or two of them were members of the committee?

By the end of the day, I realized I would crack if I didn't stop worrying. There were just too many things to worry about. I had done the best I could. It was time to let go. I would just be myself at the meeting. If I failed, I would learn from the experience. Maybe I could try again later.

I was at peace with myself.

THE BEST-LAID SCHEMES

On the eve of my meeting with the Treasury committee I went out with Louise Clayton, whom I had met in London at an a cappella concert in a synagogue. Louise was one of the singers: then twenty-one years old, an only child, and the apple of her parents' eyes. She took me to corners of London that I might never have found on my own. With her, I learned to appreciate good theater and acquired a sense of British history. In the spring of 1957 she had come to Israel for a visit.

We walked along the beach in Tel Aviv before stopping in a coffee shop. I wanted to be rested the next day, so we cut the evening short and flagged a taxicab.

The driver took a shortcut through a pitch-dark street in a section of North Tel Aviv under construction. I thought I saw something strange near an apartment building, something that flitted across my line of vision and vanished suddenly.

"Did you notice anything?" I asked the driver.

"I think I saw something."

NO WAY BACK
The Journey of a Jew from Baghdad

I looked back as we stopped the car. I could see nothing out of the ordinary, but it was so dark I couldn't be sure. Something eerie was in the air.

"Shouldn't we back up to the apartment building and see?" I asked the driver.

"Sure."

We stopped the car by the building's entrance. Our headlights threw light on the entrance, but we couldn't see past the thick hedge in front of the building. The car windows were open, but I couldn't hear a sound.

"Does anyone hear anything?" I asked.

No one did. I reached for the door handle.

"Maybe I should go out and look."

Before I got the door open, two men emerged from behind the hedge. In the headlights I could see they were wearing suits and ties. The taller of the two carried a briefcase. They brushed their suits with their hands as they proceeded to walk briskly. If these men were as respectable as they looked, I wondered, why did they have to hide behind the hedge?

The cab driver slowly followed them. Suddenly the taller man turned to face the taxi. He pulled a gun from his pocket, and pointed it at us. It was a small gun, much smaller than any I had seen in the military. The driver stopped the car. The man didn't approach us or say anything. He just stood and stared at us, gun in hand.

The sight of someone pointing a gun from such close range sent chills up and down my spine. Armed violence was not common in Israel, and I couldn't believe this was happening. The figure standing in the pale light, surrounded by darkness, didn't seem real. Were we watching a clip from a Western movie?

We decided it was safer not to confront the pair and stayed in the car. The tall man put the gun in his pocket, and the two resumed their brisk walk. We drove past and headed for a small movie theater nearby, where the driver said we would find a public phone.

The outside lights of the theater were off, but the door was open and we could see light inside. We walked in, and were startled to find a man lying motionless on the floor. I was afraid to touch him to find out if he was dead. Drawers were pulled open, a chair was overturned, and papers were strewn everywhere.

I ran to the phone and called the police. They asked us not to leave the scene.

No sooner had I hung up than the man opened his eyes, groaned and reached a hand behind his head. He blinked at us and shook his head, grimacing a little.

Bit by bit he told us his story. He worked at the theater and was alone, closing the accounts of the day, when two men wearing suits and ties walked into the theater and demanded that he hand over the cash. He refused. One of the intruders struck him on the head with a sharp object. He couldn't remember what happened next.

"Those two men were obviously leaving this place when we ran across them," I exclaimed.

The taxi driver and Louise nodded in agreement.

It was close to midnight when the police finally showed up. I was worried about my next day's meeting in Jerusalem. I needed a restful night. But now that the police had arrived, it should not take us long to report what we had seen and head home.

The police had a different plan.

"We can't release you yet," one officer said.

Release you? Were we under arrest? What was going on? We were only doing our civic duty when we reported what we had seen.

It was close to 2 a.m. when the police finally finished taking the report from the theater's employee, inspecting the drawers, tracking the footprints, and taking measurements. We could go home, but were told to show up the next morning at police headquarters downtown to identify the suspects from a line-up.

"How long will that take?" I asked.

"We don't know. But you should plan on being there the whole day."

"I have an important meeting to attend in Jerusalem tomorrow afternoon," I explained. "Couldn't it wait until Sunday?"

"We don't know. You'll have to show up at 9 am and talk to the station commander. He's the one to decide."

I was worried and angry that this snag would put an end to everything I had been trying to piece together. "The best-laid schemes o' Mice an' Men Gang, aft a-gley," I thought. I was an innocent citizen and had committed no crime, yet the police were restricting my freedom of movement.

I tossed and turned in bed. By the time I fell asleep, I had made up my mind. I wouldn't let this new hurdle stand in the way. If the station commander wouldn't permit me to leave for Jerusalem, I would just take off and worry about the consequences later.

I was at the police station at 9 a.m., tired, incoherent, and tense-- everything I didn't want to be on the day of my meeting in Jerusalem. The station commander was reluctant to postpone the line-up until Sunday, but, realizing he needed my cooperation, he compromised. I would leave for Jerusalem when I had to, but return to the station immediately after my meeting.

In the meantime, one line-up was ready. I joined Louise and the driver in the line-up room. The scene shocked me. I shuddered at the thought of mistakenly accusing an innocent man without an airtight alibi.

About a dozen young men stood in the lineup. Except for one who looked defiant, all seemed tired and broken. They must have been yanked out of their beds in the wee hours of the morning. Several avoided eye contact. One had his eyes fixed on the ground the entire time. I tried to remember the features of the two we had encountered the night before. I was never good at recalling facial details. Still I struggled to find any shred of resemblance between them and the men who had threatened us the night before. Finally, I told the station commander I couldn't in good conscience identify any as a suspect. Louise, on the other hand, pointed out two people without hesitation.

Weary with stress, I finally untangled myself from the police and boarded the bus to Jerusalem. I had a short nap on the way and woke up refreshed.

THE LINCHPIN MEETING

I was alert and focused when I walked into the committee's room. Gone were the tension and disorientation I had experienced that morning. I needed to concentrate on the critical business at hand.

The committee was made up of five men and one woman. I only knew the chairman was a Treasury official, a gruff man probably in his mid-fifties. The rest were middle aged, too, and looked tired. My case was apparently the last on the agenda for the day.

From the start, the question was: why spend dollars on funding graduate work abroad when the same could be accomplished at Hebrew University in Jerusalem? I explained the problem with Hebrew University and challenged the committee members to put themselves in my place. Would they choose to start over from scratch as freshmen at Hebrew University rather than go on to graduate school at a top institution in the U.S.? As I spoke, the woman on the panel kept nodding in agreement. She was, I thought, on my side, and I drew strength from what I perceived as her empathy. One committee member seemed to be in deep thought. The chairman was stone-faced. He proposed postponing the decision until a later date. I said I couldn't wait.

"Why are you pressuring us?" he growled, raising his voice.

I remember those words to this day. They still ring in my head.

"I am not pressuring you. I am under pressure to meet a deadline," I said.

I saw sympathetic looks on the faces of the rest of the interviewers. The chairman asked me to wait outside.

I felt serene as I sat outside. I had done the best I could and was reconciled to whatever might happen. But deep inside, I had the feeling I had made it.

Finally, the chairman called me back in. His demeanor had changed; he was smiling and actually looked humane. The committee had been impressed with my credentials and the way I had defended my application, he said. With a grin, he told me my application had been approved.

I had made it! I was ecstatic. Of course other hurdles lay ahead. But I didn't care. All had to do with money. I wanted to go out and announce my success to the skeptics, to those who had urged "realism," to those who had counseled against aiming high and to those who had exhorted me not to risk disappointment.

There was one detail to work out, the chairman said. The Treasury would authorize me to purchase $4,400, instead of the $4,800 that Harvard required. But in order to formally satisfy Harvard's requirement, the chairman would notify Bank Leumi that the Treasury had authorized $4,800, on condition I sign an agreement not to purchase more than $4,400 from the bank.

"Would you sign off on that?" the chairman asked.

This was the least of my worries. At that point I couldn't put my hands on $50, much less $4,400. It made no difference whether I were authorized to purchase $4400 or $4800. I couldn't acquire either amount.

I readily agreed to the chairman's terms.

Then I walked outside, sat on the steps of the Treasury building, put my head in my hands and sobbed.

THE MIRACLE

Bank Leumi was ready with its one-liner: "This is to certify that the Treasury has allotted to Mr. Daniel Khazzoom the sum of $4,800." The director of the bank's foreign-exchange department, Yits'hak Avital, looked happy when he handed me the letter.

"I hope to be able to call you Professor Khazzoom next time I see you," he said.

I express mailed the bank's authorization to Harvard. There was nothing else to do but wait. Would it work?

In short order, Harvard sent me its letter of admission.

I wrote to Mr. Shasha in New York to share the news with him and thank him for his magnanimity. Even though I didn't make use of his affidavit, his willingness to vouch for me had been a source of hope and strength.

I expected to be in Cambridge, Massachusetts in mid-September 1958 for the start of the school year. I had 100 liras in my bank account, but needed 950 liras ($320) to pay for my airfare.

NO WAY BACK
The Journey of a Jew from Baghdad

When my friend, Albert, learned I had been admitted to Harvard, he gave me all of his savings: 200 liras. Other friends and members of my family chipped in. The Consumers' Co-operative Society came through too, but I was still 150 liras short. There was one other possible benefactor: the Fund for the Education of Immigrants from Iraq, which had been established by Babylonian educators and leaders at the start of the exodus from Iraq to Israel.

Several times before, I had been tempted to ask the trustees of the fund for help, but I didn't have the audacity to approach them, having let them down in the past.

During my college years, several leaders of the Babylonian Jewish community ran for election to the *k'neset*. I remember particularly one of them -- Silman Sheena, a close friend of my family. He was a top lawyer and a two-term representative of the Jewish community in the Iraqi parliament. Mr. Sheena and the other Babylonian candidates worked hard to convince us that raising the issue of discrimination in the *k'neset* would contribute to a change for the better. But we, in our young and perhaps less than honest ways, did not want to vote for them and instead used every tactic to defeat them. We attended their rallies and deliberately asked provocative questions to throw the speakers out of kilter and we made harsh comments to create a scene and disrupt the rally.

And that was the worst part of it – not only did we not fight the adverse environment we found ourselves in, but we did not give our elders a chance to fight it either. We said we did not want people elected to the parliament wearing a tag representing the Babylonian Jews. We argued that that would be divisive and that we opposed divisiveness, even though the division was glaring and was there for every one to see. We strenuously proclaimed we wanted one Jewish people, not Jews with ethnic tags.

But perhaps the real reason why the people of my generation had opposed our elders was that it was too painful for us to admit to ourselves that we were already tagged, regardless. We were the people that were tagged "Second Israel"; we were the ones that the press called "Laggard Israel". Maybe it was too painful for us to stand up and be counted among the laggards. Better to act as if they did not exist.

We prevailed. None of the Babylonian candidates was elected.

Later, I came to regret what we had done. Those leaders were honest. They had the courage of their convictions. They saw discrimination and tried to wrestle with it.

Several board members at the Fund for the Education of Immigrants from Iraq were part of the same Babylonian leadership I had opposed during my years of denial. How could I now turn to them for help? That fund was the embodiment, the quintessence of the traditions of Babylonian Jewry. It reflected the worldview of the Jews of Iraq, their values and societal priorities. Having been so hostile to the preservation of those traditions, how could I justify benefiting from those same traditions, just because they now happened to serve my needs? I finally concluded that honesty and logic required me to stay away from the fund.

As I wracked my brain trying to think of sources of financial aid, it occurred to me to write to Bekhor Shitrit, the minister of police and the lone Sephardi member of the Israeli cabinet. He was the scion of an illustrious family that had lived in Israel for generations.

I had written letters to other cabinet members asking for help, but my letters were ignored. Mr. Shitrit responded promptly, assuring me that he would be back in touch, as soon as he had time to think of a way to help me.

Then my life took an unexpected twist.

Paying for the tuition and living expenses for my first two years in graduate school was, I knew, something I would have to face eventually, but I planned to tackle this problem once I had the money for airfare. But when I learned of a chance to get tuition assistance, finding the 150 liras suddenly became a pressing priority.

Harvard notified me that I was eligible for a Ford Foundation grant to attend The Economics Institute, an experimental program established that year. The Institute was intended to provide remedial instruction in English and economic theory to first-year foreign grad students. Classes, beginning the second week in July 1958, were to be held on the campus of the University of Wisconsin, Madison. The program included extracurricular activities to familiarize the foreign students with life in the U.S. -- trips to the countryside, tours of factories and farms, meetings with scholars and dignitaries, and weekends with American families.

I was excited about the chance to improve my English and become oriented to my new American environment. There was also an advantage to being in the U.S. some two and a half months before beginning the semester at Harvard. While attending the Institute, I could contact American banks about getting a school loan.

Even as I worried about my 150-lira shortfall, I rolled up my sleeves, sat in front of my Underwood typewriter, and filled out the Ford Foundation application for the Institute.

I had no idea what my chances of getting the grant were. But that didn't prevent me from daydreaming about what I'd do with the money if it came through. I'd pay the $400 tuition fee for the Institute, but would scrimp on meals and save on my other living expenses. Maybe I could get on just one meal a day. Maybe I could also share a room with other students to save on rent. If so, I'd need to borrow less, and maybe that would enhance my chances of getting an education loan from a bank. Maybe. Maybe. Maybe.

The response was not long in coming. The Ford Foundation approved a $1,000 grant for tuition and room and board, a $250 allowance for a round-trip flight from New York to Madison and a generous sum for a four-night stay in a hotel in New York.

"This is a miracle," I said when I read the Foundation's letter.

I considered hitchhiking instead of flying from New York to Madison and back. I could then save the airfare allowance. I was adept at hitchhiking. I did a lot of that when I was in the military. Maybe I could do it in the U.S. too. Why not? I might be able to save enough to pay for my first-term tuition at Harvard. That would lift a big burden off my back. Maybe. Maybe. Maybe.

But my immediate problem was coming up with the 150-lira airfare to the U.S. I couldn't use the grant money to pay for my airfare. I had to first get to New York to get the grant. Otherwise, I'd lose my chance of attending the Institute, lose the Ford Foundation award and, with it, the dream of saving enough to help with my Harvard fees. So much hinged on closing that 150-lira shortfall.

Then, unexpectedly, I received a letter from the Fund for the Education of Immigrants from Iraq. Minister Shitrit had asked them to help me cover my 150-lira shortfall. The letter pledged the fund's assistance. That would do it, I said to myself. But I was still plagued by guilt about accepting their help. How could I face them?

Two weeks later, another letter arrived. The fund had a check for me to pick up. They had sponsored a benefit dance party and had set aside my 150 liras out of the proceeds.

When I went to pick up the check, a middle-aged man at the fund smiled and said, "We're so proud of you, Danny," as he handed me the check.

I wanted to tell him how much their forgiveness meant to me, but I could only murmur my thanks while fighting back tears. When the chips were down, this community that I had dismissed for most of my time in Israel had come through with magnanimity.

I gazed at the check, and was pleasantly surprised to notice that Minister Bekhor Shitrit had countersigned it.

I thought back on my efforts to get to graduate school, on the struggle to put the pieces together, one at a time – piece, by piece, by piece. That check was another of those pieces, arguably the most important. But it had more than monetary value. It was part of my history. It epitomized the generosity of the Babylonian community and its willingness to come to my rescue, in spite of what I had done. It signified my effort to continue my education, even without the wherewithal, and it symbolized what I was and what I had been through. It carried a message that I wanted preserved as inspiration for immigrants, the poor and the downtrodden: "Don't give up on education for want of money, and don't get discouraged before you have tried. Take a risk. It is true that even if you try, you might not make it. But if you don't try, you surely will never shine."

I had to cash the check to pay my airfare. But before I did I paid to have it photographed. It was expensive, but I was not going to scrimp. That check had too much value. Without it, the whole endeavor might have failed.

To this day, the framed photograph of that check hangs proudly in my study.

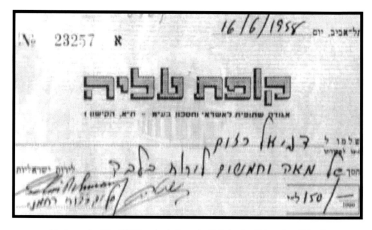

Photograph of the 150-lira check from the Babylonian Educational Fund

I lost contact with the fund, but I never forgot its mission. For years I donated to organizations in Israel dedicated to preserving the cultural heritage of the Babylonian community and educating its children.

When my friend and fellow economist, Vivi Darweesh-Lecker, of Bar Ilan University passed away in 2002, her husband Eddy told me about a fund that had established a fellowship in her memory to support doctoral and post-doctoral work by members of the Babylonian community. I was electrified. It was none other than the fund that had given me the 150 liras.

I sent the fund a check in Vivi's memory, and renewed my links with it.

A DESPERATE PLOY

Late in April 1958, while I was engrossed with my Harvard application, Uncle Moshe handed me a letter smuggled out of Baghdad. I immediately recognized my father's handwriting. *Ammu* Moshe had established communications with Baghdad through covert channels that the Babylonian Bank in Tel Aviv maintained with remnants of the Jewish community in Iraq. I learned later that he had updated my father on our activities in Israel through this channel.

My father wrote that he had acceded to my mother and brother's insistence that they leave Iraq immediately. Further, he stated that he expected me to cancel my plans to go abroad and stay in Israel to support my parents. Should I choose to stick to my plans, Baba continued, he would have no choice but to let my mother and brother leave by themselves, while he would stay behind and face whatever fate had in store for him. He ended his letter with a Judeo-Arabic saying, "Whatever is written on the forehead, the eye can't escape witnessing," a Babylonian saying that conjures up misery and destruction.

It was a devastating letter. Was everything I had been working on to go down the drain? How could my father make such demands on my future? He was casting me as the villain, responsible for his threatened separation from my mother. Blood surged through my veins, my heart pounded and I had difficulty breathing. At no other time in my life do I recall a surge of emotions such as I experienced that day.

I tried to calm down and sort through my feelings. If my father came to Israel I knew he would suffer a terrible drop in social status. I imagined he was still practicing law. But he would need a license to practice in Israel. At sixty-eight, he was almost certainly in no shape to go back to law school and start over again. His message clearly sprang from fear of what the future might hold. Maybe he imagined himself jobless and friendless in a new country, where he would no longer enjoy the prominence he had once enjoyed. He was a drowning man who would latch onto anything he could grab, even at the risk of sinking his rescuer. He must have been driven by panic, I said to myself. I should be more understanding.

Still, I despised him for maneuvering to make me responsible for the breakup of my parents' long, happy marriage. I treasured that aspect of their life, and my father knew it. During all my years in Israel, I had dreamed of the day when my parents would make it out of Iraq, alive and whole. I looked forward to welcoming them and helping them resettle. I owed that to them. But I didn't owe them my life. And that was where my father and I parted company. It was also where I had parted company with other oppressive Babylonian practices.

In Iraq, it was customary to expect sons to take care of their parents and support them in their old age. That was why most Babylonian Jews, like other Middle Easterners and Asians, preferred to have sons and not daughters. Sons were the social security for old age. My parents had five daughters and one son – myself -- living in Israel. My father wrote to me, but not to any of my sisters, asking that I dedicate my life to my parents. This was not an unusual request for a Babylonian

Jew. Many "good" sons gave up the opportunity to have careers or get married and have families of their own, because they were expected to devote their lives exclusively to their parents. People were pilloried for bucking those practices.

As I thought through the implications of my father's letter, I realized he had no power over me. I would still go ahead with my plans; he had no claim on my life. I knew that my father had no compunction about tormenting the conscience of others, if that was what it took to get his way. It was a weapon I had seen him use before to bend *ammu* Moshe to his will.

In 1950, the year that Jews were given the opportunity to register to leave Iraq and relinquish their citizenship, I was the only one in my family to do so. Later on, when Uncle Moshe decided to register to leave Iraq with Aunt Guerjiyi, he and my father discussed the matter. I was the only other person present during their conversation.

My parents had had a hard time finding suitable spouses for Jamila and Muzli, and paying off their dowries had drained their resources. Marrying off my other sisters was expected to be even tougher because so many eligible bachelors were planning to leave in the big exodus. Reyna, Helwa and Latifa were in their late teens or early twenties, which in Iraq was considered a marriageable age.

"When you go to Israel, Moshe," I heard my father declare, "take Reyna, Helwa, and Latifa with you and see that they get married there."

Ammu Moshe's eyes widened and his jaw dropped. He thought for a while.

"It's a big responsibility," he replied.

Ammu Moshe was in his early sixties. He had no children of his own, and he no doubt dreaded the prospect of being saddled with this unwelcome burden at his advanced age.

" It is up to you, Moshe," my father continued. "If you don't take care of this, the retribution for the miserable lives they would end up leading here will fall on your head."

I looked at *ammu* Moshe. He was foaming mad. His mouth was working, though no words were coming out. He finally let out a curse and left the room.

I don't know what further was said, if anything. I do know that when *ammu* Moshe and *khala* Guerjiyi came to Israel they brought Reyna, Helwa and Latifa with them.

As I thought through all of that, I realized that I couldn't just ignore my father's letter and go on with my life as if nothing had happened. I needed to get word to him that he couldn't threaten me into submission, that I had no plans to change course.

I also felt that even though my father had written to me and not to my sisters, his threat to stay behind in Iraq had implications for my sisters, as well. They needed to know about his letter, as well as the consequences of what I was about to tell him. It would affect their lives, too. Mama and Baba were the parents of us all. I thought it might do us good to hold a family meeting and exchange views on the subject.

I was uncertain how my sisters would react to my intention to stick to my plan, knowing that my parents might arrive anytime soon. My sisters knew practically nothing about my effort to gain admission to Harvard or the hoops I had been through to piece things together.

I know my sisters were proud that I held the most prominent job in my family. But judging from occasional comments I heard from them, they probably wondered why I would want to abandon the big catch I had in hand in favor of the less tangible rewards of graduate work. Nor do I believe it would have mattered much to them whether I was admitted to Harvard or to a dinky school in Timbuktu. In fairness, I don't think many in Israel knew the difference either. To most people in Israel, a university was a university. That there was such a thing as a first-rate university and a third-rate university was beyond the ken of most Israelis.

I was agitated when I told my sisters what had transpired with our father. I told them I felt awful that I might have to leave at a time when our parents would be arriving in Israel, but I assured them that I had no plans of shirking my responsibility to help, even when I was abroad. I noted I was not our parents' only child and didn't feel I was the only one who had the responsibility to support them. I shared with my sisters my sense of outrage at my father's machinations. I told them I planned to give *ammu* Moshe a letter for my father, informing him in no uncertain terms that I didn't plan to change course. I asked for my sisters' reactions.

There was a long silence, as well as sad faces. Latifa proposed that we write a letter to our father, telling him that we looked forward to having him join us with Mama and Jacob, that although I would be abroad all of their children would be there to help. Latifa proposed that we put our initials to the letter. We agreed this was the way to go.

I drafted the response in code form.

"SON, YOU LOOK SO DIFFERENT"

In May 1958, my parents and my brother Jacob left Baghdad on a tourist visa to Turkey. (Valentine had arrived eight months before through Turkey). From there they boarded a plane to Israel. Jews by then were normally barred from leaving Iraq. But depending on the whims of the regime, some were allowed to go on short visits abroad, but had to leave their assets or family members behind as collateral. The exit doors closed for good in 1958, with close to 15,000 Jews remaining in Iraq.

NO WAY BACK
The Journey of a Jew from Baghdad

As I sat in the airport awaiting my parents' arrival I was still stewing over my father's letter. Maybe it was all to the good that we wouldn't be together for very long. At the same time, I was struggling with my own sense of guilt.

Maybe my father was right. Maybe I should stay. But if I did, what would that do to my future? My preoccupation with my parents' resettlement might not leave me time to put the pieces back together. I might fall into the same trap that other "good" sons had fallen into. They watched their life go by, while they were absorbed in taking care of their parents. I didn't want that to happen to me. But I still didn't want to see my parents suffer.

It seemed doubtful that our conflict would be resolved without pain and sorrow. But the least I could do was to spend as much time as possible with them during the short time I had remaining in Israel. The first few weeks and months would be the hardest for them. But at least I spoke Hebrew, and could serve as a buffer between them and Israel's bureaucracy.

As I sat absorbed in my thoughts, the announcement came over the public address system that their flight from Turkey had landed.

I was allowed to go on the tarmac outside the waiting area when people began to disembark. The passengers had a good distance to walk to the customs area. I was not sure my parents would be able to walk that far on their own.

From the distance, I could see my mother, followed by my father. As I got closer I could see she was beaming. I rushed to her and gave her a hug. She hugged me and kissed me on both cheeks, but didn't recognize me. She asked if I was Naim, Muzli's husband. When I told her it was Daniel, she rushed to put her arms around me. Then she pulled her head back to take a closer look at me.

"You look so different, my son!" she exclaimed.

I guess I did. I was eighteen when I had left. More than seven years had passed. My father approached slowly. He looked worried, and his eyes seemed to have sunk deep in their sockets. His steps were heavy, and he had aged much more than I had expected. I gave him a big hug and held his hands to my chest, as if to reassure him that in spite of it all, I was still his son and that I would do what I could to stand by his side.

Jacob trailed behind. I went to meet him. I put my arms around him and told him I was glad to see him.

"My goodness your voice has changed. It is so different now," he remarked.

A lot of things were different now, I thought to myself. A long separation takes its toll. Still, nothing could change the fact that they were-- and remained-- my own flesh and blood. I felt a surge of joy; at the same time I felt overwhelmed with sorrow over the pain of separation that we had all endured. I couldn't respond to Jacob's observation. I was choked with emotion. He embraced me and we both broke into tears.

My parents had managed to take with them some photographs and other items of sentimental value – possibly by paying a bribe – and were allowed to take enough money to pay for their expenses during their stay in Turkey, where Baba made a sentimental visit to his law school in Istanbul. Even before we left the airport, my father reached into his pocket and handed me travelers' checks in pounds sterling that he had brought from Baghdad. I was familiar with these checks. The Iraqi authorities had stamped them "Not Negotiable in Israel." Banks in Israel did redeem them, but at a fraction of their face value. There was also a thriving black market in Tel Aviv, where "Not Negotiable in Israel" checks were redeemed at close to their face value. The difference between what the banks and the black market paid was substantial. My parents left the decision about what to do with the checks to me. I was uneasy about breaking the law by redeeming the checks in the black market. On the other hand, I felt protective of what little my parents had salvaged from their wealth. Those checks were all they had. Nothing else would be coming to them in the future. How could I justify advising them to turn them over to a bank, knowing that the bank would take advantage of them?

Jacob, September 28, '1957

Ultimately, I followed my instinct to obey the law. The loss my parents incurred was sizeable, and I wished I had the money to compensate them for it. They used their greatly reduced nest egg for the down payment on a one-bedroom apartment they bought in Ramat Gan shortly after they arrived.

My parents and my brother spent their first weekend in Israel at the apartment of *ammu* Moshe and *khala* Guerjiyi, and our first Friday night *kiddush* was a memorable experience. There were hugs and tears of joy. At long last, we were reunited. We had been so accustomed to thinking of our parents as living in danger that it was hard to believe they were now safe. But it was also painful to see the fall they had suffered— from our big house in Baghdad to makeshift accommodations in my uncle's cramped apartment hallway. None of us had the wherewithal to provide them with anything close to the physical comfort we had enjoyed growing up. We worried also about their age and endurance. It was easier for my sisters and me to adjust to a lower standard of living. We were young, and there was always hope for a better future. But what future was there for a man in his late sixties and a woman in her late fifties?

I was moved when we chanted "*shalom aleikhem, mal'akhei hashalom,*" "peace be unto you, angels of peace," that first Friday night. It had been over seven years since we had last chanted the *kiddush* hymn together. Then it was the Woman of Valor, which we always chanted for my mother. We congregated around Mama, and some of us replayed what we used to do in our younger years - playfully pushing each other to snuggle close to her.

Then it was time for the leader of the *kiddush* ceremony to hold the *kiddush* cup and recite the sanctification over the fruit of the vine. My father, who had always presided over this part of the ritual, insisted that *ammu* Moshe do us the honor this time. At the end of the sanctification, Baba bent over and kissed *ammu* Moshe's hand. I was startled. I had never seen him do that before. Maybe he wanted to express his gratitude to *ammu* Moshe for taking my three sisters with him to Israel and relieving my parents of the responsibility of finding husbands for them.

Before the week was over, my parents found their apartment in my sisters' and *ammu* Moshe's neighborhood. In settling close by relatives, they were following the pattern of the old country, where all our homes were within a short walk from one another. Their new neighborhood in Ramat Gan was sought after by immigrants from Iraq. It had many features reminiscent of Baghdad's parks: tall eucalyptus trees, a river, and rowboats.

During the month we overlapped in Israel, Baba and I never spoke of the letter he had sent me. But he never dropped his insistence that I abandon my plans to go to Harvard and stay in Israel to support him and my mother.

We were at my parents' apartment one day when he again began to badger me. It seemed he would never give up until he had worn me down and gotten what he wanted. I reiterated my decision not to change course. He looked defeated and sad. Helwa looked at him, and then turned to me.

"It hurts his feelings, can't you see?" she exclaimed.

I didn't know what to say. It was useless to carry the

conversation any further. But that incident left a heavy burden on my heart, haunting me long after I moved to America.

Jacob, who had a degree in pharmaceutical chemistry from Baghdad's Royal College of Pharmacy, was eager to find a job, and he came to me for advice. I had anticipated this request, and had already compiled a list of healthcare centers that had job openings. I suggested that we start with the prestigious Belinson Hospital, the prize on my list.

I set up an appointment for the following day and accompanied Jacob to the interview. The interviewer was so impressed with Jacob's credentials that he cut the interview short and told Jacob he could start work the following day.

This was beyond my wildest expectations. I felt relieved - a big burden was now off my shoulders. My biggest worry had been that, because of the language barrier, it might take Jacob a long time before he could find a job. Jacob was all smiles.

Mama was ecstatic. Baba was pleased with the news, but hardly effusive. He had difficulty cheering up.

My parents, April 12, 1961

Not long afterward, my father asked if I could help him find a job. I didn't know what to say. I had not done the groundwork for a job search. After writing him that I planned to leave for the U.S., I had assumed he would carry out his threat to stay in Baghdad. There was also the age factor. Immigrants much younger than him were unable to find jobs, particularly in law. But Baba was an active person, and the thought of being shelved and removed from the center of activity was foreign to him.

Having no idea where to start, I suggested that we broach the subject with the Jewish Agency.

We met with an agency official, a middle-aged, kindhearted woman. My father was tense; he looked as if he was facing the fateful test of his life. The official tried to put him at ease, speaking to him slowly in Hebrew.

My father opened a cylindrical container he had carried out of Baghdad and lovingly unfurled his law school diploma. It was written in Turkish. That was the first time I had seen his diploma. It was only then that I began to fully fathom the depth of his fall. My father had never needed to prove himself to anyone before. He had never had to brandish his credentials for anyone. His reputation preceded him. I remembered him as a highly respected professional, a leader of our community. But here he was – a broken and frightened man. He looked anxiously at the agency official to weigh her impressions, as though a defendant waiting for the jury's verdict. His humiliation was heart-rending.

My father's law diploma, written in the old Turkish alphabet

NO WAY BACK
The Journey of a Jew from Baghdad

The official seemed touched. She looked at the diploma closely. I don't know if she knew Turkish. With a sad look, she turned to me.

"I can't think of any place to refer your father, in light of his age. He is entitled to rest after a long life of work."

She turned to my father and shook his hands warmly. He seemed to have gotten the gist of it: that this was the end of his illustrious career.

My father never pursued the subject of work again. Not long after the interview, he embarked on a project to compile a Judeo-Arabic/Hebrew dictionary. Recently, while searching through his files, I came across a pile of neatly written pages of Judeo-Arabic words, listed alphabetically, with their Hebrew counterparts written next to them.

That was Baba's unfinished dictionary.

LEAVING FOR THE U.S.

I planned to spend the night before my flight to the U.S. with my parents in Ramat Gan. I took my time packing the few belongings in my room in Tel Aviv, lingering as though I had all the time in the world. How could I face my parents? Would I ever see them again? How could I leave them? I had worked so hard to reach my goal—how could I not leave? I remembered how I had felt leaving Baghdad for Israel: uncertain about the future and heartbroken to part with my family. But in Baghdad my father still had his career. In Israel he and my mother were refugees.

A photograph Mama managed to get out of Iraq
She is in our home in Baghdad, my photograph in hand,
a few days after I left Baghdad in 1951

It was late in the evening before I arrived at my parents'

apartment. The bedroom was dark; my father was already asleep. Mama sat on the balcony waiting for me. Jacob summoned my sisters to bid me farewell, and we all gathered in the bedroom where Baba slept, undisturbed by the lights and our chatter. I felt that my mother very much wanted to gather me to her and open her heart to me. But I was determined not to let her. I was distant, haughty. That intimidated her. She kept her distance.

Our seven-year separation, and the constant worry whether I was alive, had been an enormous strain on her. When we were reunited in Israel, she told me that she had cried her heart out when I left home, and that for a while she had kept my picture with her wherever she went. She had a hunch, she said, that if I had made it to Israel, I was serving in the military. So every time there were clashes on Israel's borders she was sure I was in mortal danger.

Now, there were no tears, but her anguish was obvious. I wanted to go to her, hug her and tell her I loved her, that I was sorry to be leaving and that I had missed her during our long years of separation. She had nothing except her children, and the journey out of Iraq had been to reunite with me especially. But something held me back. I suppose I was afraid if I gave in to my emotions, I might decide to stay. Then the intricate plan I had constructed for my future would unravel.

I slept fitfully that night.

The next morning, we all rose early, though no one said much. Our hearts were heavy as we faced yet another separation. Most painful for me was to watch my mother. She sat on a chair and just looked at me. Her eyes spoke of a deep sense of loss.

Mama had set the table for breakfast, but I couldn't force myself to eat. It must have been disappointing for her not to be able to nurture me one last time. But she didn't complain when I walked away from the table.

When it was time to leave, Baba and Jacob said they would escort me up the street to catch a taxicab to the airport.

"Will I ever see you again?" Mama asked.

"I will be back," I said coldly.

"You are lying," Mama replied.

In Judeo-Arabic that expression just connotes doubt, as in "It may never happen." I chose to interpret my mother's remark literally.

"Don't call me a liar," I retorted sharply.

My poor mother couldn't apologize enough. To this day, it pains me to remember how I treated her that morning. Tears streamed down her cheeks. She lifted the bottom of her dress to wipe away her tears, and she asked through her sobs:

"Why were we destined to be dispersed?"

It tore my heart to see Mama's anguish. I wish I had found the courage in that moment to open up to her and make amends for my harsh words. Instead, I just hugged her and kissed her good bye.

Throughout the years, I looked forward to the day when I would return to Israel and apologize to Mama, face to face, for my heartlessness. But that day never came; Mama died before I managed to return.

My father and brother escorted me to the main street where we would find a taxicab. I hugged Jacob. He was my friend; I had shared so much with him in our younger years. I told him how much I would miss him.

I then turned to my father and hugged him. He was standing silently, his eyes filled with tears. He looked at me sadly. How could I leave him? He was my father who loved me and had cared for me when I was a child.

"May God bless you, Baba," I said, as I choked up.

Then I turned away, got into the taxicab and slammed the door. The driver edged into the traffic and sped up.

I didn't look back.

PART THREE

NO WAY BACK
The Journey of a Jew from Baghdad

EN ROUTE TO THE UNKNOWN

By any rational accounting, I was headed pell-mell for disaster when I boarded the flight for America. I had accepted a place at one of the world's finest universities without a clue how to pay for my tuition and living expenses. I had neither family nor friends in the strange new country where I would spend the next few years. I had prepared at a mediocre college and was not at all proficient in English. Worst of all, my yearning to make a new life in a free society was being gnawed at by feelings of guilt at leaving my parents in Israel just when we had been reunited.

On the morning of July 2, 1958 I got my first glimpse of America.

As the plane flew over New York harbor, I caught sight of the Statue of Liberty. I had seen pictures of the statue and had read the inspiring Emma Lazarus poem, but still was unprepared for the size and majesty of the original. It seemed as though she was standing in the harbor waiting for me to arrive. I wanted to put my arms around her and hug her. On the other hand, I was disappointed that the huge skyscrapers that outlined the city skyline dwarfed the statue. Perhaps, I thought, this was a symbol of things to come. My problems, too, might seem smaller once I arrived in America.

"Where in the United States are you going?" the customs official asked as he inspected my passport.

"To the University of Wisconsin, Madison for the Economics Institute and then on to Harvard in Cambridge, Mass., for graduate work."

The official smiled.

"Do you know what a great school Harvard is? It is the best university in the whole of the United States. May you have a wonderful stay. Welcome to the U.S."

I still remember his smile and his firm handshake—his genuine good will. As I walked off with my suitcase, I couldn't help but contrast this complete stranger's welcome with the indifference, even hostility, surrounding my arrival in Israel. Nor could I forget the many doubters in Israel who had discouraged me from applying to Harvard.

As soon as I arrived in Manhattan, I called on Maurice Shasha, the businessman who, sight unseen and knowing no more than I was a Jew from Baghdad who wanted to do graduate work in the U.S., had been willing to sponsor me, pledging the assets of his company as security. Considering the enormity of his gesture, I wanted to tell him in person how grateful I was. As I looked into his dark, smiling eyes and felt his firm handclasp, I knew he was no longer a stranger, but a friend. I asked him why he was willing to vouch for me when we had never even met.

NO WAY BACK
The Journey of a Jew from Baghdad

"My roots are in the Babylonian community, and I love that community," he told me. "It pains me to see the disaster the community has suffered. I would do anything to help revive it. What better way than to help one of its children attend a top institution of learning."

Now Mr. Shasha went a step further.

"I would feel so much better if you would let me send you a check for $100 each month," he said. "Put the money in the bank if you like and don't use it unless you have an emergency. For my part I will rest easy knowing you have it. You can pay it back to me when you graduate."

I shook his hands, but I was too choked up to put my thanks into words.

Economics Institute – On a bus trip, heading for a major factory in Milwaukee.
The student sitting in the front row on the left is an Iraqi Kurd. He spoke out against the 1958 coup in Iraq, which took place while the Institute was in session. He received threats on his life from Arab students on campus. The authorities took him into protective custody.

HARVARD WON'T LET YOU DOWN

I spent two pleasant months in Madison at the Economics Institute. I virtually moved into its basement language laboratory, where most days I holed up from seven in the morning until seven at night, leaving only for lectures and lunch. My English was much improved by the time I got to Cambridge, and my frugality had paid off handsomely.

By living at the YMCA in Madison instead of a dorm and eating only one meal a day, I managed to arrive at Harvard with $600 in savings from the Ford Foundation grant. I went to the Bursar's office and paid $500 for my first semester's tuition and $45 for the first month at the dorm. That left $55, not much even in those days. And there were books to buy and food to pay for and monthly installments to make on the dorm.

At my first meeting with Seymour Harris, the Chairman of the Economics Department, I told him that I planned to apply for an educational loan, and confided that if I didn't get it I was uncertain about my ability to continue my graduate work.

Professor Harris turned and looked straight at me. His words were measured. "Harvard wouldn't let you down after admitting you. At Harvard you never have to give up your education for lack of money. We wouldn't let that happen."

A picture dear to my heart--I took this picture of Widener Library. I spent many days and evenings in Widener. Built in 1915, Widener housed close to three million books of Harvard's collection.

My step was lighter as I left his office that day. I was to receive $100 a month for a ten-hour-a-week research assistantship in the computing center.

A few weeks later, Rabbi Morris L. Zigmond, the director of the New England Hillel, designated me the recipient of a $200 annual scholarship that an anonymous donor had set up for a deserving graduate student. I set it aside to pay the monthly installments on my dorm, secure in knowing I'd have shelter at least through January.

When I settled into life during my first semester I worked non-stop to keep up with the enormous amount of required reading. In spite of the strides I had made, I still couldn't read English quickly. My vocabulary was still limited, and I didn't want to just skip over unfamiliar words. With a dictionary always beside me, I looked up every word I didn't understand. While this habit built my vocabulary, it greatly slowed my reading speed and disrupted my concentration.

Studying in the dorm, Perkins Hall.

To compensate, I decided to cut out time spent on anything other than classes or study sessions with fellow students. I drew up a chart on which I recorded my daily activities, looking for "waste" that I could redirect to my reading lists. "Waste" could mean a 15-minute rest on my bed, or a 10-minute break to watch the news in the dorm's common room. I went to bed later and got up earlier, finally paring my sleep down to five hours a night.

This Spartan existence was worsened by perpetual worries about money. The research assistantship and the grant from Rabbi Zigmond helped, but didn't stretch far enough. I was sending my parents $35 a month to help with their living expenses. I was importing my textbooks from England, where they cost less than half as much as in the States. My diet consisted of boiled eggs, bread, coffee and iceberg lettuce. I used a hotplate to boil the eggs and make coffee in my room, trying to ignore hunger pangs.

LONGING FOR FAMILY

As winter set in, my thoughts turned repeatedly to my parents and the difficulties they were having adjusting to their new life in Israel. I yearned just to hear my mother's voice, and late one night I felt so desperate that I threw myself at the mercy of the overseas operator.

Harvard Yard.
Daniel standing next to the statue of John Harvard.

Harvard's Littauer Center where most of my classes were held.

"I need to talk to my parents in Israel, but I am a student and I don't have the money to pay for the call. Is there any way you could help me?" I pleaded. "Is there any way we could work out the cost of the call?"

"You don't have the money and you want to make a transatlantic call?"

"Just for two minutes."

I fought back tears as I felt a flush of shame rising on my face. This was totally humiliating. I, who had never begged for anything, was asking a total stranger for a free ride.

"There is no way, sir. AT&T wouldn't allow us to do that."

I replaced the phone on the hook and walked blindly out of the telephone booth, sunk in the pain of rejection and humiliation. It was hard to ask for anything and harder to be turned down. But the hardest of all was the longing to hear my mother's voice, knowing that longing wouldn't be satisfied. I had done this to myself. I had chosen to come to Harvard instead of staying in Israel.

I was in touch with my father and brother by letter, but my mother didn't know how to write, so she could only communicate with me through their correspondence. I had been away from her for so many years while I was in Israel. And now we were separated again.

A LETTER FROM MY FATHER

These worries were not allayed by the disturbing letters I was receiving from my brother Jacob. They were full of complaints about his difficulties in Israel: There were no decent cigarettes to be had; there was no time to go out; he just hated being there. Curiously, every letter closed the same way, something like, "But don't you worry about me. I just wanted to give vent to my frustrations. I have no one to talk to. Don't fret. You just go on having a good time in America."

Those letters made me feel miserable. None of the things Jacob complained about sounded as bad to me as what I was living through. Still I was tormented to read of the hardships, and had to concede the difficulties of adjusting to a new environment, a new country. I also had to concede that Jacob's tolerance for change might be lower than mine. I was eighteen when I went to Israel. He was thirty-one. Maybe he resented my going on with my life, but didn't feel free to say so. Maybe this was his way of expressing his resentment less overtly.

Jacob was living with my parents and helping to support them. I was in the United States pursuing a graduate education. To him it probably seemed I had the better deal.

What did Jacob think I was doing at Harvard? What "good time" was he talking about? Evidently he knew nothing of how difficult my life really was. All he knew was that I was in America and he was in Israel living under conditions that he deemed intolerable.

I suspect Jacob might have been complaining to my parents, too.

A week or two after the AT&T operator had turned me down, I received a letter from Jacob, alerting me that our father was writing to me to ask me to come back. "Ignore what he says," Jacob said. "Don't pay attention to what he asks of you."

Looking back at the situation I suspect Jacob was feeling guilty. He probably had created a commotion that got out of hand, provoking my father to action. Baba probably felt that, since he himself had no way of lightening the burden on Jacob, his only alternative was to ask me to come back to help.

Jacob's letter put me in a tailspin. I had trouble concentrating on my studies in my agitation awaiting my father's letter and fearing the kind of pressure he might bring to bear. I wished his letter would just come and put an end to my anxiety.

Some two weeks later, I heard again from Jacob, noting that my father was taking a lot of time finishing his letter, and to ignore it. I was both relieved and apprehensive when our father's letter finally arrived a week or so later. He said that I should come back to Israel and help support the family. The inducement he offered was that I could then "enjoy Mama's delicious cooking."

I shoved the letter in my pocket and walked through the campus with my mind in turmoil. Was there never to be an end to it? Was my father going to continue to torment me through all my years at Harvard? Would he stop even after I graduated? I was doing what I could. I was sending money to help with my parents' expenses. To bolster my resolve, I reminded myself that my father had paid for Jacob's college education but had been unable to contribute to mine.

At the same time, my heart was heavy as I thought about the tragedy of my parents' uprooting. Had life worked out differently, Baba might now have been imploring me to come back to Baghdad. There, his prestigious position would have opened doors for me in that society. Now he was a broken man living in Israel with nothing left to offer me but my mother's cooking. It broke my heart to think about it. Still, I decided I did not want to give up my education.

I ignored Baba's request. He never broached the subject again.

NO WAY BACK
The Journey of a Jew from Baghdad

THE TURNING POINT

Life during my first year in graduate school was difficult. I lived mostly on one sparse meal a day and went without a winter coat. Gloves were beyond my means, and I flirted with frostbitten fingers on more than one occasion. I struggled with a new language and a new culture and was struck by acute homesickness when the dorm emptied during the Christmas break. And Harvard's hospital had to literally save my life when I left a post surgery infection untreated -- I did not have the money to buy the antibiotics I needed.

But all of these problems paled in the face of my continuing turmoil over my disillusionment with life in Israel.

I was fortunate that Harvard was one of the very few schools at the time that offered free psychiatric treatment to its students. I had several therapy sessions during my first year in graduate school. Sometimes I talked with my therapist about my sense of guilt in leaving my parents behind in Israel. Sometimes I talked about my sense of exhaustion at the unrelenting pressure I was under to keep up with the academic demands, all in a language that was not my native tongue. But eventually our sessions always came back to my inability to deal with the ethnic problems in Israel.

In one session I talked about my feelings of being pulled in opposite directions: On one hand, my experience in Israel as a Jew from an Arab land and my shattered dream of making Israel my homeland; on the other my sense of duty to settle in Israel at the end of my graduate work.

Speaking slowly and with his blue eyes fixed sharply on me, my psychiatrist asked, "Daniel, why do you have to go back? Why don't you just stay here?"

I bristled at his question. How could I do that? I would be a traitor. For ages, Jews had prayed for the ingathering of the exiles; during my childhood in Baghdad we prayed for that goal every day. It was ingrained in me. How could I turn my back on it? I cried uncontrollably.

But, as I dried my tears a sense of peace stole over me. I felt relieved. Suddenly, my life looked a whole lot brighter.

My psychiatrist's pointed question forced me to confront reality head on. My psychiatrist was not an anti-Semite; he was not trying to undermine Israel. His question sounded reasonable. Why did I have to return? Why live in a place where life would be a roller coaster? I liked my friends at Harvard. I liked the warmth and courtesy I had been shown by Americans everywhere, Jews and non-Jews alike: The customs official who had applauded my acceptance to Harvard on my first day in this country; the professor who had rescheduled our exams so they wouldn't conflict with Passover; the Christian minister who had invited me to a church supper—and arranged to serve me a *kasher* meal. I felt at home in America. I did not want to go back. Why feel guilty about that?

Yes, I was an exile, an outsider with foreign customs and a shaky command of English. But for the first time in my life, no one seemed to hold my differences against me. Indeed, all these positive impressions had struck a deep chord with me, seeming to speak volumes about the sensitivity and character of the American people.

That therapy session was the most critical turning point in my life. Why do you have to go back? Why don't you just stay here? Whatever emotional conflict had tormented me up until then about leaving Israel vanished. The psychiatrist's questions freed me. I was entitled to live where I was happy.

I had several therapy sessions after that. But I never felt the need to bring up the subject any more. And it never came up again in any context.

I had finally found my rightful homeland.

EPILOGUE

My financial conditions brightened after my first year in graduate school. I received fellowships from the Department of Economics during the rest of my years in graduate school. I was able to increase my financial help to my parents.

I graduated from Harvard with a PhD in Economics in June 1963. My career in academia and government took off. I taught at major universities, published widely, and gained an international reputation.

On May 22 and 23, 1973, Dr. J. Daniel Khazzoom blazed and flashed like a beacon of intellect from the witness stand in the Superior Court of Quebec. He was the last in a six-month parade of witnesses presented by the James Bay Task Force before Judge Albert Malouf and he was, in the words of task force organizer Dr. John Spence, "the most arrogant, testy, splendid and irrefutable witness" the judge had heard. For two days he turned the courtroom into an intellectual fireworks display and, when it was over, Hydro-Quebec's rationale for the James Bay project had been ripped to shreds.

Dr. Khazzoom was a forty-one-year-old economics professor at McGill, a scholar of international brilliance, and former chief econometrician for the Federal Power Commission of the United States. His speciality was to set up econometric models, the purpose of which he defined as "to quantify what the economist talks about in general qualitative terms." He had submitted Hydro-Quebec's projections for electricity consumption in the province up to 1985 to the test of an econometric model and he delivered his verdict at the start of his testimony.

"What," he was asked, "is your opinion of those projections?"

"I think they are exaggerated. I think they are out of line with anything that could be realistically expected.".

For two days on the stand, Dr. Khazzoom displayed a vast erudition about all forms of electricity usage, the economics of power utilities and the mathematical structures of his science. Though he was exhaustively and sometimes repetitively cross-examined, he never flinched from his judgement that Hydro's projections were quite unreal.

From: Philip Sykes, Sellout, Huntig Publishing (Edmonton: 1973), p. 194

One of my proudest accomplishments was being instrumental in saving the reservation of the indigenous Indians in northern Quebec. In the early seventies, the provincial government of Quebec planned to flood the Indians' fishing and hunting grounds in order to construct a massive hydroelectric project. The Indians objected but to no avail.

The impending displacement of Quebec's natives resonated with my own history; I did not want to see them being uprooted as I once was. When they sued Quebec, I joined them in court to testify on their behalf.

Using the results of a large econometric model of energy I had developed for Canada, I demonstrated in court that Quebec's rationale for the hydroelectric project did not hold water. The court's decision was not long in coming. It found in favor of the Indians.

I was touched when the Indians declared me an honorary member of their tribe

There were sad moments, too.

Mama died suddenly in 1967. The last time I saw her was on the day I left for the U.S., nine years before. The timing of Mama's death seemed especially cruel. Since my graduation in 1963 I had wanted to take a trip to Israel to see my mother and tell her face-to-face how much I regretted my rudeness toward her on the day I left for the U.S. But I kept putting the trip off. I had just accepted my first academic appointment at Cornell University. At that early stage of my career, it was a ruthless world of publish-or-perish - the pressure to publish in academic journals to demonstrate scholarly prowess. It was an intensely competitive environment. By the time I was over that hump, it was too late. Mama was gone.

Mama and I had spoken by telephone for the first—and only-- time a year before she died. That was the first time I could afford the cost of a transatlantic call. We were on the phone for a long time, and Mama wept as we spoke. She said she couldn't believe she was speaking to me. I fought back tears as I was transported back to our life together in Baghdad. There was my parents' home, and my family sitting around the kerosene heater, drinking hot tea with milk on a cold winter night. There were my bedroom and my desk, and the big picture of the snow-covered village that adorned the living room in our home. There was the synagogue I had attended, two blocks from home. I could see it all, as I listened to my mother.

And now we would never speak again.

My family and I traveled to Israel to be with Baba during Mama's first memorial in 1968. We traveled again in 1973 to spend *rosh hashana* with my father. He was going to meet four-year-old Loolwa, my mother's namesake, for the first time.

When we arrived, my father stood in the doorway for several moments staring at me, almost as if he couldn't believe I was there. I reached out to place my younger daughter in his arms but, in those first few moments, my father saw only me. I was his child, the one who lived so far away, the one he couldn't count on seeing again after I had returned to the United States five years before.

I bowed my head as my father covered it with his hand and recited in a loud, but trembling voice, the Shehehiyyanu blessing, "Blessed art Thou, our Lord, Ruler of the Universe that hast given us life and sustenance, and brought us to this happy occasion." I hugged my father, but I didn't fully appreciate what he was feeling. Now that my own children are so far from me, I understand what was in his heart.

During that visit, my father and I stayed up late, sometimes almost till dawn. Those were memorable nights, the best times I ever spent with my father. It was wonderful to listen to him recollect events in his life. His fights on behalf of the downtrodden and the poor were very much on his mind.

"I was fatherless. I knew what it was to be poor and I knew the difficulties of attending school without having enough space to do my homework. When I was elected to the Jewish Governing Council, I devoted my energies to helping the needy get an education, so they could pull themselves out of their poverty, just as I did."

Last picture I have of my father - taken on Dec 30, 1974.

Baba spoke of his dream of one day taking possession of the lot he had purchased on Mount Scopus in Jerusalem. He and other Babylonian Jews had invested in this area at the urging of Jewish emissaries from Palestine back in 1920, and they had held onto the land in times when any association with Palestine was grounds for imprisonment in Iraq.

NO WAY BACK
The Journey of a Jew from Baghdad

By the time my parents arrived in Israel in 1958, East Jerusalem was occupied by Jordan, and the Jordanians had declared investors like my father absentee landlords, according to Jordanian law.

"When Israel captured East Jerusalem in 1967," Baba told me, "I went to claim my land. I had managed to smuggle the deed out of Iraq at great risk. The Bureau of Land Management in Jerusalem confirmed my ownership, but told me I could not take possession of the land. Israel had decided to expropriate the lots on Mount Scopus."

"Do you still have the deed, Baba?"

"Yes, but what I want is possession of the land," he continued. "All those years in Iraq I risked being discovered and penalized for holding title to a piece of land in Palestine. Now that I am finally here, they want to take my lot away. I had dreamed of building our home in Jerusalem, on Mount Scopus. We had answered the call to buy land in Jerusalem. It is not fair that now we should be stripped of what we have risked our lives for."

Baba and other Babylonian landowners had appealed the government decision but the appeal was then winding through the courts.

"Who knows how it'll end?" Baba sighed. "I am clinging to the hope that one day I will be able to reclaim my land on Mount Scopus."

Baba did not live long enough to hear the court's decision.

The Appeals court upheld the government decision to expropriate the land on Mount Scopus. The government compensated the owners at pennies on the dollar, treating them as absentee landlords, even though they were all residents of Israel by then.

As Baba and I talked late into the night in 1973, I could see that his physical strength was waning, even as his memories of his former days of glory were still fresh. It was characteristic of him to dwell on milestones in his life, without expressing deep emotion or affection. Verbalizing feelings is customarily avoided in the Middle East; it is virtually taboo. I can't recall whether I ever heard my mother say she loved me; I know my father never said it. Instead, we would read one another's expressions and gestures to understand what was felt.

Now 83, my father was too feeble to come to the airport when we departed. He waved goodbye from the doorway. I looked back to see a lonely, broken and sorrowful old man. He was my father and I was again leaving him behind to face his own fate.

When we reached our apartment in Montreal, I just wanted to be alone. I retreated to the room at the far end of the apartment and gave way to my grief. That visit was the last time I saw my father.

NO WAY BACK
The Journey of a Jew from Baghdad

I was not present at the deathbed of either of my parents. I was the child who lived eight thousand miles away from them. I was the one who had left the fold. Seldom do we make choices knowing all the consequences. It saddens me not to have been with my parents during their last moments, not to have accompanied them to their last resting places.

I wish I could have followed the Babylonian custom of visiting my parents' graves every Friday during the first year following their deaths. Yet even from thousands of miles away, I had managed to do one thing for them. I had bought the graves, one next to the other, in which my parents lay. It gave me a small measure of consolation to know that my mother and father, who had loved each other so much, were again united in death. It was a gift they couldn't thank me for, and that made it all the more precious in my eyes.

My parents' Gravesites at Holon's cemetery

My father willed his Ramat Gan apartment to me and asked that I keep it in the family in Mama's memory. I have continued to maintain the apartment, and each time I visit I am transported back to the first few days I spent there, visiting with my parents after their escape from Baghdad. It was bare of furnishings except for some creaky folding chairs borrowed from my sisters. But the sparse surroundings didn't dampen the pleasure we found in each other after so many years of separation. I especially remember the surge of love and joy I felt, seeing how Mama still worried about my pants being pressed and my shirt being mended. Much later, that apartment was where my father and I at long last made peace, and where he, my wife and my daughters grew to know and love each other. After Baba's death, it provided shelter for my Uncle Sion, who had depleted all his savings to raise a dowry for his sister Nazeema. And the apartment was the place my brother and sisters gathered for comfort when we said our last goodbyes to my sisters Jamila and Reyna, who died a few days apart in 2002.

My parents' apartment in Ramat Gan, Israel –
First floor shaded window to the right

I am an American now. But parts of me remain with the ghosts of Baghdad's now-decimated Jewish community, and also in Israel, the long-dreamed-of Jewish homeland that broke my heart. During my life, my family and I moved many times - from one town to another, from one state to another, and from one country to another. We had many "homes." But my parents' apartment in Ramat Gan is the one constant in our lives. It is the one place that my family and I have known the longest. It isn't big or fancy. But it is our refuge nonetheless, an island of caring and peace in the midst of a turbulent world. I cherish the memories of those who lived within its walls.

NO WAY BACK
The Journey of a Jew from Baghdad